Library of
Davidson College

The Structure of Love
Representational Patterns and Shakespeare's Love Tragedies

Michael Hall

The Structure of Love

Representational Patterns and

Shakespeare's Love Tragedies

University Press of Virginia   *Charlottesville*

THE UNIVERSITY PRESS OF VIRGINIA
Copyright © 1989 by the Rector and Visitors
of the University of Virginia
First published 1989

Library of Congress Cataloging-in-Publication Data

Hall, Michael, 1951–
  The structure of love.
  Bibliography: p.
  Includes index.
  1. Shakespeare, William, 1564–1616—Tragedies.
2. Love in literature. 3. Sex in literature. I. Title.
PR3069.L6H35 1989   822.3'3   88-20463
ISBN 0-8139-1207-5

Printed in the United States of America

Contents

Acknowledgments   vii
Introduction   ix
1 / The Structure of Love: Then   1
2 / The Structure of Love: Now   32
3 / Creating the Heroine: The Comedies   46
4 / The Paradise of Flesh: *Romeo and Juliet*   72
5 / Magic in the Structure: *Othello*   98
6 / Words, Words, Mere Words: *Troilus and Cressida*   115
7 / The Gap in Nature: *Antony and Cleopatra*   140
Conclusion   166
Notes   171
Index   185

Acknowledgments

It is difficult even to remember all those whose help in one form or another has contributed to this book, and more difficult yet to thank them in a way that is not hackneyed. This being the case, I will accept my fate and the usual form and thank only those who have offered special help or whose influence on the manuscript has been especially great.

In the special-help category, thanks go to Dean William M. Wilson of Virginia Wesleyan College for providing various kinds of support, and to the Mednick Foundation for helping fund travel to various libraries and museums overseas. Thanks also go to Gerald Trett at the University Press of Virginia for his sensitive editing and for shepherding the manuscript through the publication process; also to Fletcher Collins and the late Walker Cowen, Director of the Press, without whose interest and encouragement this publication could not have occurred.

Among those who have read and commented on all or various parts of the text are J. R. Bennett and Cary Nelson, both of whom also contributed greatly to the development of my theoretical position, and Howard Cole, Beth Packert, Lisa Horwitz, Kathy Merlock-Jackson, and Mary Beth Mina. My most profound thanks go to Mark Rose, whose advice and teaching are apparent throughout the text, and to Dan Heaton and L. Anderson Orr, without whose careful and tireless editing the text would be much different and inferior.

Introduction

Although structural approaches to literature have grown increasingly important in recent years, they have had less impact on Shakespearean studies than on most other areas. The reasons are clear enough. First, since structuralism, semiotics, and poststructuralism all generally emphasize the study of a small section or limited aspect of a text, they are at their best with works of limited scope. And since they all in one way or another define literary expression in terms of restrictive linguistic concepts, they are also usually at their best with works most simply and obviously reflective of their traditions: that is, the least original ones.

These restrictions obviously limit the usefulness of structural approaches for Shakespearean studies, and they are further limited by their strong tendency (and that of their near cousin, reader response) to de-emphasize the importance of character and theme. Few Shakespeareans are going to be attracted to such a de-emphasis, since a large part of our subject's prestige, most of our students' favorable responses, and probably most of our own interest derive from the ability to see Shakespeare's characters and ideas as independent units that can be discussed as such. These days no one writes books about the girlhoods of Shakespeare's heroines, but neither can we be happy with theoretical positions that make character merely part of the overall semantic field—as in, for example, Barthes's influential *S/Z* and most of the works of Eco, Greimas, Derrida, and many others.[1]

This insistence on the preeminence of character and theme is part of what might be called the referential view of literature, which is that literary works have a definite meaning or meanings that can be described in terms of ideas or human characteristics or (most commonly) both, but in any case in terms of referents outside of the work in question. More simply, the referential position is that any literary work of value has a point, and that point is its characters and themes, which make sense and are interesting because we have met people and ideas much like them in the real world. This position provides the theoretical basis for the typical literary interpretation, which argues for a specific meaning based on the relationship of various aspects of a work (including historical or biographical sources) to its characters and themes.

This understanding of the nature of literature is doubtless the one ordinary readers or viewers have always held. As formal literary theory it had its birth in the works of Plato, who saw literature as an inadequate and frequently dangerous imitation of the outside world (*Ion; Republic,* 2, 3, 10; *Laws,* 2, 7); and Horace, who agreed (in general) that literature imitates the world but argued that it has its own positive function in that world: teaching us what is good and bad in a pleasant enough way to make us pay attention (*Art of Poetry*). With minor alterations, this idea that the function of literature is to teach us about the world in an aesthetically pleasing way has been and remains the standard of most critics and general readers.

The classical opposition to this view is the *Poetics,* in which Aristotle agrees that literature ultimately imitates the world, but argues that how an audience responds to what it sees is controlled by rules intrinsic to literature itself. Central to these is that the "soul" of tragedy (and by implication comedy and the epic as well) is plot, the nature of which "implies personal agents, who necessarily possess certain distinctive qualities both of character and thought" (6).[2] In other words, most of what we think of as character is an aspect of plot structure; the social status of characters, the most significant of their values, their responses, and much else are dependent on their position in a particular story and hence are most accurately understood as part of the plot. Character as an independent category is for Aristotle only whatever additional is added to the plot-dependent actions and qualities to make a figure different from others who have filled, or might fill, the same role. Like the paint an artist uses to fill out a sketch, these additions are subordinate to and in a different category from the central structure, and they make a different contribution to how the work is perceived. Hence approaching a character as if he or she were real distorts the way character is produced. For Aristotle, as for many recent critics who take structural approaches, such analysis of how literature works is the purpose of criticism; what any particular work teaches is not a significant issue.

Ironically enough, although most critics inclined to a referential approach define themselves as New Critics, that school had a structural origin. The first

New Critics specifically rejected the referential idea that literature is best seen in terms of meaning, and instead insisted on the primacy of function, or effect. As I. A. Richards puts it at the beginning of *Practical Criticism* (1929): "The all-important fact for the study of literature—or any other mode of communication—is that there are several kinds of meaning. . . . Language—and preeminently language as it is used in poetry—has not one but several tasks to perform simultaneously, and we shall misconceive most of the difficulties of criticism unless we understand this point and take note of the differences between these functions."[3] This mild manifesto is a long way from Barthes, but the two critics are alike in their belief that the referential approach gives an artificial importance to what is at best only a part of any reader's response to a literary work. Interpretations based on character and theme produce the comforting illusion that literary response can be contained and understood, but as Cleanth Brooks puts it in the "Heresy of Paraphrase" (the last chapter in *The Well Wrought Urn*, 1947), they also seriously misrepresent the nature of literature: "To repeat, most of our difficulties in criticism are rooted in the heresy of paraphrase. If we allow ourselves to be misled by it, we distort the relation of the poem to its 'truth,' we raise the problem of belief in a vicious and crippling form, we split the poem between its 'form' and 'content'—we bring the statement to be conveyed into an unreal competition with science or philosophy or theology."[4] The "heresy of paraphrase" is isolating characters and themes by retelling—paraphrasing—them, then asserting that this retelling is what the work actually "says." Such an approach exposes literature to Plato's damning criticism that if the purpose of literature is to comment on life, then surely anything a writer says could be more accurately and authoritatively stated by an expert in that field. Like Aristotle, Brooks sees literature as significant not because of what it says but how it says it.

The problem with the structural position is that the major response of almost any reader to almost any work of literature is the sense that it is telling us something about people and values. So while a referential approach may distort the nature of literary response, this kind of distortion is itself part of that response, and without it none of us feels that the work in question has been done justice.

As a result, most criticism of the last forty years follows the lead of Brooks and Robert Penn Warren in *Understanding Poetry* (1938) and seeks an amalgam of the referential and structural positions. Generally stated, most of us employ some combination of close reading, social or artistic or biographical history, psychological observations, and mythic or imagistic patterning to defend the validity of a specific content. None of us would follow our eighteenth- and nineteenth-century forebears in seeing Shakespeare's value chiefly in his "lessons" (in which they included his representation of character), but neither are we interested in criticism that ignores these lessons altogether.

This study is also built around a combination of the referential and structural positions, but with a higher than usual emphasis on the latter. Rather than make concern with the way the text works a tool to prove a novel interpretation, I will be building on more or less standard readings and concentrating instead on how the texts push us toward them. Along the way I hope to suggest a few new insights into the characters and ideas of the plays I consider, but my real interest is refining the way we understand the generation of these characters and ideas. By applying a structural concern with the way literature comes to achieve meaning to a traditional, referentially derived framework of character and theme analysis, I realize that I shall be making theoretical compromises that are untenable in much recent, especially poststructuralist, thought. Specifically, it might well be questioned why I establish a linguistic basis for one level of meaning, but simply assume the existence of another. I hope to provide a specific answer in the next few pages, but generally I make this and related compromises in the interest of contributing to the four-hundred-year-old tradition of reading Shakespeare. I wish that I could account for how all meaning in one of the plays is produced; but, that being impossible, I think there is some value in a hybrid approach. There certainly is no value in so savagely reducing the scope of Shakespeare's plays that they seem unremarkable.

My approach assumes the existence of what I call exterior and interior systems, conceptions borrowed from standard semiotic theory.[5] Anything we can recognize or otherwise understand must already be held in the mind as a system of conventionally related signs, for it is only by identifying one or more qualities or patterns as part of a larger whole that understanding occurs. Thus we can identify a certain object as a tree only because we already have a mental system to compare with the sensory image. That this mental system is made up of several otherwise independent elements is demonstrated by the fact that we can classify many kinds of images as trees. Real trees may or may not have leaves, and they can be quite small (bonsai trees); the bark can be missing or indistinguishable (as from a distance). It is even possible to identify trees just from the sound of wind whistling through the leaves, and representations of trees can be so identified in an even greater number of ways. The system that allows us to identify some things and representations as trees (or tree representations) contains a series of attributes, none of which are essential, plus various associations (shade, growth, strength, and so on) that give trees whatever significance they hold for specific cultures and individuals.

Any thing or idea that can be recognized has such a system behind it. Some are simple, some extremely complex, but in all cases the system has to be in the mind of the viewer before any comprehension is possible. For my purposes, all of these are exterior systems—exterior because they exist outside of a given narrative. They include everything a reader brings into a work: knowledge of the language in which the text is written; familiarity with ideas, values, stereotypes, and prejudices; understanding of literary conventions, such as generic distinctions, character formation, and standard plots; knowledge of conventional distinctions among various places and times; and so forth.

Simple narratives, such as children's stories, use only a few well-established exterior systems, and they use them in such a straightforward way that little sophistication on the part of the reader is required. But complex narratives depend on their readers to respond in a predictable way to a large number of exterior systems and to a large portion of the signs within them. Not only must the readers associate each sign with the proper system or systems, but each system itself must be understood in a nonidiosyncratic way. For example, holding hands is usually employed as a sign of innocent sexuality and affection; a reader who rather thinks of germs and disease will not be able to respond coherently to a work in which that sign appears.

Actually, few of us could make such a mistake, for whatever our personal attitude toward handholding, we have all been exposed to the communal system, and thus when exposed in a work of art to characters holding hands, most of us would delimit our response or at least give precedence to the public elements, that is, those that we have learned from other works of art and from other public communications. Most sign systems have both personal and public elements, but because those of us who are not psychotic force the private ones into a background, supplementary role, we are able to respond similarly (although not identically) to works of art. And because the public aspects of these types are learned from public sources, it is possible to generalize about their constitution by referring to their use in various documents of the society.[6]

Interior systems, which include characters and anything else intrinsic to the specific work, are built out of exterior systems which the author expects his or her audience to share. They develop in the course of the narrative and have no existence outside of it. Thus a specific character is constructed out of elements taken from various exterior systems, which together give him or her the illusion of reality. Through act 2, "Malvolio" is a particular actor using distinctive gestures, a kind of clothing, and a set of statements and actions—all of which come to suggest one another and to induce us to see a consistent character. The sudden introduction into this system of the opposite of many of these elements makes "Malvolio" hilariously unstable and forces us to restructure the system. Usually, characters, ideological structures, settings, "possible worlds" (the nature and rules of wherever stories are set), and other interior systems avoid such disjunctions, but their independent establishment is an essential task of any narrative, since finally it is the interior systems that give a text whatever reality it achieves.

This distinction between exterior and interior systems is useful for several reasons, but one is that it helps illuminate the basis of a frequent criticism of structuralist and semiotic analyses: that they fail to distinguish good literature from ordinary. Such a problem is inevitable in criticism that concentrates exclusively or almost so on how exterior systems are constituted and used in literature in general. Studies such as Northrop Frye's *Anatomy of Criticism* (1957) and Vladimir Propp's *Morphology of the Folktale* (1958) make no pretense of complete analyses of individual works, and hence do not concern themselves with how these systems are transformed by specific uses. Some others do seem content merely to show the ordinary roots of extraordinary works, but as when the same failing occurs with various other kinds of criticism, the problem is with the critic rather than the approach.

A more justified criticism, from my perspective, is that almost all structuralists and semioticians (Barthes is the best counterexample) define exterior systems as logically organized and logical in their relationships to other systems. Frye, for example, postulates a precise structure of complementary character-plot systems, and many others produce carefully drawn boxes, triangles, circles, and (for lack of a better term) flowcharts.[7] Although some of these are quite compelling, they cannot possibly be accurate accounts of systems that have developed over a substantial period of time, as is the case with all exterior systems of particular consequence to narrative. These systems have been under construction for centuries and usually millennia, and each has been modified dozens of times by substantially different cultures and periods. The resulting systems are not necessarily and probably not even possibly logical, and they can no more be described by a mathematically precise diagram than can a long-established town or city.

The exterior systems that generally control narratives are better seen as clusters of signs which have been associated with each other over a long period of time but which do not necessarily have any "center" or any other consistent structure. Our present system for understanding romantic love was in the fifth century B.C. mainly a vehicle for justifying homosexual liasons between men and adolescent boys. Menander and the playwrights of the Roman republic who followed him introduced heterosexual relationships into the system and also associated the New Comic plot and characters with it. Later Roman writers such as Catullus, Ovid, and Horace gave the system many of its overtones of unnaturalness and violence, and the Christian ascetics who followed profoundly altered its use of sexuality. Subsequent periods (as I will demonstrate in chapters 1 and 2) have made equally substantial additions, the result of which is a disorganized and sometimes contradictory conglomeration of disparate elements. This formlessness and illogic make it difficult for most people to define romantic love in a satisfactory way, but the almost universal ability to recognize and manipulate the system in a variety of contexts shows that it is nevertheless very firmly implanted in most of our minds. There is, then, no true denotation or other absolute hierarchy within exterior systems, and there is no metaphor that can accurately give them a consistent structure.

This study will describe the public elements of a related series of exterior systems, then show how these systems are manipulated, combined, and opposed to help form the interior systems that control our response to a group of Shakespeare's plays. The systems I have chosen are among the most commonly and prominently used in Renaissance literature: those employed to represent sexual relationships, including romantic love. Since these systems mutually define one another—it is impossible to define true love without reference to relationships based on seduction, domination, and lust, and the roles of lover and lady have meaning only when opposed to those of seducer, whore, rapist, and witch—these systems form a typology, allowing me to refer to the individual systems as types.

Nineteenth- and twentieth-century criticism has consistently de-emphasized the significance of sexuality in Renaissance thought, usually by sentimentalizing romantic love and separating it from the conflicting types that were used to define it. But even a casual look at the literature shows how important the subject must have been to the reading and playgoing public. Non-comic explorations of the difference between love and various other kinds of relationships are an important concern in every book of both *The Courtier* and *The Faerie Queene;* in every one of Shakespeare's plays, as well as in almost all plays in general; and in every Renaissance sonnet sequence, pastoral romance, and epic. Although, as we shall see, there were many who condemned romantic love, almost all literature takes its value for granted and concerns itself only with whether given relationships fit within this or some other type. In short, the nature of sexual relationships was of exceptional importance throughout the Renaissance, and it is of exceptional importance in Shakespeare's plays, especially those I will examine.

Our own understanding of sexual relationships has been heavily influenced by twentieth-century psychology, and partly as a result we usually see sexuality in terms of the individual psyche and various vague notions of natural development. Even romantic love, which is very highly conventionalized and has been since the ancient Greeks, seems to us a natural expression. We worry ourselves considerably over whether particular relationships are true or false love, thinking the answer reflects an inner reality that is uncontrolled by the barrage of nearly identical representations of each of these types.

We may be right. It is certainly possible that love is a natural emotion that the conventional qualities accurately describe. The important point for this study, however, is not whether love exists or how it develops, but rather that almost all of us recognize its representation though the use of certain conventional qualities (sweaty palms, obsessive interest, etc.) and narrative forms (especially New Comedy, in which a relationship is threatened by some outside force). Whatever the actual status of love and other kinds of sexual relationships, each of the types through which we understand and represent the subject has its own history and independent existence.

Like the Elizabethans, we learn the constitution of these systems through many sources. One is the literature and art of periods before our own (including, of course, the Renaissance), but more importantly we find conventionalized representations of various kinds of relationships a constant fixture of our world. It is difficult to find a popular song or novel that does not allude to these types, and they are equally fundamental to all of the forms of drama, from the most hackneyed soap operas to the most serious plays and movies. All of us thus have considerable practice in their recognition and obviously receive considerable enjoyment from their continual representation.

I do not mean to imply that contemporary (or Renaissance) representations reproduce exactly the types upon which they are based. Significant literature (or film or any other narrative form) always recasts familiar exterior systems into unique and hence seemingly lifelike interior ones. But at the core of any portrayal of a sexual relationship is inevitably a familiar and easily interpreted type (or occasionally types), for otherwise we would have no way to begin to understand the relationship or the characters in it. In just the same way that we begin our understanding of real people by placing them in categories that will eventually seem far too limiting, so we must start to build character on a typical base. As Frye puts it,

Hence when we speak of typical characters, we are not trying to reduce lifelike characters to stock types, though we certainly are suggesting that the sentimental notion of an antithesis between the lifelike character and the stock type is a vulgar error. All lifelike characters, whether in drama or fiction, owe their consistency to the appropriateness of the stock type which belongs to their dramatic function. That stock type is not the character but it is as necessary to the character as a skeleton is to the actor who plays it.[8]

The "sentimental notion" Frye wants to discredit is that characters in literature exist independently of the traditions from which they emerge. For him, as for Aristotle, characters are made interesting and believable through the addition of individuating traits, but without their typical basis they could not be understood at all. The types that Western culture has elaborated for conceptualizing sexuality serve this function for all characters, ideas, and plots related to this subject.

Although the basic elements (that is, the ones that cause us most readily to think we understand the nature of a relationship) usually have interesting histories, I will begin my detailed examination of the types only with the sixteenth century, adding brief descriptions of earlier developments where appropriate (chapter 1). My intention is not to provide a comprehensive history but rather to explain how each of the types important in the sixteenth century was generally understood at the time of its incorporation into Shakespeare's plays.

Even though my interest is in the response of modern readers and audiences to specific plays, the systems through which people in the sixteenth century conceptualized sexual relationships are nevertheless essential, for reasons having to do with the nature of major systems. Such systems develop organically, growing more complex but seldom eliminating what has gone before. Greek and Roman societies shared many types, but those in the latter were made more complex by the inevitable addition of Roman elements to the preexisting Greek types. Some Greek elements disappeared, but in general it is very difficult for living systems to shed outdated elements as long as the culture for whom they were not outdated continues to be studied. The Romans read Greek literature and told themselves stories largely originating there; thus the particular Greek forms of many systems continued to influence the Romans, just as they continue to influence us.

As a result of this continuing influence, Greek representations of sexual relationships seem realistic to us in a way that representations from, say, ancient Babylon or medieval India do not. We also feel at home with the representations of sexual relationships of several other cultural moments, including the Elizabethans. The fact that we see the sexual relationships in Shakespeare's plays as realistic and familiar shows that we still understand at least the basic elements of each system in much the same way as did playgoers in the sixteenth century. We are not Elizabethans, but it is only because there is much of the Elizabethans still in us that we are able to read their works. And so looking at the types they used establishes at least the starting point of any modern response that can make sense of a play.

That Shakespeare's plays reflect commonly held understandings of sexuality is shown by their popularity. Shakespeare himself doubtlessly had numerous essentially private associations related to sexual relationships, for like every member of his audience he had the experiences of his own life to draw on, as well, perhaps, as local or regional variations. Any of these private elements of the systems that found their way into the plays would have been misinterpreted or ignored by most of the original audiences, and just as contemporary playwrights change parts of plays that somehow fail to work, Shakespeare probably revised the most obvious ones away. Some less significant ones almost certainly remain in the texts, where they are ignored as a kind of noise by most readers. Evidently, however, Shakespeare usually struck familiar chords for the members of his original audience; hence their types must be the ones controlling his plays. And since we in the twentieth century can still make sense of the same plays, we must be responding in at least basically similar ways.

We are not responding identically, however, for various recent changes in the types have moved the reading of almost any modern reader away from that of the original audience. These cannot be major, structural changes, for if they were, the relationships built on the affected types would seem defective or perhaps even unintelligible. But even minor changes can have a substantial effect. For example, most aspects of romantic love are common to both us and the Elizabethans, but we assume a much higher intellectual capacity for women than they did. As a result, we must be seeing Shakespeare's bright heroines differently than did the original audience, and we must in general be viewing romantic love differently than did a society that habitually saw women as grossly inferior. Similarly, changes in the relationship of lust to love have changed our understanding of romantic love. For the Elizabethans (as we will see), lust was an inevitable but troubling and dangerous companion to love, but the basic nineteenth-century type for representing true (i.e., romantic) love excludes lust as an attribute, partly because of the popularity of several older theological and philosophical positions, and partly because of such contemporary movements as the redefinition of women as supermoral, sexless creatures and the attempt to insure a "proper" canon for the rapidly widening reading public. Different social movements have this century reassociated sexuality and love, indeed have made them inseparable, thereby changing the type again. But the basic elements predate the particular manifestations in any of the three periods, and they have not been changed by either the total separation or the necessary connection of love and lust. These elements include the valuation of sexual love as the most significant of human relationships, the association of some form of mysticism with the relationship, the use of the idea that love makes a person better and more complete, and the use of the modified New Comic plots and characters that have come to be associated with the type. None of these have changed or probably can change.

It is not within the scope of this study to examine all of the changes relating to sexual relationships that have occurred in the nearly four centuries since Shakespeare flourished. Nor does such an analysis seem to me essential: any changes must have been relatively minor or we would not still be able to enjoy and respond to the plays. My second chapter, then, is not intended as an inclusive account of post-Elizabethan representations of sexuality but rather as a brief review of how the types most significant in Shakespeare's plays have adapted to more recent times. Though this chapter chronicles various minor changes, its main point is to show the continuity of the types: despite constantly adapting to new situations, their core structures remain much the same as they have for hundreds and usually thousands of years.

The remaining five chapters examine the way in which these types help control our ability to respond to a group of comedies and to four tragedies: *Romeo and Juliet, Othello, Troilus and Cressida,* and *Antony and Cleopatra*.[9] These chapters will show how the types plus other familiar external systems are used as the raw material of the internal systems that account for what we perceive as each play.

Any discussion of reader response raises the question of what reader is having the response. While this is not the place fully to consider the history of this complex and central issue, it does seem clear that the major theoreticians in this area have recently been investing less authority in the text and more in the reader. Norman Holland and David Bleich use psychoanalytic concepts to attempt to uncover the motivations and deep structures that control reading.[10] Stanley Fish has abandoned his earlier text-centered position and moved toward poststructuralism, with its denial of any objective meaning in the text and consequent turn to the self as a culturally constituted constantly signifying text.[11]

My position is more conservative, deriving as it does from structuralist and semiotic principles these critics are now post of. I agree that despite readers' and critics' desire to do so, no text can adequately be controlled by a meaning or meanings; like Richards and Brooks, as well as Derrida and Miller, I see this desire to paraphrase as seductive and fulfilling, but deceptive. But it does not follow that because the old Platonic-Horatian model is inadequate, no consistent and demonstrable control on the signification process remains in the text. Active control is exercised constantly, but on the levels of language and exterior systems, not through the paraphrases of characters or themes that readers inevitably form.

The exterior systems through which any individual is able to conceptualize and hence communicate with the surrounding world have personal, familial, and perhaps regional elements, in addition to the public ones shared by the culture at large. Although these private elements influence the ability of readers to respond to representations, it is apparent that competent readers strive to read as much as possible on whatever level of generality they perceive links them with the author. Readers occasionally spin off into galaxies of personal signification, but mostly they try to figure out what the work or author is trying to say—that is, they try to restrict their processing of information to what they perceive as the public level of systems. The exterior systems do not themselves exercise any actual control, and the reader can always choose an idiosyncratic train of signification, just as he or she can choose to take a word in a private way. But the more competent the reader, the more likely it is that such choices will be conscious ones, and the public path eventually retraced or followed simultaneously with the private one.

So most of the time readers choose to suppress private responses in favor of what they perceive (sometimes incorrectly, of course) as correct public ones. Frequently, more than one kind of public response is possible or essential, as with puns or other kinds of ambiguity, but in such cases the control is still with the text, or more precisely, with the reader's willingness to interpret the text through the nonprivate sections of whatever exterior systems the reader believes he or she holds in common with the author.

Once the reader has associated a particular exterior system with a part of a text, it then becomes the basis for the interior systems that account for most of the experience of reading. The creation of these interior systems is the most basic task of any narrative, for they are what give the text a sense of individual identity. There obviously is substantial control on how these systems are formed, for otherwise all readings would be random. But it is equally obvious that reading on this level is far less controlled, as the disparity of interpretations in classrooms and scholarly journals shows. What happens is that while competent readers restrict their reading of exterior systems to make communication possible at all, the pleasure of the text is lost without the exercise of limited freedom on the next level. Thus partly because of the greater indeterminancy of this part of the reading process, and partly because many of the controls that do exist have not been delineated, at least in a precise way, definition of response on the level of interior systems must be a somewhat speculative endeavor.

My analyses of individual plays will be concerned mostly with how a group of exterior systems (my typology of sexual relationships) are recognized and incorporated into interior systems. To the extent that the typology and its application are adequate, I believe that my method will account for how any competent reader deciphers the text to the level of exterior systems. The movement from here to the creation of the interior systems is much less certain, and at this point I rely heavily on the way others have read the plays, assuming that standard readings reflect the creation of basically similar interior systems.

Each of my analyses, then, will define a response that moves from likely for all competent readers (the use of the exterior systems) to possible for some (the formulation of the interior systems). I will defend the former with my typology, the latter with standard readings and the methological tools used to create them. My hope is that such a procedure will shed light both on the plays and on the process we all go through to interpret them, both in ordinary and in critical reading.

There is certainly much more to the reading process than exterior and interior systems. The former especially must, in both their existence and structure, serve important functions for the societies that created them and the individuals who give them use. This study, however, does not attempt to determine the motivational origin of the types I describe, the needs their representation serves, or (except briefly, in the chapter on *Antony and Cleopatra*) the possible deep structures controlling the way they are constituted and employed. Nor is it concerned with the epistemological status of the text and mind. These are very important issues, and I make no pretense here of contributing to the developing arguments about them.

I will be using two terms in what may seem an idiosyncratic manner. *Narrative* is traditionally used to describe literature that is told rather than performed, but like other recent structuralists and semioticians I will be stretching the term to include drama and any other form that represents a story. Although there are many differences between drama and the novel, as there are between any narrative forms, they are more like each other than like any other kinds of communication. Since there is no preexisting term for all the ways of telling a story, *narrative* has had to grow (if somewhat illogically) to fill the need.

By *heroic* characters I mean those whom readers perceive as stronger (in whatever way) and more significant than themselves and than other characters in the narrative—the same as those inhabiting Frye's "high mimetic" mode. This perception cannot be created unless the conflicts within a narrative are between characters who both fit this definition, for a struggle between a hero and a clown or a hero and an ordinary person would be ridiculous rather than heroic. The villains in heroic literature have to be of the same status as the heroes, and hence I call both heroic characters, though only one is the real hero.

The Structure of Love
Representational Patterns and Shakespeare's Love Tragedies

1

The Structure of Love

Then

When Shakespeare and other dramatists looked for models for representing sexual relationships they found a series of well-defined but contradictory types. By the late sixteenth century each of these types was firmly associated with one or more narrative or expository forms, within which other types would make little sense. The marriage of a lecherous young woman and an impotent, tyrannical old man in a fabliau is essential to a form in which we laugh at all the characters; representing either party as genuinely abused and worthy of our sympathy would radically change the structure of the story. Similarly, the woman in a Petrarchan sonnet sequence has to be represented as unyielding to give any reason for those sonnets in the first place, and she has to be worth the effort lest the man's complaints seem absurd or even perverse. But Elizabethan drama in its 1590s form had not been stable long enough to have many fixed traditions, including fixed ways of representing sexual relationships, and as a result its dramatists were in the enviable position of being able to choose among all the existing types.

The type most common in various kinds of expository writing, as well as in some forms of narrative, is what I will label the Ascetic type, after the late Roman social and philosophical movement that provided most of its modern form. As we shall see, our descendant of this type has become much more positive, but the sixteenth-century version served as the chief vehicle for representing the danger and irrationality of sexual passion. Asceticism, which continued to be a cornerstone of Christian theology throughout the sixteenth century, posits a double standard of morality in which the life of the world is accepted and regulated but given a lower moral position than the life

2 / *The Structure of Love*

of the spirit. The focus of this double standard is usually sexuality, which patristic literature views as the most powerful fleshly temptation, and hence our main inducement to abandon spirit and God for world and Satan. As Augustine puts it, the "standing proof" of the extraordinary power of sexuality is that it alone has the power to defy the will and seize control of both body and will:

> But the peculiarity of that passion of lust which we are here discussing is that the soul can neither sufficiently control itself so as to be free from lust, nor in any way control the body when lust takes over the control of sexual excitement in defiance of the will.... Our soul is ashamed because our body, which by its lower nature is subject to the soul, defies the higher nature; whereas in the other passions which resist the soul, there is less shame because, being conquered by a part of itself, the soul can still claim victory for itself.[1]

With sexuality so dangerously independent, it is not surprising that early ascetic commentators attack it, and since most of the writers were male and all of them had the rich traditions of Hebrew, Greek, and Roman misogyny to draw on,[2] it is also not surprising that the ascetics used aspects of these older deprecations of women for their representations of sexual relationships. Adding condemnation of sex itself—which is not a part of the earlier traditions—the ascetics created a type in which intense sexual relationships are foolish because in them a man gives in to his physical desires, demonstrated by his attraction to what is really an unattractive, subhuman creature. The reduction of women to beasts is not an end in itself, but rather a way of portraying relationships with them as unattractive. Hence when Tertullian writes to his "best beloved sisters," his main message is that they should avoid anything that makes them attractive to men, since they are "the devil's gateway," and "all ages are perilled" by their physical allure. And when Chrysostom writes to a man contemplating marriage, the focus is on the irrationality of viewing women as beautiful:

> If you consider what is stored up inside those beautiful eyes, and that straight nose, and the mouth and the cheeks, you will affirm the well-shaped body to be nothing else than a whited sepulchre; the parts within are full of so much uncleanness. Moreover when you see a rag with any of these things on it, such as phlegm, or spittle you cannot bear to touch it with even the tips of your fingers, nay you cannot even endure looking at it; and yet are you in a flutter of excitement about the storehouses and depositories of these things?[3]

Of course, the Church could not condemn women and sex altogether, for both scriptural and practical reasons, but even the *Summa Theologia*, written hundreds of years after the Early Fathers and with as moderate, reasonable a tone as possible, has a very hard time finding anything good to say about either. Aquinas supports marriage because of the necessity for reproduction, but he finds little other value in it for the properly oriented man. After all, how can a woman, who (following Aristotle) is no more than a malformed man, weak in reason and highly susceptible to sin, be useful for more than her reproductive function? Even the female part of reproduction is inferior, since the woman only provides the matter to which the male gives human form, and aside from it, Eve gave Adam nothing that another man could not have more suitably provided. The sexual desire that leads men to reproduce is not evil, according to Aquinas, but since this desire leads to the suspension of rational and temperate intellectual activity, the more reasonable and godly a man is, the less use he will have for women and sex.[4]

Naturally, since women are less reasonable than men, and sex is an irrational, animal desire, women are the more lustful gender. And since lust is Satan's primary weapon for destroying men, women are his natural accomplices, or at least his unwitting tools. For John Bromyard, writing in the fourteenth century, Satan makes the jewels women wear seem attractive so that when a woman dances or walks through a town, "she inflames with the fire of lust—it may be—twenty of those who behold her, damning the souls whom God has created and redeemed at such a cost for their salvation. For this very purpose the Devil thus adorns these females, sending them forth through the town as his apostles, replete with every iniquity, malice, fornication and the like."[5] More ominously, Kramer and Sprenger's *Malleus Maleficarum* (which was eventually used as the authority for prosecuting thousands of accused witches) ends its discussion of why women are more prone to witchcraft than men: "To conclude. All witchcraft comes from carnal lust, which is in women insatiable. . . . Wherefore for the sake of fulfilling their lusts they consort even with devils."[6]

Such an extreme tone is uncommon among significant sixteenth- and seventeenth-century writers, but the view that sexual desire is dangerous and irrational is not. In many cases this Ascetic understanding is defended less in terms of ascetic philosophy than stoicism, which (briefly stated) held that the only true evil in the universe is the chaos of a passionate mind. Such portrayals are less likely to show sex and women as Satan's lure, but they still represent sexual passion as a weakness any rational man should attempt to avoid as much as possible. More's Utopians, for example, admit that pleasure is derived

when the body's parts are renewed and refreshed by food and drink, or when some excess in the body is discharged, as in bowel movements, procreation, or rubbing and scratching some itch. Such sensual pleasures, however, are not delightful in themselves, but only as they resist the encroachment of sickness.... So it is better to reject these pleasures of sense than to be captivated by them. If any man thinks he is happy in the midst of these pleasures, then he must confess that he would be the happiest of men if he should spend his whole life in an unending round of hunger, thirst, itching, followed by eating, drinking, scratching and rubbing.[7]

Noting that "it is impossible to love and be wise," Francis Bacon follows in this same tradition. For him, "great Spirits and great Businesse do keep out this weake Passion," but for those who cannot quite reach this goal of heroic reasonableness, Bacon advises that "they doe best, who if they cannot but admit *Loue,* yet make it keepe Quarter; and seuer it wholly, from their serious Affairs, and Actions of life."[8]

Bacon's contemporary, Robert Burton, is generally more fearful of the consequences of sexual passion than either More or Bacon, though he at first declares that the whole subject of love melancholy is "too light for a divine, too comical a subject, to speak of love-symptoms, too phantastical, and fit alone for a wanton poet, a feeling young love-sick gallant, an effeminate courtier." But after indicating his disdain, he goes on to assert that passionate love is really "burning lust, a disease, phrensy, madness, hell [which subverts] kingdoms, overthrows cities, towns, families; mars, corrupts, and makes a massacre of men; thunder and lightning, wars, fires, plagues, have not done that mischief to mankind, as this burning lust, this brutish passion."[9]

Despite Burton's worries, the main idea in the Ascetic type is not so much evil as weakness: love reflects an inability to control one's sensual nature and a poverty of true nobility, rather than inveterate sinfulness. Men in love are fit for laughter, not fear, and their proper literary place is in comedy, which according to Heywood treats either clownishness or "else it intreates of love, deriding foolish inamorates, who spend their ages, their spirits, nay themselves, in the servile and ridiculous imployments of their mistresses."[10]

As a result, in an Ascetic relationship the woman is presented in terms of traditional misogyny—unreasonable, inconstant, devious, and tending toward lust and sin—and the man as exceedingly foolish for loving her. In *Euphues: The Anatomy of Wit,* for example, Lucilla is beautiful and knows all the courtly rhetoric, but she is congenitally inconstant and finally gives her much-sought virginity to a man who is physically deformed, doltish, and poor. Before she makes this ridiculous choice, Euphues damages his friendship with Philautus by trying to steal Lucilla from him, but despite this violation of his friend's trust, Euphues is portrayed less as evil than as weak and immature. Because he is "of more wit than wrath and yet of more wrath than wisdom," Euphues allows his sensual passions to get the better of his rationality. Only when he has seen Lucilla's inconstancy does he realize that friendship with another man is more reasonable, constant, and valuable than a love affair with a woman. Euphues and Philautus are finally reconciled by their mutual revulsion from Lucilla and their pledge to remain constant to each other and to the manly activities of government and learning.[11]

A related example is the tale of Jocundo and the king of Lombardy in *Orlando Furioso,* in which the two principals' wives swear constancy to their husbands but take a "beggar's brat" and a dwarf as lovers. After a long search, Jocundo and the king are forced to conclude that their wives "are as chaste and honest as the best" and that they were foolish in the first place to upset themselves about a frailty their wives could not help.[12]

The complement to this extremely negative view of sexual relationships appears in dozens of stories of selfless, Griselda-like wives and of female martyrs (including many saints whose devotion is to their faith rather than an earthly husband). The relationships in these stories are as positive as those discussed earlier are negative, but in fact both project the same view of what sexual relationships should and should not be like. Both suggest a positive view in which a woman understands her irremediable weakness as a female, and thus never tries to dominate her man, who in turn makes every decision, never shows more than a master-slave affection for his woman, and holds absolute power, even to abuse. Both likewise imply a negative representation in which a weak man's lust causes him to give control to a woman, whose inconstancy, lust, and general depravity bring shame or destruction upon one or both of them.

The Ascetic type, then, appears in two complementary forms. Though most sixteenth-century literature still read primarily represents sexual relationships through other types, the Ascetic was much the most commonly used type throughout the period. There were scores of tracts, sermons, and stories all through the period taking one side of the question or the other, as indicated by the titles of a few representative works: the anonymous *The deceyte of women, to the instruction and ensample of all men, yonge and olde, newly corrected* (1560); Thomas Deloney's *The Garland of Good Will* (1593); Thomas Bentley's *The Monument of Matrones: conteining seuen seuerall Lamps of Virginitie* (1582); Peter Colse's *Penelopes Complaint: Or. A Mirrour for Wanton Minions* (1596); and Anthony Givson's *A Womans Woorth, defended against all the men in the world* (1599).[13]

As popular as the Ascetic type (including both its positive and its negative representation of relationships) was in the sixteenth century, it had relatively little impact on heroic literature, partly because other types of relationships were more fashionable. A more compelling reason, however, is that the central figures in heroic literature are always strong characters, though some are good, some evil; otherwise, a heroic struggle would be impossible. Any kind of relationship, sexual or otherwise, that is defined primarily in terms of the weakness of one or both parties is thus inappropriate to this mode. There is a world of difference between Lucilla and Goneril, or Griselda and Rosalind: the women developed in terms dictated by the Ascetic tradition are weak (in most ways) and inconsequential, while the heroic ones are much stronger and much more interesting.

Put another way, the system of signs that makes up the Ascetic type does not include a narrative pattern that can be used to create strong characters, except to the extent that obedience and chastity are strengths in the positive form of the type. In the more common negative form the system specifically associates weakness with both male and female. As a result, literary representations based mostly on this type, such as the medieval fabliaux, are mostly comedies in the classical sense of the term: works that treat the foibles of lower-class and middle-class characters.

Thus the only significant function the Ascetic type can serve in heroic literature is as a partial or discredited interpretation of otherwise strong characters. In *The Changeling*, for example, Beatrice-Joanna is partly characterized as lustful, inconstant, and weak—all feminine attributes of the Ascetic type—but she is also described as a strong woman unwilling to give up the man she loves for one chosen for her by her father. Eventually, the tragedy of the play is that she becomes the Ascetic creature that De Flores asserts throughout to be her true identity. His lust for Beatrice-Joanna is sustained by the knowledge that there are "daily precedents" of women "beyond all reason" loving men as deformed and repulsive as himself (1.1.76–88), and he defines her switch from Alonzo to Alsemero in terms not of true love winning out over parental pressure but of inveterate female inconstancy. After watching Beatrice-Joanna and Alsemero talk, he tells us:

> I have watch'd this meeting, and do wonder much
> What shall become of t'other; I'm sure both
> Cannot be serv'd unless she transgress; happily
> Then I'll put in for one: for if a woman
> Fly from one point, from him she makes a husband,
> She spreads and mounts then like arithmetic,
> One, ten, a hundred, a thousand, ten thousand,
> Proves in time subtler to an army royal.
> (2.2.57–64)[14]

For him, women can only be defined in terms of Ascetic irrationality, inconstancy, and geometrically expanding lust. But if Beatrice-Joanna were always represented in terms of this type, the play would have little emotional interest for us, since we would never in any way identify with the central character; it is only because we sometimes see a stronger character that we are able to view the play as tragic.

A more familiar use of the Ascetic type is a partial characterization in the Duchess's relationship with Antonio in the *Duchess of Malfi*. That relationship seems interesting to us as readers because it is initially described in terms of three very incompatible types, which taken together make it seem complex. The most obvious of these is what I will later define as the Petrarchan type, the type that allows the relationship to seem like true love. This type is stressed throughout the play, but one excerpt from the Duchess's oft-quoted wooing speech will illustrate the point:

> Go, go brag
> You have left me heartless—mine is in your bosom,
> I hope 'twill multiply love there.
> (1.1.452–54)[15]

Like any other Petrarchan lover, her love is genuine, and she feels she cannot survive unless it is reciprocated.

The next type used early in the *Duchess* is not directly related to love at all but rather to political power. As the Duchess tells us before she even mentions Antonio,

> If all my royal kindred
> Lay in my way unto this marriage,
> I'd make them my low foot-steps.
> (1.1.341–43)

The Duchess in this speech sounds a little like Tamburlaine, presenting herself as an overreacher, unbound by the established hierarchies. In these terms her relationship with Antonio is merely a means for her to assert her absolute independence from the authority of her brothers or anyone else.

In the same speech she goes on to compare her violation of her brothers' interdiction to soldiers achieving "almost impossible action" when most pressed by danger, but she then ends with a comment that radically subverts all of the previous overreacher and military imagery: "Let old wives report / I winked and chose a husband" (1.1.348–49). This ten word comment is an excellent example of how quickly a Renaissance author can draw upon his audience's knowledge of the Ascetic type, and how willing these authors are to do so even immediately after a contradictory characterization. Far from the fearless overreacher or the inspired Petrarchan lover, the Duchess of this portrayal is just as lustful and irrational as any other widow represented in terms of this type, willing to have anyone as mate, provided that she has him immediately. If this were the only Ascetic representation of the Duchess, her ascription of it to "old wives" rather than herself would deflate its possible significance. But the Duchess describes herself in much the same way later in the scene:

> This is flesh and blood, sir;
> 'Tis not the figure cut in alabaster

> Kneels at my husband's tomb. Awake, awake, man!
> I do here put off all vain ceremony,
> And only do appear to you a young widow
> That claims you for her husband, and like a widow,
> I use but half a blush in't.
>
> (1.1.454–60)

Widows are always lustful from the Ascetic point of view because they, unlike daughters and wives, are not under the control of men and can thus express their natural inclination. If the Duchess were represented exclusively in terms of this understanding, she would not seem strong and independent enough to elicit sympathy, and the plot could never produce any real pathos. But like most Renaissance plays, the *Duchess* uses the Ascetic only sporadically, as a means of making a character seem more complex and "human." Although unable to generate a heroic plot, the Ascetic stands on the periphery of many, and the economy with which it is suggested indicates that the Ascetic view of women and sexual relationships was never far from the Elizabethan consciousness.

Another type that was never far from the Elizabethan mind is the Seduction, which as the name implies is the type for representing relationships defined primarily by a man's attempt to convince a woman to have sex with him. The reverse of this ancient type is possible, as when Scilla pleads with Glaucus in "Scilla's Metamorphosis," or when Venus "like a bold-fac'd suiter 'gins to woo" Adonis in *Venus and Adonis*,[16] but in such cases part of the erotic content is that the usual pattern is being reversed. The reader, in other words, interprets the interior gender roles in terms of a preexisting exterior orientation, which is that the male will sue and the female resist. Most representations of sexually aggressive women are through the Ascetic, where the insatiability of women is a cliché, or the Emasculating, the type associated with Circe and other castrating women.

In general, the Seduction type has changed very little for us, so the elements of this exterior system continue to seem obvious. The male is always false, especially in his use of rhetoric, even if in some earlier or later part of the narrative his love for the woman is represented as true (and hence shifted into a different type). This falseness is such an integral part of the type that we read it into a character's words regardless of their possible validity in another context. Thus when Leander tells Hero that "My words shall be as spotlesse as my youth, / Full of simplicitie and naked truth" (*Hero and Leander* 1.207–8),[17] we read the claim as a lie and expect more to follow, not because he has lied before, but because the situation—that is, the Seduction type—demands that we view it so. Few would disagree with his statement a few lines later that

> Virginitie, albeit some highly prise it,
> Compar'd with marriage, had you tried them both,
> Differs as much, as wine and water doth.
> (1.262–64)

But whether the statement is true is not the issue as we approach this or similar arguments; when part of a Seduction relationship, such rhetoric is always read as false, as a maneuver in a battle rather than a claim of truth.

Another defining element of the type is that the relationship is represented as comic and nondestructive, rather than tragic and evil. Many relationships, of course, especially in Victorian literature, represent the woman as genuinely harmed and often destroyed by being duped into sex, but while such relationships follow some aspects of the Seduction type (such as the woman's initial unwillingness and the man's falseness), in most respects they are part of another system, the Rape. This type, which is used in such sixteenth-century works as *The Rape of Lucrece* or *Comus* (where no harm actually comes to the Lady, but its potential is powerfully evoked), creates a relationship that seems perverse and destructive, not erotic, or at least not erotic in any usual way. Seduction relationships, on the other hand, do not seem perverse and do seem erotic and humorous because the woman is not represented as hurt in any significant way. Either she successfully resists advances that we know all along are doomed to failure, such as Hammond's courting of Rose and Jane in the *Shoemaker's Holiday* or the female speaker's rejection of male rhetoric in Campion's "Think'st Thou to Seduce Me Then"; or—more commonly—she really wants the sex after all, even if she does not know it at the time the seduction is occurring. The woman's ultimate willingness to have sex allows us either to identify with the male as he leads the woman to what is actually good for her, or to see the whole struggle as artificial, as a mating dance in which the woman's coyness is as false as the male's arguments. Marlowe's Hero is a good example; she thinks she should continue to refuse Leander, especially inasmuch as he turned up naked and uninvited on her doorstep, then chased her into her bed. Nevertheless

> Treason was in her thought,
> And cunningly to yeeld her selfe she sought.
> Seeming not woon, yet woon she was at length,
> In such warres women use but halfe their strength.
> (*Hero and Leander* 2.293–96)

Campion's "I Care Not for These Ladies" describes a similar woman,

> Who, when we court and kisse,
> She cries, forsooth, let go:
> But when we come where comfort is,
> She will never say no.[18]

Behind this view of female coyness is, of course, the misogynistic ideas that women do not know what they want, that they should be controlled by men, and—ultimately—that they are sexual animals who violate their own natures by refusing sex. These ideological foundations show themselves most clearly in the rudimentary Seduction relationships in fabliaux, such as the "Miller's Tale," where Alisoun, who is earlier compared to a variety of animals, is seduced partly by Nicholas's absurdly limited arguments, but mostly by his clever strategy of having "prively caught hire by the queynte" as a preface to his pleas.[19]

Similarly, in the *Decameron*'s "Third Day, Tenth Story," Rustico seduces Alibech by convincing her that sex is the way insistent male devils are forced back where they belong, fiery female hells, and she responds not with outrage, but with an ever-increasing need for devils. In another context, we might view this relationship as a horrible violation of a girl's trust, but the presence of various comic elements (such as the religion-sex puns) leads us to conceptualize the relationship in terms of the Seduction type, and hence we read the girl's initial trust and virtue as no more sacrosanct than Rustico's clever argument.

Even closer to the idea that women want and enjoy sex even when forced is the Seduction relationship in the "Reeve's Tale," where the daughter's response to waking up to find one of the students raping her is to fall in love with him and help him completely humiliate her own father. Since she is not represented as harmed by the relationship, we read it as Seduction rather than Rape, and thus most of us are able to view the story as one of Chaucer's funniest—despite the horror of the student's actions in almost any other context.

Besides false male rhetoric and female coyness, the most repeated elements of the Seduction type in the sixteenth and seventeenth centuries are the carpe diem motif and the pastoral setting, the former as a part of the false rhetoric and the latter as another way of insuring our perception of the seduction as nondestructive. The carpe diem motif, of course, is not necessarily associated with Seduction relationships in Latin or Medieval literature, but its repeated use in this way in the Renaissance so identified the old Epicurean idea with sex and general excess that its original orientation was lost. *England's Helicon* alone contains dozens of poems employing all four elements of the Seduction type (all of the poems in this anthology have a pastoral setting), among them Marlowe's shepherd imploring a nymph (a term implying sexual eagerness) to live with him and be his love, and her reply (probably provided by Ralegh) that

> If all the world and love were young,
> And truth in every sheepherd's tongue,

> These pretty pleasures might me move
> To live with thee, and be thy love.[20]

Herrick's speaker advises virgins to gather rosebuds while they can and Corinna to get out into the May morning, Marvell's twists the form by insisting that it is the lack of a timeless pastoral paradise that makes immediate sex necessary, and Donne's (in "Elegy XIX") makes the woman's body the pastoral paradise. Jonson's Volpone uses all of the form but the pastoral setting to try to seduce Celia, and Shakespeare uses all four elements (but with the sex roles reversed) in *Venus and Adonis,* and all but the setting in many sonnets (but especially in the first seventeen) and in various comedies. The Seduction type appears in virtually all extended pastoral lyrics and romances, as well as in the lyrics and plays of almost every significant author. Though much more limited in scope than most other types, the Seduction is nevertheless an exceptionally common Elizabethan representation of sexual relationships, and because of the type's short and sharply defined list of elements, is probably its most easily identifiable.

The Ascetic finds its home in sermons, philosophical treatises, and fabliaux, and the Seduction is the type of pastoral romances and some fabliaux. Neither, however, produces characters who are heroic enough to structure the relationships in Renaissance romance-epics. Four other types serve that function, all of them derived ultimately from the classical epics and their representation of a hero as one who earns his renown by constantly striving to complete a sufficiently heroic task. In the type most clearly based on the epic understanding of heroic character, the Epic, a sexual relationship is represented as one of the rewards for heroic action. That is, one of the ways texts employing this type indicate to the reader that an action of the central character is positive (heroic) and complete is by providing a sexual relationship as one of his rewards. Because sleeping with a woman is not an object the hero strives for, but rather a symbol of his completion of a task she neither gives nor participates in, there is never any sense that the male is dominated by the female or by his sexual desire, and hence no reason to view the relationship as perverse or dangerous.

All three classical epics build toward such a sexual reward, represented as a future or resumed marriage. Odysseus wants to return to Penelope, but his relationship with her is described in terms not of love or even sexual passion but of property: she, his kingdom, his home, and his son are all his possessions, and he looks at them as the rewards he will be granted for winning his numerous battles. Aeneas' future relationship with Lavinia is even less passionate and more obviously a reward, and even in the *Iliad,* which depends less on a single hero than the others, the Greek objective is the recovery of Helen.

Since the central figures in Renaissance romance-epics are always influenced by the Petrarchan glorification of love, they are never exactly like their classical counterparts, but the same absence of sexual passion as a motivating force is still evident. Britomart, for example, is first motivated to take up arms by her desire to find her true love, a situation that could not have occurred before the development of courtly love. But while she is on her several adventures, Spenser has her seldom mention or even think of Artegal: it is this singleminded devotion to a project not involving love that is the mark of the Epic type. A better example in the *Faerie Queene* is the Redcrosse-Una relationship: these two characters seldom indicate any love for each other before the last canto, but there is never any doubt that they will eventually marry. And perhaps the best example of an Epic relationship occurs near the conclusion of the *Lusiads,* where the goddess Tethys offers herself as reward for Vasco da Gama's successful mission, and provides an island full of frolicsome nymphs for his crew, all of which is justified as "compensation in full for all their arduous experiences." Camoëns goes on to state explicitly the centerpiece of the epic and Epic view: "It is thus that life reserves to the latter end its reward for deeds of outstanding bravery and daring: only when fully earned can it carry with it resounding fame and a great and glorious name."[21] Sex, according to Camoëns, is not a positive goal in itself; it is simply the natural and acceptable reward—like public acclamation or a material gift—for a completed mission. When enjoyed as a reward for success, sex is compatible with that eternal goal of the epic figure, resounding fame. But when enjoyed before completion of the goal it is, as we shall see, contrary to both the idea of the epic hero and the progress of the epic plot.

The Epic representation of positive sexual relationships is ideally suited for heroic literature because it allows the participants to be associated with strength, but it is also very limited by its inability to develop relationships fully before the conclusion, when it is time for the rewards to be doled out. Whatever intellectual, social, and political reasons there may have been for the development of courtly love, its way of representing sexual relationships, which I will call the Petrarchan type, solved an obvious narrative problem by expanding the role positive relationships could play in a heroic narrative. And the Petrarchan type solved the problem by making a single change in the Epic system: instead of insisting that a sexual relationship be generated by some desire unrelated to it, the Provençal school allowed sexual love rather than ambition or love of Christ to be the desire that generates and thus organizes the heroic actions that define epics and romances. Chrétien de Troyes's Lancelot is so much in love with Guinevere that he scarcely remembers his own name and is willing to abase himself even for the chance of helping her. To view such a character as other than ludicrous and base would have been impossible before the development of courtly love. But in *Lancelot,* as in the numerous romances which imitated it, such singleminded devotion to a woman is not only honorable at the onset but is the source of increased honor throughout the text; love dominates Lancelot, but it is also love that gives him direction and gives him the strength to conquer his foes.[22]

By making love and honor compatible, courtly love rejects the ascetic view that sexual passion is always destructive to honor. This rejection is not as complete as it seems, however, for courtly love still does not make sexual attraction positive in itself. Rather, like any other passion, it is good only to the extent that it leads a man to glory and personal improvement. Like anger or pride in martial ability, sexual passion can be destructive if pursued for its own sake. Not all sexual relationships are positive and honor producing, therefore, and thus one of the necessary tasks for the Provençal writers was to distinguish among the many possible kinds.

The clearest such categorization is that of Andreas Capellanus, who in the *Art of Courtly Love* lists the types of women a man might meet when he turns his attentions to love: "The most laudable are those women who when anybody asks for admittance, learn by dilligent inquiry what he deserves who seeks to come in by the open door and how good a character he has; and after they are fully convinced of a man's worth they admit the worthy ones with all honor, but drive the unworthy ones away from Love's palace." Those "common women who never refuse any man" are much less admirable, while the least acceptable are those who "never open to anybody who knocks but deny to everyone an entrance into Love's palace."[23]

Andreas's assertion that chastity is worse than whorishness is typical of the playful rebelliousness of the Provençal school, but the structure of the typology, if not Andreas's exact description of each member, is generally applicable to the basic narrative pattern of all courtly love literature. In this pattern, a lover falls in love with a lady (either through his own volition or the actions of Cupid), struggles in some way to win honor and her favor, and finally enjoys a suitable reward for his labors.

For Andreas and others in the Provençal tradition, the reward is twofold: first the lover is ennobled by love, and second, he wins the sexual favors of his lady. Of these, the first is much the more important, because it is ennoblement that gives love the positive value it lacks in the Ascetic type. *Lancelot,* for example, develops the idea that love is a noble order, selection to which is a sign of virtue and special worth. And Andreas's speaker and his various characters are often explicit about how love makes a man more noble, as in this list:

Now it is the effect of love that a true lover cannot be degraded with any avarice. Love causes a rough and uncouth man to be distinguished for his handsomeness; it can endow a man even of the humblest birth with nobility of character; it blesses the proud with humility; and the man in love becomes accustomed to performing many services gracefully for everyone. O what a wonderful thing is love, which makes a man shine with so many virtues and teaches everyone, no matter who he is, so many good traits of character!

(p. 31)

Later, a character seeking his lady's love declares simply that "all men agree that no one does a good or courteous deed unless it is derived from the fount of love." But when he tells his lady that she should grant his suit so that he will be impelled toward noble deeds, she replies that "before you ask for such a gift you must exert yourself to do the deeds which are considered worthy of the rewards you are asking for" (pp. 40–41). The two characters' attitudes reflect the typical structure of twelfth-century courtly love relationships: a man who serves love in serving a woman will be ennobled in a very important way, but only when he has produced worthy deeds will the lady grant a sexual reward.

The sexual conclusion, then, is the symbol of the lover's ennoblement, and the lady who causes a lover to perform the deeds that prove his nobility then rewards him appropriately, allows the full development of the desire-struggle-reward pattern and earns Andreas's highest accolade. A whorish woman, on the other hand, allows a lover to go straight from desire to reward, thereby excluding the most important part of the process, the ennobling service to love and the lady. And the woman who disdains love altogether, is more perverse still: she either cuts off the narrative at the desire stage, or, if she permits a man to serve her, allows the proof of worthiness without any possibility of the appropriate reward.

The Italian followers of the Provençal writers made one substantial ideological change in the Petrarchan type, but they did not alter the basic desire-struggle-reward structure that determines how the type will fit into narratives. The change, for Dante, Petrarch, and others of this later tradition, is to make the lady at least partially a symbol. Consequently, the lover's reward for serving both the lady and the idealization she represents is often some sort of religious experience instead of sex. Beatrice eventually brings Dante before the face of God, and Petrarch hopes (in sonnet 61 especially) that Laura's pity on his lifetime of mostly virtuous love for her will be rewarded by her acting as a Mary-like intercessor between the poet and Christ.

This partial idealization of the lady was made complete by the Florentine Neoplatonists, whose ideas filtered into mainstream literary thought mainly through Castiglione's *Il Cortegiano*. For them, "love is nothing but a certain desire to enjoy beauty," and the beauty of a particular woman is caused by an "effluence of the divine goodness." If a man can reasonably contemplate this beauty without allowing his sensual nature to lead him to lust, he will be rewarded by movement up the Neoplatonic ladder of love toward a vision of divine beauty itself:

> The soul, aflame with the most holy fire of true divine love, flies to unite itself with the angelic nature; and not only completely abandons the senses, but has no longer any need of reason's discourse; for, transformed into an angel, it understands all things intelligible, and without any veil or cloud views the wide sea of divine beauty, and receives it into itself, enjoying that supreme happiness of which the senses are incapable.[24]

This view of the proper sexual relationship is a long way from that of the Provençals, but Andreas's typology still holds. Dante and Petrarch consider sex as an improper reward for the service of love and a lady, but had Beatrice and Laura refused to act as the intercessors with God that both poets saw them as serving, they would have resembled Andreas's most dangerous woman, the one who unnaturally refuses to allow or acknowledge the ennobling of her lover. The Neoplatonists likewise depend on the lady to make herself available for contemplation, and they are so afraid of beautiful but lecherous women that they define away their existence by asserting beautiful women to be by nature virtuous.[25]

While Andreas's, Dante's, Petrarch's, and Castiglione's courtly lovers all work for specific, if dissimilar rewards, English courtly love sonnet sequences offer no such definite conclusions. English sequences, in fact, move wildly from one tradition to another, sometimes imaging the lady as an ethereal being whose resolute chastity will help move the lover to moral and spiritual betterment, then in an adjacent sonnet viewing her as the quarry in a Seduction game. Similarly, the same lover can be despondent or happy, assertive or servile, true or false. The obvious reason for this variability is that writing courtly love sonnets was not as serious an activity for the English writers as for Dante and Petrarch. By the 1590s there had been several hundred thousand sonnets written on the Petrarchan model in Europe, so that by the time the tradition began to flourish in England, sonnet writing was a way of demonstrating wit and literary competence, but no longer a form that could be used without calling attention to itself. The Petrarchan model was much more hackneyed for the Elizabethans than detective stories are for us; as a result, the better Elizabethan sequences never take themselves completely seriously and seldom allow their speakers to remain long in any particular stance.[26] Instead, the speakers make rapid and unannounced changes, helping make these sequences seem more like collections of poems than unified narratives.

But despite this seeming independence, both the individual poems and the sequences as wholes are still narrative in form and still closely related to the structure of earlier courtly love literature. English sonnets are part of a highly conventionalized genre, or put in different terms, sixteenth-century love sonnets are a sign system in which the constituent signs are used so commonly and so exclusively with that form that the use of even a single sign is often enough to suggest the whole system. Hence a single image in a sonnet comparing a woman's eyes to the sun implies much more about the relationship between the narrator and the woman than could an image outside of the system, such as, say, a comparison of the woman's agility to that of a fine horseman. The latter is a true metaphor in the sense that it impels us to determine a similarity between woman and horseman, that is, establish an interior system different from any exterior one we brought to the text. The eyes-sun image, on the other hand, is a sign within a preestablished exterior system, and when we read it in a sonnet we know that the narrator has at some time in the past fallen in love with the woman and is at present trying to impress her, an action that will lead to his betterment as an individual and perhaps to some demonstration of her affection, even if only a smile. Even if the sonnet itself does not tell us when the narrator fell in love, or how he is trying to impress her, or what reward he will eventually receive, all of the elements of the desire-struggle-reward pattern are nevertheless implied by the use of an image closely linked to the system. No courtly love sonnet can escape from its narrative heritage.

The narrative pattern behind sonnets is important because it is through this pattern that alternative views of the courtly relationship are possible. Most English sonnets are either descriptions like the hypothetical example above or simple complaints against the lady's resolute disdainfulness, the staple subjects of the Petrarchan type.[27] Other, more interesting, sonnets and groups of sonnets play upon a useful contradiction in the courtly tradition as received by the Elizabethans: although all courtly relationships exist in terms of the desire-struggle-reward pattern, the most positive relationship in the Italian tradition is in some respects very close to the most negative relationship of the Provençal tradition. Specifically, the chaste woman of most Elizabethan sequences is analogous to Beatrice, Laura, and the Neoplatonic mirror of the divine, but she is also the Provençal refuser of love, the unnatural frustrator of all courtly activity. Thus a relationship dominated by a chaste woman can and usually does imply the fulfillment of the narrative pattern, but always implicit is the possibility of viewing the relationship as a perverse frustration of it.

The difference between the positive and negative views of the courtly relationship is the possibility of reward: there must be some kind of potential reward for the persevering lover if the relationship is to be seen as normal. In most sonnets, this reward is some sort of vaguely implied self-improvement that the lover can expect, but in each of the major sequences, more specific rewards are developed. One way of looking at these sequences is in terms of these rewards, for as they change so does the particular relationship being developed. *Astrophel and Stella* and *Delia*, for example, both open with sonnets intimating that the lover's reward is the sequence itself. As Daniel's speaker puts it, "Oh had she not been fair and thus unkind, / My muse had slept, and none had known my mind" (sonnet 6).[28]

Later, however, the speakers of both sequences imply the possibility of a sexual reward, especially Astrophel, who more than once (see sonnet 69, for example) seems convinced he is about to enjoy his lady sexually, only to be crushed shortly thereafter. Thus the lady is first the inspirer of created beauty, certainly consistent with movement up the Neoplatonic ladder, but then a sex object, for the Neoplatonists a sure sign of sensuality and movement away from God. In other cases, the reward strikes a middle position or at least one different from either of these. A good example is sonnet 41 of *Astrophel and Stella*, where the lover tells us that when "Stella lookt on, and from her heavenly face / Sent forth the beames," he became the best soldier in the field. Similar examples abound.[29]

Of the rewards listed above, sex is by far the least common, for the Stellas and Delias of the courtly world hardly ever smile, let alone offer stronger encouragements. The result of this resolute chastity is countless vague complaints, but also an occasional specific characterization of a relationship as perverse. The first Englishman to employ this type of courtly relationship is Thomas Wyatt, who produced several poems that in effect demand sex as the price of further attention by the lover (numbers 34 and 45 for example).[30] Sidney employs the same type when he has Astrophel happen upon the sleeping Stella:

> Have I caught my heav'nly jewell,
> Teaching sleepe most faire to be?
> Now will I teach her that she,
> When she wakes, is too too cruell. . . .
>
> See the hand which waking gardeth,
> Sleeping, grants a free resort:
> Now will I invade the fort;
> Cowards *Love* with losse rewardeth.
>   (song 2, stanzas 1 and 4)[31]

The tone of this poem is playful, and Astrophel does not, of course, abuse his lady, though he does steal a kiss and call himself "Foole, more foole, for no more taking." The fact that force could even be suggested, however, indicates the fundamental difference between the relationship here and in sonnet 41. Rape is never a noble action, and Astrophel's consideration of such a method of providing a reward for his desire and struggle indicates the perversity of the relationship in this particular representation.

The source of this perversity is delineated in the fifth song, where Astrophel asserts that Stella is a witch, then goes on to explain the accusation:

> But murder, private fault, seemes but a toy to thee,
> I lay then to thy charge unjustest Tyrannie,
> If Rule by force without all claime a Tyran showeth,
> For thou doest lord my heart, who am not borne thy slave,
> And which is worse, makes me most guiltlesse torments have,
> A rightfull Prince by unright deeds a Tyran groweth.
> Lo you grow proud with this, for tyrans make folke bow:
> Of foule rebellion then I do appeach thee now;
> Rebell by Nature's law, Rebell by law of reason,
> Thou, sweetest subject, wert borne in the realme of Love,
> And yet against thy Prince thy force dost dayly prove:
> No vertue merits praise, once toucht with blot of Treason. . . .
> What, is not this enough? nay farre worse commeth here;
> A witch I say thou art, though thou so faire appeare;
> For I protest, my sight never thy face enjoyeth,
> But I in me am chang'd, I am alive and dead:
> My feete are turn'd to rootes, my hart becommeth lead,
> No witchcraft is so evill, as which man's mind destroyeth.
>
> (5.55–66, 73–78)

The Stella of this song is unnatural because she has refused to offer the appropriate reward once the lover has proved himself, that is, admit she is a subject of the "realme of Love" and give in to Astrophel. The argument is a common one for Petrarchan lovers, but the mention of a metamorphosis suggests specific literary witches, such as Alcina of *Orlando*.[32] The result is a relationship that seems perverse, for Astrophel's rooted feet and leaden heart show he is losing his manhood, which for the Renaissance is usually conceived in terms of active qualities—bravery, physical and intellectual strength, courtesy, the performance of heroic deeds. Stella (in this poem) is Astrophel's Alcina, and her evil has incapacitated his feet, heart, and mind, leaving him as little a man as the trees, stones, and beasts that Alcina's victims become. The relationship portrayed in this song is the opposite extreme of Andreas's ennobling service of love; love here has no value and in fact destroys the value that existed previously, stripping the lover even of his manhood and humanity. Or, in the terms with which we have been dealing, the Stella of this song is worse even than Andreas's refuser of love, for she has dominated her lover to the point where he desires but can no longer struggle, and thus not only fails to gain nobility but loses what he had to begin with. Like the knights turned to inanimate objects on Alcina's island, the Astrophel of this song views himself as under the unnatural command of a Circe-like witch. Circe figures will be discussed in detail shortly, but for the moment it is enough to note that a courtly relationship in which the lady is portrayed as frustrating the conclusion of the narrative pattern is fundamentally different from a relationship in which the lady's resolute chastity leads the lover to ennobling deeds or a higher rung on the ladder of love. The basic situation—a woman eternally refusing the sexual advances of a man—is the same for both, but one truncates the narrative pattern and calls into question the lover's manhood, while the other allows for some sort of completion and reaffirms manhood through whatever ennoblement the completion provides.

This structural ambiguity provided Shakespeare with a narrative device often employed in the plays, as I shall demonstrate in subsequent chapters, but two of his most innovative uses of this device occur in his sonnet sequence. Since the lover's irrationality and inability to keep an even keel in the stormy sea of his own tears is a cliché of the form, complaints such as Astrophel's are hard to take seriously, especially given the occasional non-Petrarchan poems suggesting the lover's desire to rape or seduce his lady. In his first seventeen sonnets Shakespeare avoids making his speaker clichéd or a special pleader by making the lady a man and the narrator an observer rather than the main participant. The result is a more rational-sounding complaint against unnatural chastity than can ever occur in the normal context. Sonnet 10, for example, describes the young man's refusal to marry as self-murder and irrational hatred of everyone, including the self:

> For shame deny that thou bear'st love to any,
> Who for thyself art so unprovident.
> Grant, if thou wilt, thou art belov'd of many,
> But that thou none lov'st is most evident;
> For thou art so possess'd with murd'rous hate,
> That 'gainst thyself thou stick'st not to conspire.
> (ll.1–6)

There is nothing in these lines that is not also used by Sidney's and Daniel's self-serving lovers, but since the context here is considerably different from that of the ordinary Petrarchan sonnet, the argument suddenly seems sensible and moderate. No one fills the place of the lover in this poem, and the resulting lack of self-interest in the argument makes the young man's chastity seen genuinely perverse.[33]

20 / *The Structure of Love*

Perhaps a more interesting attempt to make perverse a Petrarchan-like relationship occurs in the "Dark Lady" sonnets. The lady of these sonnets is the opposite of her counterparts in other sequences in that she is not beautiful and is identified with unfaithfulness or even whorishness. Shakespeare sometimes emphasizes the ways in which the Dark Lady is different from the ordinary, as in the light parody of Petrarchan conventions in number 130 ("My mistress' eyes are nothing like the sun"), but in the next sonnet, it is similarity to the perverse interpretation that is the subject:

> Thou art as tyrannous, so as thou art,
> As those whose beauties proudly make them cruel;
> For well thou know'st to my dear doting heart
> Thou art the fairest and most precious jewel.
> Yet in good faith some say that thee behold,
> Thy face hath not the power to make love groan;
> To say they err I dare not be so bold,
> Although I swear it to myself alone.
> And to be sure that is not false I swear,
> A thousand groans, but thinking on thy face,
> One on another's neck, do witness bear
> Thy black is fairest in my judgement's place.
>   In nothing art thou black save in thy deeds,
>   And thence this slander as I think proceeds.

The fictional stimulus for this poem is an assertion by some of the speaker's acquaintances that his lady is not attractive enough to make a suitable love object. It is easy to imagine Lancelot's reaction if someone had called Guinevere's beauty into question, but this lover, even though he is sure his lady is as tyrannous, fair, cruel, and jewellike as the best, dares not even say the accusers lie, and can only groan silently to himself. The speaker's timidity, especially his use of groans for this purpose, marks him as a parody of the typical Petrarchan lover, but the parody goes much deeper than that of the previous poem. In this case we know that the lady really is unattractive and that the lover really is doting when he thinks her beautiful, a doting that has caused black instead of fair—evil instead of good, and ugliness instead of beauty—to gain the upper hand in his "judgement's place." Rather than ennoble and strengthen him, love has corrupted the speaker's reason and left him unable to act, even in the face of one of the most provocative insults a Petrarchan lover can receive.

But the most uncomfortable aspect of the poem is not the lover's emasculation but his concluding rationalization of the insult against his lady. In asserting that his lady is black only in her deeds, the speaker means that she has been tyrannous and cruel, like all Petrarchan ladies. The asserted similarity between this relationship and the normal one is thus reemphasized, for were the lady's deeds the same sexual refusals as those of every other Petrarchan lady of the nineties, and were her described beauty consistent with what the speaker claims, the sonnet would be almost completely within Petrarchan conventions. But we are led to believe that the lady's evil deeds involve unfaithfulness and that her unattractiveness is genuine, thereby suggesting that the lover had devoted himself to an unworthy object. His confidence in his own normality and correctness, however, tends to reinforce the comparison between his and the normal Petrarchan relationship and to imply that ultimately both are equally perverse: in either case a man degrades himself by service to a woman whose pride leads her to an unnatural tyranny over men. As sonnet 129 suggests, such service is merely "an expense of spirit in a waste of shame."[34]

English courtly love sonnets, then, offer a single situation, but two opposing interpretations of it. A sexual relationship in this tradition always involves a woman dominating a man, but this domination can be viewed as the spur that will produce increased nobility for the male and perhaps a future return to the usual male-dominated relationship, or it can be viewed as a corruption of the natural order, in which the female rebels against her normal social position and love itself, while the male demonstrates his own weakness and ignobility by allowing such a situation to continue. I will call these two contradictory types the Petrarchan and the Emasculating types, the latter because it is the male's emasculation that always defines the chief evil of this type.

When they appear in sonnets, each of these types is highly conventionalized and thus easily recognizable. Shakespeare's use of the Petrarchan and Emasculating types in his plays does not come primarily from sonnet sequences, however, but rather from the other half of the courtly love tradition: romances and other narratives in which love is secondary to or represented through other activities. The primary adaptor in this regard is Chrétien, who took firmly established romance traditions and imposed upon them the tenets of courtly love. What he did for romances, Boccaccio and then Chaucer did for shorter narratives, providing among many Ascetic fabliaux a few examples of Petrarchan love in action.

For all three authors the traditional form through which the Petrarchan could best be represented was New Comedy. Instead of Roman New Comedy, in which the woman is usually a possession fought for by two men, Medieval and subsequent New Comedy almost always presents the woman and one of the men as sharing a true, that is, a Petrarchan, love that is threatened by some outside force. For Chrétien and his successors, this outside force is usually a distant and evil knight who has captured the lady, a situation providing the opportunity for numerous adventures on the way to his castle and then for a final clash between hero and villain. Thus in *Lancelot* the hero must endure a variety of trials and win numerous battles before he can even get to Meleagant's castle; only when Meleagant has been defeated are the lovers allowed their reunion. In the shorter tales, the blocking force is usually closer both in distance and relation, such as Isabella's brothers or Palamon's best friend (or Arcite's, in what is in effect a double New Comic plot), but in each case it is basically a New Comic struggle that is being played out, made genuinely new by the addition of Petrarchan love to the older pattern of males struggling for a woman. By Shakespeare's time, New Comedy automatically suggested Petrarchan love, and the two were (and still are) inextricably mixed: New Comedy suggests Petrarchan values, and Petrarchan relationships reproduce the New Comic structure inasmuch as the lady's haughtiness (indicating the lover's lack of proof) represents a blocking force that must be overcome. Indeed, in many cases—again *Lancelot* is an excellent example—both a villain and the lady's haughtiness must be overcome before the final union can be achieved.

Unlike the Petrarchan type, the Emasculating is very old and appears in many kinds of narratives. It is also closely related to the Ascetic, for both types surely have their origin in the male fear of female sexuality. The earliest influential representative of a woman enslaving men through sexuality is the Circe episode in book 10 of the *Odyssey*. In this self-contained narrative, Circe turns into swine a group of Odysseus' men who have been attracted by her beautiful song and the marvelous web she is spinning. Odysseus seeks to rescue his men and is able to avoid their fate partially because he has been forewarned and given a magic root. In a less literal sense, however, he avoids destruction because his response to Circe is the opposite from that of his men. Instead of allowing himself to be seduced by the comfort and ease promised by the song and web, he charges upon the witch with drawn sword; amazed by this show of strength and determination where all others had shown weakness and a willingness to be misled, Circe embraces Odysseus' legs, swears she will not try to castrate him once they are in bed, releases his men, becomes his lover, and helps him continue on his journey and into the next episode. Though only a part of the larger narrative, the Circe episode is a complete enactment of the desire-struggle-reward pattern in that Odysseus desires to rescue his men, struggles with the witch for possession of them, and takes as his reward not only the men, but the witch herself. As part of the reward, the sexual relationship with Circe is acceptable, and since Odysseus is preparing to continue toward his ultimate goal at the same time that he and Circe are lovers, their relationship is acceptable in the Epic context of both the episode and the narrative as a whole. In fact, Odysseus' taking Circe as a lover is structurally identical to his taunting the wounded Cyclops at the end of book 9: each is the legitimate and well-earned reward for a completed mission.

Odysseus' response to Circe exemplifies the Epic ideal, but the Circe episode nevertheless became the model in later epics for improper sexual relationships. These relationships always involve an abrogation of the epic mission in which a witch casts a spell on the epic hero, the success of which shows his weakness. As in Emasculating relationships within sonnet sequences, those in epics (or later, epic-romances) always portray a man kept from development by the unnatural domination of a woman. In the sonnet sequence version, however, the woman is merely unnatural and uncourtly, whereas her epic counterpart is an actual witch, using magical powers to help control her man. The descendants of Circe usually are also strongly associated with promiscuity, and they are isolated from society (rather than living in court or a pastoral utopia), on a distant island or mountaintop. But despite these differences between the leading ladies, the Emasculating relationship is basically the same in both the courtly love and epic traditions: in both a man is portrayed as losing his ability to act and hence his manhood because of a servile and humiliating attachment to a perverse woman.

Emasculating relationships dominated by a Circe-like figure are quite common in post-Homeric epics. The one most influential on later authors is Dido and Aeneas in the *Aeneid*, a relationship so dangerous that Jove himself seeks to break it up. When his messenger, Mercury, arrives to tell Aeneas of his proper duty, he finds the hero no longer dressed to fit the role:

> And lo! his sword was starred with yellow jaspers,
> and a cloak hung from his shoulders ablaze with
> Tyrian purple—a gift that wealthy Dido had wrought,
> interweaving the web with thread of gold.[35]

Dido is made much more sympathetic (i.e., no longer a Circe figure) by the end of the episode, but at this point, she is portrayed as clearly preventing Aeneas from completing his mission. Aeneas' sword, of course, carries the same phallic associations as Odysseus', but his is decorated with Dido's jewels instead of being ready for battle, an obvious metaphor for the inappropriateness of its owner's activities. It is also a metaphor for his rejection of his mission in submitting to Dido, who like Circe has caught a sailor in a web of gold.

Similar are the "golden bracelets" with which Alcina has tied Rogero in *Orlando Furioso*, whose degeneration has been much more severe than Aeneas':

> His locks, bedew'd with waters of sweet savour,
> Stood curled round in order on his head,
> He had such wanton womanish behavior,
> As though in *Valence* he had long bene bred:
> So chang'd in speech, in manners, and in favor,

> So from himselfe, beyond all reason led,
> By these inchantments of this am'rous dame
> He was himselfe in nothing but in name.
>   (5.47)

Another well-known variation on the same theme occurs in *Gerusalemme liberata*, where a "soft but surely holding chain" made of "woodbines, lilies, and of roses sweet" (14.68) represents Armida's perverse captivation of Rinaldo, who like Aeneas and Rogero before him is dressed in "wanton habit" and has allowed his sword, symbolic of manhood and the masculine activities of the epic mission, to be defaced:

> His sword, that many a Pagan stout had shent,
>   Bewrapt with flow'rs hung idly by his side,
> So nicely decked that it seem'd the knight
> Wore it for fashion sake, but not for fight.
>   (16.30)[36]

And in book 2 of the *Faerie Queene* Acrasia's current lover has hung upon a tree "His warlike armes, the idle instruments / Of sleeping praise" (2.12.80). Elsewhere, Redcrosse and Artegal are temporarily emasculated when they allow the establishment of unnatural sexual relationships.[37]

All of these Circe figures, as well as the Edenic gardens they occupy, have as one of their main sources the late-Latin and medieval gardens of love, beginning with the epithalamia of Statius and Claudian and ending with the courtly love gardens of Andreas, Jean de Meun, and others. At the center of these gardens is Venus, and unlike her Circe-figure descendants, this Venus is a positive figure, who in the Latin epithalamia is responsible for creating sexual desire in the bride-to-be and in the courtly love literature with creating desire in everyone. By the beginning of the Renaissance, however, a much more negative view of Venus and her overt sexuality had been firmly established, and it became possible to view both Venus and her gardens of love in terms of Circe and the unnatural enslavement of men. Commenting on Venus' exchange of clothing with Mars, for example, the tapestry in Busirane's castle makes Mars the victim in a standard Emasculating relationship:

> How oft for *Venus,* and how often eek
> For many other Nymphes he sore did shreek,
> With womanish teares, and with vnwarlike smarts,
> Priuily moystening his horrid cheek.
>   (F.Q. 3.11.44)

This view of Venus is of considerable importance to Shakespeare, most obviously in *Antony and Cleopatra,* but Venus as Circe figure is not the only Venus to be represented, either in that play or in the sixteenth century in general. There are, in fact, several types of positive Venuses, and all of them somehow relate to the goddess's fertility function in the epithalamia and medieval gardens. The same exchange of clothing that seems perverse when Venus is viewed in terms of the Emasculating type becomes positive, sometimes in the same description, when Mars and Venus are used to represent discord and concord. In this case, Venus' victory represents the triumph of peace, marriage, and generation over the forces of war, dissolution, and death. Or the union of Mars and Venus can be used to represent the mysterious union of natural opposites, the discordia concors that is the paradoxical heart of the universe. Thus when Renaissance authors and artists represent Venus wearing Mars' clothes or Mars chained to Venus' throne, the representation often carries contradictory messages: one implying condemnation of the relationship by associating it with Circe figures and the other holding it up as a glorification of generation and peace or as a model of the paradoxical unity of the universe.[38]

Pictorial representations of the Venus-Mars relationship, such as Botticelli's *Venus and Mars,* are usually set in a garden, thereby creating one more example of a garden centered around a woman entertaining her lover. But despite such positive examples as Camoëns's Island of Venus (with Tethys and Gama at the center) and Spenser's Garden of Adonis (Venus and Adonis), most such gardens in Renaissance romance-epics are portrayed as negative. Part of the reason for this is the difficulty in justifying such relationships in terms of the epic tradition, for unless they occur at the conclusion, as does the Island of Venus, any such relationship will seem like a perversion of the male's proper role in life, as well as a glorification of physical desire. The problem is that both the Epic and the Petrarchan types portray sex as valuable only as the symbol of one kind or another of a completed mission which has made the man more noble. In the sense that they offer no way of viewing sex as positive in itself, these types are not altogether different from the Ascetic, and it is not surprising that neither can easily produce positive representations of such exclusively sexual relationships as that of Mars and Venus.

The late-Elizabethan author, however, had at his disposal a newer way of portraying sexual relationships, one that would eventually allow Shakespeare to take advantage of the oppositions inherent in Venus and her gardens. By the end of the sixteenth century, the old ascetic view of marriage and human sexuality as necessary but generally regrettable facts of life was coming under considerable political and ecclesiastical attack, since it was justifiably associated with Roman Catholicism. One of the ways the emerging English Protestant church defined itself was by denying the Catholic view that celibacy is superior to marriage, the result of which was a sudden increase in the Elizabethan valuation of all aspects of marriage. The most obvious indication of this changed attitude is the large number of commentaries on marriage that began to appear in the 1590s. These include Henry Smith's *Preparative to Marriage* (1591), Samuel Hieron's *The Marriage-Blessing* (1614), a series of tracts by Thomas Gataker, William Gouge's *Of Domesticall Duties* (1622), and William Whately's *The Bride-Bush* (1617) and *The Care-cloth* (1624). These and many others preach that sexual desire is natural and good, that its satisfaction in the divinely ordained matrimonial bond is a glorification of God, and that its suppression through chastity is, for all but a chosen few, hypocritical and perverse. William Perkins makes the case most practically and succinctly when he asserts that the "deeds of matrimonie are pure and spirituall . . . and whatsoever is done within the laws of God though it bee wrought by the body, as the wipings of shoes and such like, howsoever grosse they appear outwardly, yet are they sanctified."[39]

The increasing value that the English placed on marriage, plus the extraordinary popularity of Petrarchan relationships in literature, quickly led to the reconceptualization of marriage partly in Petrarchan terms. For Puritan writers especially, the idea of love at first sight seemed attractive, for such an occurrence could easily be ascribed to divine selection. Daniel Rogers, for example, declares that God preserves marriage by causing "a secret sympathy of hearts to live in the brests and bosomes of some men, and some women, that are to live in the married estate, (whereof no reason can bee given, save the finger of God)."[40]

William Whately adapts the courtly lover's transfixion by his lady's beauty by finding that a husband who finds his mate "more comely, handsome, beautifull . . . than perhaps shee is (making her vertues carry a greater shew to his eue, by looking upon them through the spectacles of love), . . . is a thing so far from blame, that it deserveth rather commendation." For Whately, a husband and wife who are "so mutually blind with the liking each of other, as not to bee able to see some things that are amisse each in other" show a "praiseworthy blindness." The same author also gives an overall account of love in marriage that shows how far some Englishmen had come from the usual Ascetic-dominated view of marriage. Writers such as Bacon and Burton, as we have seen, view sexual love as foolish and possibly leading to all sorts of disasters. But Whately, writing at about the same time, has a different perspective; for him, "love seasons and sweetens all estates; love breaketh and composeth all controversies; love overruleth all passions; it squareth all actions; it is in a word the king of the heart, which in whom it prevaileth, to them is marriage itself indeed, viz. a pleasing combination of two persons into one home, one purse, one heart, and one flesh."[41]

The effects on literature of the Protestant celebration of sex, marriage, and love are too extensive to be fully considered here, but of particular importance to Shakespeare's love tragedies is the effect on poetic imitations of the ideal world. Many sixteenth-century poets took their visions of the ideal world quite seriously, for it is these visions that they believed set them apart from philosophers, historians, and other learned men. When Sidney writes that the philosopher "bestoweth but a wordish description, which doth neither strike, pierce, nor possess the sight of the soul so much as the other doth,"[42] he means partly that poets are more clever with words than philosophers, but also that only poetry can reach directly to the soul without the need of being first understood by the reason. It is able to do this because every person's soul has embedded in it the memory of what was lost at the Fall. Thus, by creating a golden Edenic world, poetry outdoes even Nature herself, who can only produce a brazen one, the remnant of the fallen ideal. Both the ascetic and the Neoplatonic traditions place human sexuality and this golden world on opposite poles, since for both sexual desire is an undeniable reminder of our corrupted flesh. But when the Elizabethans began to see sexuality as natural and divinely sanctioned, this absolute opposition was broken, and sex became a possible subject for idealization.

There are, of course, many other such subjects, as the windless, seasonless, deathless, and strifeless paradisical gardens demonstrate. But since so much literature tends toward the celebration of fertility—usually through a concluding marriage or the revitalization of society through the death of a lawbreaker—idealized sexuality is potentially a more natural and evocative subject than almost any other, and a few authors attempted to use it. One of Spenser's contributions to this new (in English literature) type was the Garden of Adonis, his view of the creative center of the universe, "the first seminarie / Of all things, that are borne to liue or die" (3.6.30). Unlike almost all other Renaissance gardens built around a woman and her lover, this one does not condemn lust and the abandonment of the heroic quest. Rather, like the late Latin epithalamia it partially copies, this garden openly celebrates fertility and intercourse. It is the place where

> Franckly each paramour his leman knowes,
> Each bird his mate, ne any does enuie
> Their goodly meriment, and gay felicitie.
> (3.6.41)

And, in direct contrast to the very negative portrayal of Acrasia and her lover in the previous book, the central pair in this garden are positive, with sexuality the main vehicle for producing the sense of otherworldliness and idealization:

> There wont faire *Venus* often to enjoy
> Her deare *Adonis* ioyous company,
> And reape sweet pleasure of the wanton boy;

> There yet, some say, in secret he doth ly,
> Lapped in flowres and pretious spycery,
> By her hid from the world, and from the skill
> Of *Stygian* Gods, which doe her loue enuy;
> But she her selfe, when euer that she will,
> Possesseth him, and of his sweetnesse takes her fill.
>
> (3.6.46)

Such a woman as a positive figure would be impossible for Ariosto or Tasso, and perhaps impossible for English authors writing only a decade earlier.[43]

An even more remarkable example of this idealization of sexuality is the ideal but intensely physical image of the union of Amoret and Scudamour at the original conclusion of book 3:

> Lightly he clipt her twixt his armes twaine,
> And streightly did embrace her body bright,
> Her body, late the prison of sad paine,
> Now the sweet lodge of loue and deare delight:
> But she faire Lady ouercommen quight
> Of huge affection, did in pleasure melt,
> And in sweete rauishment pourd out her spright:
> No word they spake, nor earthly thing they felt,
> But like two senceles stocks in long embracement dwelt.
>
> Had ye them seene, ye would haue surely thought,
> That they had beene that faire *Hermaphrodite,*
> Which that rich *Romane* of rich marble wrought,
> And in his costly Bath causd to bee site:
> So seemd those two, as growne together quite,
> That *Britomart* halfe enuying their blesse,
> Was much empassiond in her gentle spright,
> And to herselfe oft wisht like happinesse,
> In vane she wisht, that fate n'ould let her yet possesse.
>
> (3.12.45–46, 1590 edition)

The Hermaphrodite is a classical symbol of perfection, a suggestion advanced by the lovers' lack of any earthly or sensual feelings. But at the same time that she is like marble, Amoret (Scudamour too, no doubt) is thoroughly overcome with "affection" and "pleasure," and her soul has been "pourd out"—a term with frequent sexual implications throughout the *Faerie Queene*. This obviously sexual "sweet rauishment" is here intended not only as a positive but as an ideal vision so powerful that even the exemplar of chastity, Britomart, is excited. Amoret, as her name suggests, is as tied to sexual love as Britomart is to chastity, but even at the conclusion of Britomart's book, sexual love is dominant. And the sexuality in this love is deliberately and forcefully emphasized.[44]

The most overt mystifier of sexuality was John Donne, who like Spenser uses classical imagery to create a sense of ethereality at the same time as frank sexuality:

> Call us what you will, wee'are made such by love;
>   Call her one, mee another flye,
> We'are Tapers too, and at our owne cost die,
> And we in us finde the'Eagle and the dove;
>   The Phoenix ridle hath more wit
>   By us, we two being one, are it.
> So, to one neutrall thing both sexes fit.
>   Wee dye and rise the same, and prove
>   Mysterious by this love.
>   ("The Canonization," ll. 19–27)[45]

Cleanth Brooks explains this poem's equating of religion and good sex in terms of Donne's "language of paradox," and various others have attempted to disarm the association by showing Donne's indebtedness to Leone Ebreo's *Dialoghi d'Amore* and to other important medieval and Renaissance works.[46] As useful as these views may be, they also show that we are less comfortable with viewing sex as an ideal than were at least some Elizabethans. For them, the connection is unusual but not so unthinkable as to require an explanation. They simply treat sex much the same as any other earthly activity or object that can be idealized, comparing it to better-established idealizations. In the passage from the "Canonization" above, Donne compares the sexual union (the dying tapers and mutual death and resurrection) to various ideal unions, classical and Christian. The eagle and dove suggest both the debate between Righteousness and Mercy that produced Peace and the discordia concors of Mars and Venus. The fly and the Phoenix are each creatures associated in the Renaissance with hermaphrodites and resurrection myths. Hermaphroditic images, especially, are closely associated with marriage and the state of mankind in the golden age in the classical, Christian, and Jewish traditions. Finally, the "neutrall thing both sexes fit" may be the Platonic love that extends beyond the ephemerality of life and the corrupted earth.[47]

The use of sexual imagery to describe spiritual events is a commonplace of philosophy, literature, and art throughout the Middle Ages and Renaissance. What is new is the directness with which Donne, Spenser, and other Elizabethans make the analogy. In fact, the two examples quoted assert the actual rather than the metaphoric ideality of sexual consummation; it is not an analogy for anything. The ability to make such an assertion is the direct result of the Elizabethan refusal to follow absolutely the Ascetic denigration of marriage and sexuality and the concomitant understanding of sex as a natural function of our God-given bodies and, if kept in the correct context, a glorification of him. Spenser and Donne are much more radical in their approach than the Puritans, but all show the influence of a common tradition. The sign of this tradition in literature is another relationship type—the Etherealized—in which sexuality is one of the primary qualities that identify the relationship with some ideal state, a positive in itself, not a symbol for something else.

The Etherealized completes the list of the major systems through which Elizabethans conceptualized sexual relationships. The Rape type, briefly mentioned earlier in this chapter, is of considerable importance in much Elizabethan literature, even that of high status (see for example the fisherman and Florimel in the *Faerie Queene* 3.8), but Shakespeare generally uses it only in passing, as when Celia fears that she and Rosalind might be attacked on the road to Arden (*Titus Andronicus* and *Cymbeline* are obvious exceptions). In any case, its structure is obvious.

The other six—Ascetic, Seduction, Epic, Petrarchan, Emasculating, and Etherealized—are all commonly used in Shakespeare's plays, but not usually in the common way. Most writers are careful to keep the types separate, generally by employing only one in any particular narrative. More complex narratives sometimes provide multiple relationships that are not all represented in the same way, or a single relationship that is seen in contradictory ways by different characters: for example, the "Pot of Basil" story (in several variations), where the blocking characters incorrectly see the lovers in terms of the Ascetic type. A still more sophisticated use of types is that employed in some stories and in the better sequences, where a relationship is portrayed in various ways as the narrative progresses, sometimes with supplied mechanisms for linking the types (Artegal and Britomart in the *Faerie Queene*), sometimes without (*Astrophel and Stella*).

Shakespeare uses all of these methods, but in addition he uses love much as he uses many other exterior systems (such as ideas of honor or of individual initiative vs. position within a hierarchical framework): he takes advantage of the differences and contradictions inherent in models current for him, opposing and combining them to force us into interior systems that are substantially different from the exterior ones that constitute them. Rather than create relationships in which we advance from one type to another, such as Artegal and Britomart, Shakespeare sometimes makes a single representation in terms of signs drawn from contradictory systems, forcing, in effect, the simultaneous apprehension of more than one type. Spenser asks us to see Britomart's love as Petrarchan, then as Epic; Shakespeare sometimes asks us to see two types at the same time. But the types come first, for without a commonly understood group of systems there would be no way even to begin complex representations. There has to be at least one common system for there to be any communication at all, and there have to be several before complexity is possible. These seven types provided the basis for conceptualizing and representing sexual relationships in the sixteenth century; like hundreds of other exterior systems and like English itself, they are part of the raw material the playwright wrought.

2

The Structure of Love:

Now

The seven types discussed in the previous chapter (Ascetic, Seduction, Rape, Epic, Petrarchan, Emasculating, and Etherealized) were all commonly used in sixteenth-century literature, and contemporary readers would have conceptualized sexual relationships largely in their terms. Any particular reader would have added his own individual or perhaps regional elements to the communally held core that constitutes each type. But that the communal core would have been the basis for understanding a narrative representation is evident from the fact that the plays made and make sense at all: if comprehension were based on the private elements of types, it would be impossible to create a complex narrative that could hold together for a large number of readers. Even leaving aside private additions, however, we twentieth-century readers have three and one-half centuries between us and the types as Shakespeare knew them, and the communal changes that have occurred during this time affect to some extent the way we can understand the relationships used in his plays. Our understanding is different not because the sixteenth-century types have been destroyed—if that were the case we could not read Shakespeare at all—but because their current descendants have changed in many minor and a few major ways.

By minor changes I mean those that do not affect the narrative and other structural relationships within a type. For example, the usual reward in the Petrarchan type has been intercourse (twelfth-century Provençal), increased spiritualization (Italian Renaissance), a smile (English Renaissance), a promise of marriage (Victorian), intercourse again, and finally some sort of commitment or self-revelation not identified with either intercourse or marriage.

These changes in rewards have led to obvious differences—such as the lack of overt sex in most nineteenth-century novels, and its superfluousness in many recent ones—but the basic structural relations within the type have remained constant. Discussing all minor changes since the sixteenth century is impossible in a brief space, but a discussion of the most apparent ones, plus the few major changes, can help show how our response to the types used in Shakespeare's plays differs from what it would have been for his contemporaries.

The type most changed for us is certainly the Ascetic, which has been significantly altered by the association of love with marriage. Sexual love, as we presently represent it, derives from Petrarchism, which in the sixteenth century is often opposed to the Ascetic. But Petrarchism had always been associated with premarital relationships, as well as with literary ones; people in the sixteenth century may have read and fantasized about Petrarchan lovers, but when they describe real life and marriage it is almost always in terms of the Ascetic. As people began to think of love as something which not only could apply to them but which would define their relationship with their spouse until death and even beyond, the framework within which they could make that conceptualization was forced to change to something that was neither wholly Ascetic nor Petrarchan.

The driving force behind this change was, as noted in the previous chapter, Puritanism, though Puritan writers often thought of themselves as setting true love in opposition to the lust of Petrarchan writers. For example, Milton tells us in *Paradise Lost,* that married love is not the same as a Petrarchan "Serenate, which the starv'd Lover sings / To his proud fair, best quitted with disdain" (4.755–56, 769–70),[1] but his initial description of Adam and Eve nevertheless contains many Petrarchan elements, as well as the Ascetic ones usually associated with his writing:

> [They were] Not equal, as their sex not equal seem'd;
> For comtemplation hee and valor form'd,
> For softness shee and sweet attractive Grace,
> Hee for God only, shee for God in him.
>
> (4.296–99)

That Eve is made to serve her husband means that her model should be Griselda, but the idea that her beauty is her most important feature, especially connected as it is here with God's grace, suggests the Neoplatonic idea that love of a woman is valuable because her beauty is a metaphor for God's. After describing Adam's manly features, Milton goes on to Eve:

> Shee as a veil down to the slender waist
> Her unadorned golden tresses wore
> Dishevell'd, but in wanton ringlets wav'd

> As the Vine curls her tendrils, which impli'd
> Subjection, but requir'd with gentle sway,
> And by her yielded, by him best receiv'd,
> Yielded with coy submission, modest pride,
> And sweet reluctant amorous delay.
>
> (4.304–11)

Again, Eve is properly submissive to her husband, but Griselda figures do not ever employ "sweet reluctant amorous delay": that is the technique of Petrarchan ladies, who delay sexual rewards until their men have earned them. Evidently, Eve responds when Adam demonstrates the worthiness of his rule, but in the meantime her beauty has a constant, positive, Petrarchan influence on him:

> hee on his side
> Leaning half-rais'd, with looks of cordial Love
> Hung over her enamor'd, and beheld
> Beauty, which whether waking or asleep,
> Shot forth peculiar graces.
>
> (5.11–15)

Eve is eventually represented in terms of the negative Ascetic type, but here, before she has fallen, neither the positive Ascetic nor the Petrarchan is enough for Milton: marriage for him and for his Puritan fellows had to be understood in terms of both.

New in the seventeenth century, this view was standard dogma in the nineteenth, and consequently shows up in all of the numerous marriage manuals of the time. For example, a Hurst self-help text written by M. Lafayette Byrn and titled *The Book of Nature* (1875), in arguing against any kind of sexual relationship other than married love, proclaims that "the lawful love of man for woman, and of woman for man, is the best and holiest affection of which our nature is susceptible; it is also the strongest and most enduring, and ... proceeds from God Himself."[2] B. G. Jefferis and J. L. Nichols's popular *Search Lights on Health: Light on Dark Corners* (1895), which like the *Book of Nature* and most other marriage manuals eventually defends its moral and theological positions with what it regards as scientific thought, tells its readers that

> love, if pure, unselfish, and discreet, constitutes the chief usefulness and happiness of human life.... Without love there would be no organized households, and, consequently, none of that earnest endeavor for competence and respectability, which is the mainspring to human effort; none of those sweet, softening, restraining and elevating influences of domestic life, which alone fill the earth with the glory of the Lord and make glad the city of Zion.[3]

Making marriage the best of human relationships, indeed the origin of everything good in society, had the inevitable result of dramatically improving the status of women (at least in terms of their representation in literature and other media), since they are the gender responsible for producing the sweetness, softness, restraint, and elevation that allow men to "endeavor for competence and respectability." Rather than licentious animals intent on subverting any lawful authority, married women in the nineteenth century are habitually represented as secular saints—angels of the hearth untainted by sexuality or the other corruptions of the male, working world, and hence able to sustain and improve the morality of their sons and husbands. As Jefferis and Nichols put it, "Woman's love is stronger than death; it rises superior to adversity, and towers in sublime beauty above the niggardly selfishness of the world. Misfortune cannot suppress it; enmity cannot alienate it; temptation cannot enslave it. . . . It ever remains the same to sweeten existence, to purify the cup of life, on the rugged pathway to the grave, and melt to moral pliability the brittle nature of man" (p. 116). Similarly, Joseph Johnson's *Willing Hearts and Ready Hands* (1869) holds that "man craves for his help-mate as the counterpart of his being; denied which, and he becomes dwarfed and stunted in true manliness; the refined and humanized aspirations of his better nature are blunted and destroyed; denied heart affection and heart repose, he loses the healthy incentives of life, he becomes blighted in purpose and purposeless in object—he is alone in the world."[4] More succinctly, William Walling, in *Sexology* (1904), declares that "in proportion as man rejects the salutary influence of woman, the human race is rude and savage."[5] No one would argue that this new view of the function of women in society is in any sense liberated, but the difference between it and the position of Chrysostom or even most sixteenth-century authors is striking indeed.

The result on the Ascetic of this new view of marriage and women was the grafting of Petrarchan elements onto both its positive and negative representations. The positive form, which has been clearly secondary to the negative, became the most common way in which the Ascetic appeared, but only after adopting the Petrarchan ideas that women can be more moral and can be closer to God than men and that female love can improve the male who allows himself to be influenced by it. Retained from the older positive form are its strong association with marriage, as opposed to courtship (which continued to be the province of the Petrarchan), as well as characterization of the woman as submissive (the male has to choose to be influenced by her love), asexual (like Griselda), aware of her intellectual inferiority, and never wanting to involve herself in any activity outside of her role. This combination of the Petrarchan lady's ability to produce spiritual improvement and the Griselda figure's unquestioning acceptance of her role produced the Angel of the Hearth that the examples in the previous paragraph portray, as well as this description by Bryn, who after declaring that "there is no state of life more honorable, useful and happy, than that of a wife and mother," goes on to explain that

> what a true man most wants of a true wife is her companionship, sympathy, courage, and love. The way of life has many dreary places in it, and a man needs a companion to go with him. . . . He has some stern battles to fight with poverty, with enemies, and with sin; and he needs a woman that, while he puts his arm around her and feels that he has something to fight for, will help him fight; that will put her lips to his ear and whisper words of council, and her hands to his heart and impart new inspirations. All through life—through storm and through sunshine, conflict and victory, and through adverse and favoring winds—man needs a woman's love.
>
> (p. 82)

The woman of this portrait dares no more than whisper and hope to provide inspiration for her man, who is the only one who actually has any interaction with the world; but unlike her ideological grandmother, Griselda, she is essential to her man's survival: without the constant regenerating influence of her love, he would be lost in the sinister, depraved, male world.

This powerful new view of women helped make overt misogyny—the foundation of the negative Ascetic representation—increasingly unfashionable, since it now contradicted the standard view of female character. As a result, both misogyny and its vehicle were in effect driven underground, finally to reappear as the representation of women who violate their Angel of the Hearth role. Some women violate their role by letting their households and husbands degenerate, either through incompetence, such as Dora in *David Copperfield* (1850), or perversity, such as Mrs. Varden in *Barnaby Rudge* (1841). More common, however, are misogynistic representations of women who attempt activities reserved for men, such as the title character in Tennyson's *The Princess,* or Argemone in Kingsley's *Yeast,* who "had four new manias every year; her last winter's one had been that bottle-and-squirt mania, miscalled chemistry; her spring madness was for Greek drama."[6] When she eventually falls in love, Argemone gives up her superficial learning and declares that she "will study no more, except the human heart, and only that to purify and ennoble it." Similarly, responding to a women's rights meeting, an editorial in the *New York Herald* of September 7, 1853, condemned the participants as "unsexed" by their determination to

> be allowed to step out of their appropriate sphere, and mingle in the busy walks of every-day life, to the neglect of those duties which both human and divine law have assigned to them. . . . It is almost needless to say that these women are entirely devoid of personal attractions. They are generally thin

maiden ladies, or women who perhaps have been disappointed in their endeavors to appropriate the breeches and the rights of their unlucky lords. . . . They violate the rules of decency and taste by attiring themselves in eccentric habiliments, . . . making that which we have been educated to respect, to love, and to admire, only an object of aversion and disgust.[7]

While clearly misogynistic, this statement is far from the closely organized, universally applicable descriptions of medieval misogynistic literature; most of the elements of the old system (especially those having to do with the untamable lust of women) have been dropped, along with the extension of the description to most or all of the sex, and now women are represented as horrible and disgusting only to the extent that they step out of their positive role. Put another way, the negative half of the Ascetic type largely disappears in the nineteenth century, and is replaced by a mere negation of the greatly strengthened positive half—exactly the opposite of the situation in the Middle Ages and Renaissance.

Like many Victorian models, the Angel of the Hearth has been under considerable attack throughout the twentieth century. As a part of overall satirizing of romance and bourgeois lifestyles, such major male writers as H. L. Mencken, Sinclair Lewis, Ernest Hemingway, D. H. Lawrence, and William Faulkner have often resurrected old types in order to deny that women have the inclination or ability to fill the role. Mencken, for example, employs straightforward medieval misogyny to assail women who hide their natural ugliness by using makeup and other deceptions; they are "ungraceful, misshapen, badly calved, and crudely articulated, even for a woman," and even with embellishments project only "a certain hollow gaudiness, a revolting flashiness, the superficial splendor of a prancing animal."[8] Given this view of women, it is not surprising that he disapproves of intense relationships with them. In contrast, Hemingway approves of intense relationships, but only with somewhat more erotic versions of Griselda, such as Maria in *For Whom the Bell Tolls* (1940): "I will do anything for thee that thou should wish. . . . understand always that I will do what you wish. But thou must tell me for I have great ignorance."[9] He uses the Circe figure for women who try to be anything more than completely passive, as is the case with Margaret Macomber in "The Short Happy Life of Francis Macomber" (1938), and with some portrayals of Brett in *The Sun Also Rises* (1926).

Lawrence and Faulkner also attack the Angel of the Hearth with basically pre-Victorian types, but they also reflect the most significant post-Victorian understanding of sexual relationships: our belief, inspired by Freudianism, in the overwhelming place of sexuality in the psyche of both sexes. Since her "deepest consciousness is in the loins and belly," a woman for Lawrence is happy only when her man can "rip all her nice superimposed modern-woman and wonderful-creature garb off her" and "reduce her once more to a naked Eve" so that she can "yield to her own real unconscious self, and absolutely stamp on the self that she's got in her head."[10] Accordingly, his positive relationships usually are strongly sexual, but otherwise much like Griselda and Walter: for example, Annable and his second wife (he having deserted the first one for not behaving like a Griselda figure) in *The White Peacock* (1911), and Mellors and Connie (who wants to be dominated by a strong man and "free of the dominion of other women") in *Lady Chatterley's Lover* (1928).[11] Women who do not fit into this type of relationship are almost always Circe figures for Lawrence, and some of his strongest and most positive men fight back by refusing to settle down with or impregnate their women (Lilly in *Aaron's Rod,* the central males in "Tickets, Please" and "St. Mawr"), since, as he explains in *Studies in Classic American Literature* (1923), writing of *The Scarlet Letter,* "the greatest triumph a woman can have, especially an American woman, is the triumph of seducing a man: especially if he is pure. . . . Because the greatest thrill in life is to bring down the Sacred Saint with a flop into the mud. Then when you've brought them down, humbly wipe off the mud with your hair, another Magdalen. And then go home and dance a witch's jig of triumph. . . . And then stand meek on the scaffold and fool the world."[12]

Faulkner never comes quite this close to the Emasculating type, instead staying very close to the old negative Ascetic type. His women are often like Eula in *The Hamlet* (1931), who is a "primal uterus" whose only consciousness is what "supplied blood and nourishment to the buttocks and breasts." Despite her stupidity, however, she is "swarmed over and importuned, yet serene and intact and apparently even oblivious, tranquilly abrogating the whole sum of human thinking and suffering which is called knowledge, education, wisdom."[13] Unlike Circe figures, Faulknerian women are not malevolent or even conscious of why they act as they do, but their unremitting sexuality is a constant threat to men, who unfortunately are unable to resist the urge to idealize and devote themselves to these creatures. According to the novelist character in *Mosquitoes* (1927), women in general are "merely articulated genital organs with a kind of aptitude for spending whatever money you have; so when they get themselves up to look exactly like all the other ones, you can give all your attention to their bodies."[14] Temple, in *Sanctuary* (1931), has little care for any particular male and eventually has little reserve about expressing her sexuality; in the beginning of the novel she goes out with anyone who asks her for a date ("She'd just dress, and after a while somebody would call for her"), and eventually demands of a patron in a restaurant "Let's hurry. Anywhere . . . Please. Please. Please. Please. Don't make me wait. I'm burning up."[15] Belle, in *Sartoris* (1929), who is "cannily stupid," acts on the man who loves her "like a rich and fatal drug, like a motionless and cloying sea in which he watched himself drown."¹⁶ And Caddy Compson, in *The Sound and the Fury* (1929), is unable to control her sexuality and not much concerned with trying; her brother is destroyed, like innumerable of his Ascetic ancestors, not by her, but by his own foolish need to idealize women.

These powerful repeated representations by important authors have had the effect of refamiliarizing our century with much the same Ascetic and Emasculating types as Shakespeare knew, but they are hardly the norm. Indeed, all of these authors perceived themselves as writing criticism of their society, which continued mostly to employ Petrarchism and the Angel of the Hearth translation of the Ascetic, especially in the most popular media, movies and television. The motion picture version of *Gone with the Wind* (1939), for example, gives us a perfect Angel of the Hearth in Melanie, whose complete devotion to her husband, even to the point of risking death so that his sexual desires can be satisfied, helps preserve him against the destructiveness of both Reconstruction and Scarlett. This type lacks conflict and thus is difficult to use as the focus of a narrative, except where a character must be taught to fit the role, as in *Topper* (1937), and *It's a Wonderful Life* (1946); it appears most often as the moral touchstone around which a plot develops, as in many adventure films (for example, *Shane*, 1953) and in innumerable television situation comedies, among them *The Adventures of Ozzie and Harriet* (1952–66), *Father Knows Best* (1954–62), *Leave It to Beaver* (1957–63), and *The Dick Van Dyke Show* (1961–66). Shopworn and old-fashioned as the type seems to many, it still remains the norm, even and perhaps especially for those who want to reject and replace it. No matter how much we try to understand marriage (that is, represent it to ourselves) in new ways, Ward and June Cleaver help the old remain alive for most of us.

One way in which the Angel of the Hearth version of the Ascetic has clearly changed since *Leave It to Beaver* is in the amount and type of sexuality permitted the wife. Indeed, the relaxation of sexual restrictions, at least on premarital sex, has become so common that representations of women who remain virgins until marriage now seem unrealistic—that is to say, premarital virginity, once an essential element of the type (indeed, the Angel of the Hearth originally suggested a sort of postmarital virginity as well), is now being restricted from it. Female marital infidelity is still impossible within our version of the Angel of the Hearth, and is always represented as an aberration within any true marriage. But the sexual desire that precipitates the infidelity now seems normal, and thus we are able to see as realistic a relationship that continues after the aberration is removed, as is the case in the motion picture version of *The World according to Garp* (1982). Eventually, perhaps, sex outside of the relationship will seem a normal part of a realistically portrayed marriage, rather than an increasingly common and increasingly minor threat to it; that seems the most likely course.

Redefinitions of allowable sexuality certainly have changed the surface elements of the Angel of the Hearth version of the positive Ascetic. But since sexlessness or other kinds of restrictions are related to the core of the type primarily as symbols of fealty to the husband, their alteration or elimination will not substantially change the type so long as other symbols of this hierarchical relationship are developed to replace them.

A more potent threat to the primacy of the Ascetic as the basic way of representing marriage is the idea that a good wife need not restrict herself to traditional female activities. Many motion pictures of the thirties, forties, and fifties paved the road for this probably inevitable change in the type. Their deviation from the tradition was to represent positive women competing with and holding their own against men, either through battles of wit, as in *The Philadelphia Story* (1940) and many other screwball comedies, or invasions of the male world of business; for example Joan Crawford plays the owner of a trucking firm in *They All Kissed the Bride* (1942), Rosalind Russell a star reporter in *His Girl Friday* (1940), and Katherine Hepburn a lawyer in *Adam's Rib* (1949) and an athlete in *Pat and Mike* (1952). Like Rosalind in *As You Like It,* however, the female characters in these movies always indicate the primacy of love and—more importantly—the primacy of their devotion to their man over any career, and thus do not threaten the basic structure of the positive Ascetic, as modified in the nineteenth-century: the representation of the woman as defined primarily by her devotion to her husband and children, who are made better by this influx of feminine love.

Since the meek housewife role is symbolic of this devotion, eliminating the role but not the devotion that lies behind it challenges a peripheral element of the type, but, as with the decline of sexual restrictions, leaves the central structure intact. When the devotion itself is eliminated and positive representations are nevertheless attempted, as in some recent novels by women, such as Erica Jong's *Fear of Flying* (1973) and Lisa Alther's *Kinflicks* (1976), and in such movies as *Annie Hall* (1977) and *Kramer vs. Kramer* (1979), neither the Ascetic nor any of its descendants can serve as the conceptualizing base. And since no other single type is possible for such portrayals either, combinations of elements from various types have to be combined ad hoc and carefully defined for the reader. Eventually, a new, feminist relationship type may solidify itself and replace the Angel of the Hearth, at least for some readers, as the normal type. Such a type, denying a primary commitment of either husband or wife to a marriage, will be much farther ideologically and structurally from the medieval Ascetic than is the Victorian version, and it will certainly complicate and change the way we can understand Ascetic representations in Shakespeare and other authors. At present, however, our Ascetic is not so different from Shakespeare's that his uses of it will seem incoherent. Novice readers may have some problems, but the similarity of the two systems allows the rest of us to modify our reading to try to see the relationships in Shakespeare's terms; we are not forced to accept an alien system, but rather one that is not quite the same as any of its current descendants.

The metamorphoses of all the other sixteenth-century types has been far less substantial. Elements of Petrarchism have been adopted into the Ascetic, and the Petrarchan can now appear in many more contexts than it could for Shakespeare; but the core of the type has not changed at all. A Petrarchan relationship is still one in which a definite state, love, leads the lover (still usually male) to idealize and devote himself to the person he loves, who loves him in return but nevertheless resists his importunities so that he will be forced to improve and make himself more worthy of her response; both lovers are thus made better and more complete by the relationship. The elements signifying the state of love, which are not fundamental parts of the type, have become less absolutely defined as the type has moved away from its base in sonnet sequences, but even so, many of these original elements are still very strongly associated with the type: lovers are still often portrayed as full of sighs and tears, distracted, without appetite, nervous, moody, and generally unable to function in the world (except, of course, when called upon to do some heroic deed). As the "all shook up" speaker of a 1957 Elvis Presley song puts it, his "hands are shaky" and his "knees are weak" because of love, which has also left him with the mysterious ailment of "itching like a man on a fuzzy tree."[17]

With the increasing number of female readers and authors has come more concentration on the female part of the relationship, as well as provisions for much more female activity, especially within the New Comic plots that continue to form the narrative basis for most Petrarchan relationships. But the sex roles within the type have not changed in any substantial way: the concentration is still on how the male is improved by love—often now on what the woman does to effect this change—but still mostly on the man's change. *Pamela* (1740–41) details the heroine's emotions in minute detail, but the point of most of them is to show how her purity and willingness to suffer for her ideals finally turn Mr. B--'s lust into true love. In *Pride and Prejudice* (1813), Elizabeth initially refuses to admit her attraction to Darcy because she is deceived about his character and actions; he loves her from the beginning, but before she will accept him, his love must mature (helped along by her disdain when he first proposes and on many other occasions) to the point that he can ignore class differences and simply accept his love, which he demonstrates by rescuing Elizabeth's sister. In *Great Expectations* (1860), on the other hand, Dickens satirizes both bourgeois society and Petrarchism by showing that Pip's love for Stella does what it is supposed to do—makes him a gentleman—but that being a gentleman is not the positive state that Pip took it to be. *Goodbye, Columbus* (1959) uses much the same form. Kurtz's love for his Intended in *Heart of Darkness* (1902) leads him to try to civilize Africa, and Gatsby's for Daisy in *The Great Gatsby* (1925) commits him "to the following of a grail," a quest that dominates the rest of his life and finally is the one thing that separates him from the "rotten crowd" that make up the rest of the book.[18]

The Epic type has changed even less than the Petrarchan over the last four centuries; its representation of women as the prizes for which males struggle is a central element in innumerable adventure stories this century. Westerns almost invariably have used plots in which virtuous, beautiful (and hence valuable) women are threatened with harm, usually some form of rape, by a villain who is also carrying out some other nefarious scheme (rustling cattle, driving out sheepherders); a final gun battle prevents both and wins the woman as bride for the conquering hero. Examples may be found in the novels of Zane Gray, such movies as *The Virginian* (1929), *My Darling Clementine* (1946), and *High Noon* (1952), and many episodes of television westerns, though in the last the need for new plots with the same hero forces the concluding marriage to be reduced to a kiss or some other less permanent reward. Many war, spy, horror, or other adventure forms use much the same plot, as in the novels of Ian Fleming and their motion picture adaptations, and in *Birth of a Nation* (1915), *The Thief of Bagdad* (1924), *King Kong* (1933). More sophisticated adventure narratives use the same Epic structure with only relatively minor changes. *North by Northwest* (1959) and *Notorious* (1946) both make the heroine less than completely virtuous and the hero less than completely committed either to her or to his mission, while *Psycho* (1960) tricks us into thinking the Janet Leigh character is the heroine and hence liable to great threat but not death (and certainly not death early in the film), before producing the real heroine and an otherwise conventional presentation of the plot. *Star Wars* (1977) and *Raiders of the Lost Ark* (1981) mask ordinary Epic representations by making the heroines more earthy and much more active than is usual, a technique favored by many other recent movies and novels, especially those related to science fiction. In all, however, the concluding battle is still largely between the two main male characters, and the heroine remains one of the prizes signifying victory.

Many of the same narratives employing the Epic also use the Emasculating, as has been the case since the *Odyssey*. A good example is Rosa Klebb in Ian Fleming's *From Russia with Love* (1957; movie, 1963). Numerous other well-known Circe figures come readily to mind as well, testifying to the wide popularity of this representation of women and sexual relationships. Besides Scarlett O'Hara and Margaret Macomber, there are the evil, man-destroying femmes fatales in *Double Indemnity* (1944), *The Maltese Falcon* (1941), *East of Eden* (1955), and—most evil and Circe-like of all—*The Blue Angel*

(1930). Lina Wertmuller's *Swept Away* (1973) and *Seven Beauties* (1974) both have central Circe figures, the former employing the popular plot twist of the witch's reformation from ball-breaker to devoted slave of her man (just as in the *Odyssey*). Norman Mailer's "The Time of Her Time" (1959) uses the same device, then reverses the type again when the recently orgasmic, and hence recently reformed, woman calls her lover a latent homosexual as she walks out the door. Mencken, Hemingway, Lawrence (whose Mellors, in *Lady Chatterley's Lover,* describes some women as having "beaks between their legs"),[19] and Faulkner all use the Emasculating, and so do Sinclair Lewis, James Thurber, and Henry James (for example, the Marquise de Bellegarde, in *The American,* 1877, or some representations of Maggie in *The Golden Bowl,* 1905). Maggie in Tennessee Williams's *Cat on a Hot Tin Roof* (1955) obviously fits the pattern, but the mother in *Glass Managerie* (1944) is ultimately just as castrating; Edward Albee's portrayal of a castrating mother in *The American Dream* (1961) is more virulent than either. Philip Wylie's *Generation of Vipers* (1942) is a philosophical attack on mother worship and women in general, from an Emasculating perspective; it claims that "the male is an attachment of the female in our civilization," the result of which is "a new all-time low in political scurviness, hoodlumism, gangsterism, labor strife, monopolistic thuggery, moral degeneration, civic corruption, smuggling, bribery, theft, murder, homosexuality, drunkenness, financial depression, chaos and war."[20] Obviously, the Emasculating is not a type in any danger of extinction.

The twentieth-century version of the Seduction type is very closely related in form to its sixteenth century ancestor, but the situations in which it can be used have changed significantly. The pastoral form, whose deliberate denial of any correlation to the real world helped strip any threat from the type, is dead, and its various fantasy replacements have not made Seduction as significant a part of their landscape (with some exceptions, such as William Morris's *Water of the Wondrous Isles,* 1895). On the other hand, the pornographic and semipornographic forms of the nineteenth and twentieth centuries have almost always made the Seduction type their central element, often in conjunction with the Rape. Typically, such narratives represent the woman as sincerely resistant to and threatened by the actions of the male (the Rape), but once under his control unable to control her sexual passions. The overall pattern and especially the conclusion are identical to the sixteenth-century version; the only change is the Rape suggestion of serious consequences, evidently added to increase the reader's vicarious sense of power and to justify rape fantasies. Watered-down versions of this combination sometimes appear in more popular media, for example the rape scene in *Straw Dogs* (1972) or the description of rape as the "silver lining" of being attacked by the psychopathic killer in *Frenzy* (1972). Interestingly, many historical romances, which are usually written and almost always read by women, contain a scene in which the heroine loses her virginity unwillingly, but to the man she loves and will eventually marry; as in male pornography, her reluctance melts once coition has begun, but the purpose seems to be avoiding the moral problem of the heroine's seeking sex, rather than justifying rape. But the portrayal is still Seduction, or Rape followed by and redefined by Seduction.

Besides these specialized representations, the Seduction type also appears as a part of many other narratives, usually as a contribution to comic tone. Used in this way, it is an essential part of virtually all movies about high school and college students, from the beach party movies of the late fifties and sixties to *American Graffiti* (1973), *Animal House* (1978), and *Fast Times at Ridgemont High* (1982, a film that experiments with reversing the Seduction sex roles). The use of the Seduction as a comic element has also become a staple of most television comedy series produced since the introduction of *M*A*S*H* (1972–83), *The Mary Tyler Moore Show* (1970–77), and—especially—*Happy Days* (1974–80). The comic image of a male's insincere rhetoric being rebuffed by female sarcasm (or some other form of refusal) is popular in many other media as well.

The last of the Renaissance types to develop, the Etherealized, is also still present, but the purpose for its use is now significantly different. In the sixteenth and seventeenth centuries the Etherealized was employed as a method for evoking a heavenly ideal through a human activity, following the standard Renaissance critical doctrine that the highest purpose of art is to show man the divine within himself. Glorification of sex in the twentieth century, on the other hand, is usually related to "sexual liberation," which is itself a part of our overall idealization of personal freedom and fulfillment, usually as defined by Freudian and other psychological theories. The modern Etherealized, therefore, uses slightly more individualized lovers and draws its ideals from psychologically sanctioned sources like myth or the collective unconscious, but the basis of the type, representing sex as having significance beyond the ordinary human world, is unchanged. "The Time of Her Time" (1958), for example, is a story almost exclusively about inducing an orgasm in a woman who has never had one; the description of the success (closely related to a similar description in *Lady Chatterley's Lover*) links the woman to a more primitive, natural state than the aggressive, independent, contemporary one that the narrator tells us has left her frigid: "She gave at last a little cry of farewell, and I could feel a new shudder which began as a ripple and rolled into a wave, and then it rolled over her, carrying her along, . . . and finally she was away, she was loose in the water for the first time in her life."[21] A related association of female sexuality to an idealized past occurs in Marie Stopes's *Married Love* (1918), which as the first marriage manual to stress the naturalness of female sexual desire, found it necessary to give that desire value through use of the Etherealized: "Welling up in her are the wonderful tides, scented and enriched by the myriad experiences of the human race from its ancient days of leisure and flower-wreathed love-making, urging her to transports and to self-expressions were the man but ready to take the first step in the initiation or to recognize and welcome it in her."[22] Erica Jong, in *Fear of Flying* (1973), follows an account of the various sociological and psychological forces conspiring against satisfying male-female relations with a Donne-influenced description of the intermingling of souls in perfect, Etherealized sex: "The zipless fuck was more than a fuck. It was a platonic ideal. Zipless because when you came together zippers fell away like rose petals, underwear blew off in one breath like dandelion fluff. Tongues intertwined and turned liquid. Your whole soul flowed out through your tongue and into the mouth of your lover."[23] Though she has little else in common with Jong, Marabel Morgan, in *The Total Woman* (1973), also slips into the Etherealized when she needs to idealize intercourse: "Spiritually, for sexual intercourse to be the ultimate satisfaction, both partners need a personal relationship with their God. When this is so their union is sacred and beautiful and mysteriously the two blend perfectly into one. Intercourse becomes the place where man and woman discover each other in a new dimension."[24] Perhaps the final, best evidence of how ingrained is the Etherealized idealization of sex in our society is that all of these descriptions, different as their perspectives are, sound more familiar than a description of intercourse as a simple act, performed by most adults throughout the world and hence of no more significance than any other similarly common act.

The Etherealized is no more ingrained, however, than the Ascetic or the Emasculating, each in some way its polar opposite, or its near cousin, the Petrarchan. All of the major types continue to be used, both in ways reminiscent of the sixteenth century or earlier, and in ways that reflect modern social changes and perhaps point the way toward substantially new types. As is the case with most language-based systems, our ability to represent sexual relationships is becoming more complex as we continue to employ old types at the same time that we are continually creating modifications. Just as old words die much less quickly than new ones are created, usually with new senses or combinations of the old, so our vocabulary for conceptualizing sexual relationships is expanding. But the old types are still alive for us, and as is the case with so many other vocabularies, Shakespeare's plays still speak more interestingly than any other voice.

3

Creating the Heroine:

The Comedies

Shakespeare's comedies have been so frequently presented and enjoyed that most of us find it hard to keep in mind how revolutionary they were in their own day. For us, characters such as Rosalind and Beatrice seem wonderful and alive, and with some allowances for "outdated convention," perfectly realistic. Realism, however, is itself only a series of conventions, changing from age to age, and nowhere is this more convincingly shown than in the case of Shakespeare's heroines, who now seem realistic only because through them Shakespeare helped create and popularize the conventions of female characterization that now, through long repetition, seem to imitate actual women.[1]

Before Shakespeare, Western representations of women are, with a few noteworthy exceptions, relatively simple. Or put another way, earlier works almost always rely on a single type to define the characters of their women. Comedies and fabliaux, restricted to foolish and generally lower-class characters, portrayed women as shrews, gulls, teases, or cuckolders, in no case worthy of much respect from the audience. Saints' tales and other works in the moralistic, homiletic tradition showed women as nonsexual, heroically virtuous, and thoroughly passive. Epics and romances gave us Circe figures and (after the development of courtly love) all of the other permutations of the Petrarchan type. There was significant variety, but outside of a few exceptions, female characters were never represented except in terms of a single type.

A good play in which to see the difference between Shakespeare and earlier authors is *As You Like It,* which besides being one of the best of the comedies is also one of the ones taken most directly from a source: Thomas Lodge's *Rosalynde* (1590).[2] Lodge's Rosalynde and Rosader have much the same history as Rosalind and Orlando: they meet and fall in love at the wrestling match; they meet again in the forest with Rosalynde disguised as a boy and serving as a proxy for herself; they marry in the end and are returned to power. Rosader, like Orlando, is heroic and uses trees to disseminate love poetry, while both heroines are beautiful beyond compare and observe other love relationships while playing out their own.

Rosalynde and Rosalind seem similar because of plot duplications and because each is represented mostly in terms of a single type: the Petrarchan. Besides being beautiful and noble, each turns her future lover into stone when he first falls in love (p. 171; 1.2.249–60); and while both Rosalynde and Rosalind immediately fall in love as well (p. 174–75; 1.3.1–39), each makes her lover prove himself before giving him encouragement: by deeds (the wrestling match and getting food for Adam) and by words (the love poetry and direct assertions of love).

The difference is that Rosalynde remains wholly Petrarchan and Rosalind does not. Rosalynde, for example, responds to her banishment with stoicism and passivity; just like Guinevere and countless other Petrarchan heroines, resistance to any affront except attempted rape is left to the rescuing and revenging lover. But whereas her predecessor stands silent and "amazed" (p. 177), Rosalind goes on the offensive and demands the fault for which she is expelled, asserting that "Treason is not inherited," and even if it is, "What's that to me? My father was no traitor" (1.3.61, 63). Similarly, in the same scene, Rosalynde describes her use of male clothing in purely utilitarian terms, while Rosalind uses the occasion to assert her equality to many men:

> Were it not better,
> Because that I am more than common tall,
> That I did suit me all points like a man?
> A gallant curtle-axe upon my thigh,
> A boar-spear in my hand, and—in my heart
> Lie there what hidden woman's fear there will—
> We'll have a swashing and a martial outside,
> As many other mannish cowards have
> That do outface it with their semblances.
> (1.3.114–22)

The central thesis of Petrarchism is that love of a woman can spur a man to demonstrate his innate heroism, but Rosalind here refuses to play her part or even to admit its existence: for her, the lack of heroism in men is a matter for scorn rather than lamentation or corrective action. The characterization of Rosalind does not at this point contradict any of the tenets of Petrarchism, but it is not based exclusively on that type.

A more obvious and sustained difference in presenting the two heroines is their response to Rosader-Orlando's love complaints. When Rosader, in typical Petrarchan fashion, moans that his fortunes are too low to interest his lady, she (disguised as Ganimede) makes an equally typical reply: "Feare not, man, womens looks are not tied to dignities feathers, nor make they curious esteeme where the stone is found, but what is the vertue. Feare not Forrester, faint heart never wonne faire Ladie" (p. 201). In other words, Petrarchan ladies are interested in heroic nature and deeds, not the current bank balance. Later, in response to hearing one of Rosader's poetic tributes to herself, she responds ironically but still fully within her tradition: "Believe me (quoth Ganimede) either the Forrester is an exquisite painter, or Rosalynde faire above wonder: so it makes me blush to hear how women should be so excellent, and pages so unperfect" (p. 203). Since the type through which she is entirely represented holds that Petrarchan ladies are indeed "excellent" and "faire above wonder," Rosalynde does not really question that she herself might fit such a definition; rather, she simply states the truth that as a page she hardly measures up.

Rosalind's responses to Orlando, on the other hand, are often completely out of the Petrarchan tradition. After sarcastically asserting that he is too well dressed to be a lover, and must therefore be in love only with himself, she goes on to satirize the state she claimed to be in earlier in the scene: "Love is merely a madness, and I tell you, deserves as well a dark house and a whip as madmen do; and the reason why they are not so punish'd and cur'd is, that the lunacy is so ordinary that the whippers are in love too. Yet I profess curing it by counsel" (3.2.400–404). These images immediately suggest the Ascetic view that love is irrational and a type of disease, and Rosalind goes on to tell us the major reason why: women are not worthy of the worship men give them. Pretending to be the woman Orlando loves, she will therefore

> grieve, be effeminate, changeable, longing and liking, proud, fantastical, apish, shallow, inconstant, full of tears, full of smiles; for every passion something, and for no passion truly any thing, as boys and women are for the most part cattle of this color; would now like him, now loathe him; then entertain him, then forswear him; now weep for him, then spit at him; that I drave my suitor from his mad humor of love to a living humor of madness, which was, to forswear the full stream of the world, and to live in a nook merely monastic. (3.2.410–21)

Any competent reader will immediately see this catalog of antifeminist stereotypes as ironic, not a true account of Rosalind's character, but the point is that, however we arrange them hierarchically, Rosalind is clearly identified with two diametrically opposed types in a way that her predecessor never is. In *Rosalynde,* as in all straightforward Petrarchan narratives, the Ascetic simply does not exist, thereby allowing the reader to conceptualize the central relationship solely in terms of one type. As a result, the interior codes through which we see Rosalynde, Rosader, and their love as particular entities existing within a single work are in all significant ways identical to a single exterior one, the Petrarchan type. In the passage of *As You Like It*, on the other hand, we are forced to incorporate two major contradictory exterior codes into our interior ones, which we accomplish by simply defining one type as true and correct and the other as foolish and the object of ridicule. This hierarchy is not complicated, and certainly is not threatening to the primacy of the Petrarchan, but it still produces a set of interior codes more complex and individual than those Lodge employs.[3]

Repeated often enough, a satire of the Ascetic within a Petrarchan framework would itself become an element of the Petrarchan type. Indeed, the reverse was already firmly established by Shakespeare's day, for almost all Ascetic narratives written in the sixteenth century somewhere make fun of Petrarchism, usually by making the diseased lover behave and speak in ways associated with that type. Nor was Shakespeare the first to make Petrarchism the base and the Ascetic the joke. But Shakespeare does not stop in *As You Like It* with a simple hierarchy; instead he creates several places where the Ascetic associations are not ironic. Certainly the most striking of these for Shakespeare's original audience must have been Rosalind's frequent involvement in bawdry, sometimes of a fairly graphic nature. For example, Celia suggests that Rosalind might enjoy wrestling with Orlando (1.2.24–25), and Touchstone's parody of Orlando's verse paints a Rosalind who is thoroughly sensual:

> If a hart do lack a hind,
> Let him seek out Rosalind.
> If the cat will after kind,
> So be sure will Rosalind.
> Wint'red garments must be lin'd,
> So must slender Rosalind.
> They that reap must sheaf and bind,
> Then to cart with Rosalind.
> Sweetest nut hath sourest rind,
> Such a nut is Rosalind.
> He that sweetest rose will find,
> Must find love's prick and Rosalind.
>   (3.2.101–12)

It is hard to imagine anyone saying of Beatrice or Laura or Stella (or Rosalynde) that all a man who wants the "sweetest rose" must do is bring a "prick and Rosalind" together. Nor does Rosalind herself abstain from the fun, answering Orlando's assertion that "who could be out, being before his belov'd mistress?" with "Marry, that should you if I were your mistress, or I should think my honesty ranker than my wit" (4.1.83–85). Poor Orlando is so completely Petrarchan himself and so wrapped up in what he thinks is a mock wooing that he cannot understand what he should be out of to keep his lady honest, and Rosalind must provide him a hint. This little exchange thus provides a good example of the confusion and comic possibilities created by characters operating in different types: Orlando is portrayed in terms of the Petrarchan, in which the lady is never associated with sexuality; the Rosalind of this passage is operating in the Ascetic world, where sex and love are either matters of humor or condemnation.[4]

This same juxtaposition of the Petrarchan and Ascetic can be seen in other places in the play as well, especially in the various lower-class relationships that form subplots of the main one.[5] Two of these involve Touchstone. The first is established when Silvius and Rosalind both declare their loves—the former ludicrously ("O Phebe, Phebe, Phebe!") and the latter in a manner with which we can sympathize. Touchstone, oblivious to our desire to view the two differently, proceeds to parody both by parodying himself in a fictitious relationship with "Jane Smile":

I remember when I was in love, I broke my sword upon a stone, and bid him take that for coming a-night to Jane Smile; and I remember the kissing of her batler and the cow's dugs that her pretty chopp'd hands had milk'd; and I remember the wooing of a peascod instead of her, from whom I took two cods, and giving her them again, said with weeping tears, "Wear these for my sake." We that are true lovers run into strange capers; but as all is mortal in nature, so is all nature in love mortal in folly. (2.4.46–56)

His "strange caper" of breaking his sword on the stone representing his adversary for Jane's love is a parody of a Petrarchan lover's adventures, just as his desire to kiss the cow's udders parodies the familiar Petrarchan conceit of loving whatever has been close to the lady (usually a rose or her gloves), and Jane's chapped hands the lily-white ones of Petrarchan ladies.

Similarly, the Seduction account of the relationship of Touchstone and the dim-witted, foul-visaged Audrey calls into question both the Petrarchan type, whose terminology Touchstone parodies in his attempt to achieve his object, and the various Petrarchan lovers inhabiting the same forest. While Silvius, Rosalind, and Orlando are all describing their relationships as exceptional and spiritual, Touchstone reverses both with a straightforward Ascetic explanation of sexual attraction: "As the ox hath his bow, sir, the horse his curb, and the falcon her bells, so man hath his desires; and as pigeons bill, so wedlock would be nibbling" (3.3.79–82). Even in the final scene, which otherwise seems a bastion of Petrarchism, Touchstone still insists on viewing not only his own, but all of the other relationships as well, in similar terms: "I press in here, sir, amongst the rest of the country copulatives, to swear and to forswear, according as marriage binds and blood breaks" (5.4.55–57). For him, all relationships are mere sex, whether this sexuality is admitted or hidden behind a Petrarchan fiction. Because Touchstone is identified as a clown and is full of jokes, his thoroughgoing and consistent Ascetic view never seems oppressive (Jaques, with a much lighter message, nevertheless seems much more threatening). But his view is always present, and never once is devalued, as happens with Rosalind's parodies of Petrarchism, by some indication that he really believes in love after all.

The Phebe-Silvius relationship, on the other hand, is sometimes played in a serious Petrarchan manner. Or more accurately, it is sometimes played as a serious Emasculating relationship, since Phebe refuses to play along with Silvius' Petrarchan sentiments and then reduces him to such humiliating tasks (instead of the heroic ones Petrarchan love should spur) as carrying her love letter to Ganymede. Rosalind forcefully suggests this type when she demands of Phebe

> Who might be your mother,
> That you insult, exult, and all at once,
> Over the wretched?
>
> (3.5.34–36)

Eventually Phebe recognizes her mistake in Ganymede, gives her love to Silvius after all, and thereby brings the relationship to a proper Petrarchan conclusion.

At the same time that Phebe and Silvius are represented in terms of these complementary types, both the characters and the types are constantly subverted by the Ascetic. Most obviously, the rural dress and speech of the two lovers (Rosalind's more cultured accent is noted at 3.2.341–42) associates them with the lower class. Because lower-class characters are inevitably associated with weakness, not only through the Ascetic but through almost every other system that represents them before this century, Phebe and Silvius do not seem capable of being the strong characters implicit in both the Petrarchan and Emasculating types, and thus seem ridiculous Ascetic parodies of the types they suggest. This ridiculousness is underscored by Phebe's love for Ganymede-Rosalind and by Phebe's evident physical difference from the Petrarachan lady Silvius sees in her, a fact alluded to by Rosalind in the most straightforward Ascetic representation of the relationship:

> But, mistress, know yourself, down on your knees,
> And thank heaven, fasting, for a good man's love;
> For I must tell you friendly in your ear,
> Sell when you can, you are not for all markets.
>
> (3.5.57–60)

Phebe's evident homeliness separates her from either the Petrarchan or Emasculating types, and the implication that acquiring a husband is a woman's most important task, as well as the metaphor of marriage-sex as a market commodity, return us to the hard, cold world of the Ascetic.

Even Rosalind and Orlando's love for each other is sometimes presented as an Ascetic parody of Petrarchism. Orlando especially is often silly enough to suggest self-parody, giving us puffed rhetoric and action from beginning to end, as when he breaks into the Duke Senior's dinner with drawn sword and "Forbear, and eat no more," only to be told that he is silly and uncivil, and that dinner has not begun yet anyhow. Similarly, his love poetry, unlike that of his predecessor Rosader, is absurd and entirely worthy of the derision Touchstone, Celia, and Rosalind heap on it. Rosalind too sometimes slips into the Ascetic role of ludicrously excessive lover, as when she responds to the news of Orlando's presence in the forest by asking ten questions in six lines and demanding that Celia "Answer me in one word" (3.2.219–24). Later, an otherwise convincingly Petrarchan assertion of her love calls itself into question with a strange concluding metaphor:

Ros. O coz, coz, coz, my pretty little coz, that thou didst know how many fathom deep I am in love! But it cannot be sounded; my affection hath an unknown bottom, like the bay of Portugal.
Cel. Or rather, bottomless—that as fast as you pour affection in, it runs out. (4.1.205–8)

Love compared to a bay is hardly a common Petrarchan metaphor, and the juxtaposition of "affection" and "bottom" carries just enough suggestion of bawdry to make the whole statement slightly comic—and thus suggestive of the Ascetic view that all lovers are fools.

Besides acting out a straightforward Petrarchan role and parodying both Petrarchism and the Ascetic, Rosalind also follows her friend Touchstone in making sincere Ascetic definitions about sexual attraction. The best known of these is her assertion that the great tragic love stories of the past have been shams, that in actuality Troilus and Leander died ordinary deaths having nothing to do with love: "Men have died from time to time, and worms have eaten them, but not for love" (4.1.106–8). A few lines later, Rosalind follows Orlando's predictable Petrarchism with another evidently sincere correction, then immediately shifts to self-parody:

Ros. Now tell me how long you would have her after you have possess'd her.
Orl. For ever and a day.
Ros. Say "a day," without the "ever." No, no, Orlando, men are April when they woo, December when they wed; maids are May when they are maids, but the sky changes when they are wives. I will be more jealous of thee

than a Barbary cock-pigeon over his hen, more clamorous than a parrot against rain, more new-fangled than an ape, more giddy in my desires than a monkey. I will weep for nothing, like Diana in the fountain, and I will do that when you are dispos'd to be merry. I will laugh like a hyen, and that when thou art inclin'd to sleep. (4.1.142–56)

What is the point of this mixture of types? Perhaps the best explanation is C. L. Barber's—that the satirizing of the ideal world by Rosalind, Touchstone, and Jaques gives the play a sense of both realism and pathos, the latter because the satire makes us see that the ideal can never exist for us or (as Rosalind notes) even for the characters themselves.[6] Many others have used Rosalind's conflicting views of love as the basis for a portrait of her in terms of "psychological realism," that is, describing Rosalind as if she were a real person, in this case one truly in love but also aware of the impermanence of that emotion, or of the inaccuracy of Petrarchan conventions as definitions of love, or of the necessity of giving up part of her identity and most of her freedom with marriage.[7]

Such interpretations seem perfectly natural to us, since we are used to the game of turning contradictory or at least divergent traits into psychologically coherent characters. Indeed, when we are presented characters who too closely fit a recognizable type we dismiss them as one-dimensional, stereotyped, or obvious; we want to see each character as an individual whose personality can never quite be pinned down, just as a real person supposedly cannot be described only in terms of one or even a combination of types. This method of understanding has the great advantage of making literature more challenging and complex, and also of making it seem to be drawn from life itself, but it does not have much to do with how a character or story comes to have meaning in the first place. Psychological coherence is the system we employ when a character does not stay within the boundaries of a single type; its function is as the framework for integrating certain other exterior structures (Freudianism and other psychological systems, systems of morality, Marxism and other political systems, etc.) into the single interior system that allows us to perceive him or her as a unified whole. The contradictory traits that trigger its use, however, are always taken from established literary forms (else they would have no meaning to a wide audience); thus it is the underlying types that determine how the character is perceived, as opposed to the thematic-psychological question of why the character acts as he or she does.

For the Elizabethans, however, the psychological coherence game was not as fully developed as it is for us, and more importantly, it was not a mode of understanding associated with comedy, which before Shakespeare almost never crosses types so contradictory as the Petrarchan and Ascetic, or with female characters, who before Shakespeare are almost never represented in terms of mixed types. Why the change? One reason may have been to take advantage of the increased erotic potential of the kind of mixed-type heroine Shakespeare creates in plays like *As You Like It*. By adding the sexual interest and awareness implied by her Ascetic jokes to the chastity and general value implied by the Petrarchan, Shakespeare makes Rosalind seem both sensuous and virginal, thereby combining the most alluring features of both the whore and the goddess. Similarly, the satirizing of Touchstone-Audrey, Silvius-Phebe, and even Orlando makes Rosalind seem by far the strongest character in the play; nevertheless, she repeatedly asserts that her major ambition is to marry Orlando. Thus she fulfills an erotic fantasy for all of us who have ever wanted either to win the queen of the ball or to be her.

Another reason may be that the socially and sexually mixed audiences of the Elizabethan popular theater demanded a more complex representation of women.[8] Certainly, however, the mixing of types did not occur because the audience demanded a more realistic representation of women than Petrarchism afforded. Indeed, the reason Petrarchan writers before Shakespeare adhere so closely to their model is that significant deviation would have seemed unrealistic both to them and to their readers. They knew, of course, that real women are not as sexless as Petrarchan ladies, just as we know that real sex is often routine and seldom an overwhelmingly important part of a person's life; in both instances realism is defined by literary and other narrative types, not by the world itself. In any case, whether because of the quality of Shakespeare's plays or because of some more basic change in the society, or both, what seemed realistic in 1580 changed, and by the turn of the century, Shakespeare was regularly producing mixed-type heroines in both comedies and tragedies. While the old types continued to be used by some other playwrights, including the classically inclined Ben Jonson (not surprisingly most remembered for his male characters), others routinely and often badly adopted the Shakespearean type—as in Heywood's *A Woman Killed with Kindness*, where Ann is initially a strong Petrarchan lady (though one who has already given herself to a deserving lover), then almost immediately an Ascetic animal who cannot control herself or resist even the weakest Seduction rhetoric. By the end of the seventeenth century, the Restoration stage was dominated by Shakespearean revivals and contemporary plays with heroines of the Shakespearean mixed type.

Eventually, this type became the basis for women in Richardson's and Fielding's novels, which in turn helped form the women of Victorian novels. In the nineteenth century, the type was forced into its first significant change by the increasing number of female writers and readers and by the extreme goddess-whore separation seen as realistic during most of this century. The Victorians did not, however, simply return to the Petrarchan type; they changed instead the sexual awareness and aggressiveness of Shakespearean women into strong pronouncements of love and, occasionally, aggressive husband-stalking (Austen, the Brontës, Thackeray); unlike their Petrarchan forebears, Victorian Petrachan ladies almost always declare their love (if only to the reader) and often take positive steps to bring it to fruition.

The twentieth century, of course, is most obviously notable for not only returning sexual awareness and aggressiveness to women but for making sex a prime focus with both male and female characters. Nonetheless, while numerous feminist and other writers are groping toward substantially new types, it is still the basic Shakespearean mixed type that seems to us most natural and real. Contemporary fictional women are seldom virgins and may have many sex partners, but current writers and readers even now tend to insist that positive female characters seek a love that transcends sex. At least as significant—and most exasperating for those seeking to develop new types—is the fact that it remains difficult to represent women for whom love and sex are not the dominant considerations, even though they are probably not any more dominant in real women's lives than in men's. Men can be represented as primarily warriors, sports figures, scientists, and so on, because we have long had narrative forms that make such representations possible. But because women have throughout Western culture been represented only in narratives (or parts of narratives) that focus on sexual relationships, it is still not possible easily to portray women except in terms of types associated with that subject.

As noted, there have been numerous changes in the Shakespearean type during the nearly four hundred years since its development, but the basis of the form has always been an amalgam of the intelligence, aggressiveness, and overt sexuality of Ascetic women, with the chastity, seriousness, and value of Petrarchan ladies. In the tragedies, the use of types is much more complex, but before I discuss the function of love in those works, a short look at love and women in a few more comedies will further illustrate how Shakespeare created the modern type by combining traditionally antagonistic elements of older ones.

The earliest of Shakespeare's plays to portray its heroines in terms of a radical mixture of types is *Love's Labor's Lost*. More noted for language and ideas than characterization, this play nevertheless marks Shakespeare's first breakthrough into what became his standard method of characterization of women. As in *As You Like It*, the upper-class relationships in *Love's Labor's Lost* are built primarily on the Petrarchan model. The "little academy" that excludes women so that reason might thrive is, on the surface, an Ascetic creation, since it asserts the triviality and potential danger to any serious activity posed by women. Men who deny that they can be overcome by love are, however, a staple of Petrarchan literature (Chaucer's Troilus is a good example), so such a declaration in this play—especially one as excessive as the Prince's—leads us to view the opening passage in terms of the Petrarchan type and to expect that the would-be academicians will soon be professing undying love. In other words, the description of the academy is a satire of the Ascetic view, drawn from the perspective of Petrarchism.

While the men maintain a distrust of love up until the moment they see the women, none of the women ever makes a similar comment and all are in love almost from the time we meet them, as we and the Princess can see from their descriptions of their respective men:

> God bless my ladies! are they all in love,
> That every one her own hath garnished
> With such bedecking ornaments of praise?
> (2.1.77–79)

The Princess herself soon falls in love with the King, but unlike the men, the women do not declare their love, waiting instead for the men to prove themselves. Like the women in most sonnet sequences, they help this process along by denying that the men are really sincere in their love. Eventually they end the play by insisting that each man undergo a trial of his love, a conclusion that runs contrary to usual comic form, as Berowne observes, but which is very much in line with Petrarchism in general.

While the frame of the play is thoroughly Petrarchan, most of the dialogue is so bawdy that a whole book has been written on the subject.[9] Many of the double entendres directly concern the four women, as when Boyet ("the old love-monger") and Katherine joke about the relationship of her lips to a common pasture. Later, Boyet assures Rosalind that there will be no shortage of horns when she marries, and she responds that he is a cuckold already (4.1.108–17). In his assertion that her affliction is lower than the forehead, she responds that if so he cannot "hit it." He then continues the jest with Maria, exclaiming that this unhittable mark should then "have a prick in't," which leads to more bawdry and finally to Costard's apt (if unintentionally so) comment:

> By my soul, a swain, a most simple clown!
> Lord, Lord, how the ladies and I have put him down!
> O' my troth, most sweet jests, most incony vulgar wit!
> When it comes so smoothly off, so obscenely as it
>   were, so fit.
> (4.1.140–43)

Even though the men eventually talk too "greasily" for the women, it is the women who begin the double entendres, and they certainly stay around longer than any simple Petrarchan lady would (if such humor were ever a part of Petrarchan narratives). In this passage as in several others, each woman is portrayed more in terms of the "wench" Rosalind once calls

Katherine (5.2.25)—more like the bawdy, husband-cuckolding lower-class women who populate fabliaux—than like sexless Petrarchan ladies.

Besides the bawdry, there are several other non-Petrarchan elements in the play, two of especial note. First, Berowne's transition from Ascetic academic to Petrarchan lover is much muddied by his speech conceding to love:

> O, and I, forsooth, in love! I that have been love's whip,
> A very beadle to a humorous sigh,
> A critic, nay, a night-watch constable,
> A domineering pedant o'er the boy,
> Than whom no mortal so magnificent!
> This wimpled, whining, purblind, wayward boy,
> This senior-junior, giant-dwarf, Dan Cupid,
> Regent of love-rhymes, lord of folded arms,
> Th' anointed sovereign of sighs and groans,
> Liege of all loiterers and malcontents,
> Dread prince of plackets, king of codpieces,
> Sole imperator and great general
> Of trotting paritors (O my little heart!),
> And I to be a corporal of his field,
> And wear his colors like a tumbler's hoop!
> What! I love, I sue, I seek a wife—
> A woman, that is like a German clock,
> Still a-repairing, ever out of frame,
> And never going aright, being a watch,
> But being watch'd that it may still go right!
> (3.1.174–93)

Berowne admits to love here, but hardly in the Petrarchan sense; rather he portrays himself as the typical Ascetic lover: unmanly for devoting himself to a childish, immature passion, and exceedingly foolish for worshiping so low a creature as a woman. And lest we think his passion for Rosalind is somehow high-minded anyway, he goes on to note the "two pitch-balls stuck in her face for eyes" and then to play on the Elizabethan double meaning for eye (vagina) with "Ay, and, by heaven, one that will do the deed / Though Argus were her eunuch and her guard" (3.1.198–99). For Berowne in this passage, love is only desire and irrationality. If this view were made the dominant one, all of the love relationships would seem ridiculous, and the play would be a farce instead of a comedy; by only using such a view sporadically (and never again so obviously), Shakespeare makes both the relationships and the women in them seem ambivalent and complex—still positive, but somehow different and more sophisticated than either their Petrarchan or their Ascetic models.

A second major departure from Petrarchism concerns the actions of the women. A good deal of the criticism of the play has centered on why the women so abuse the men they are in love with, the consensus being that they want to pull them away from the artificial world and toward the more positive natural one, a view that fits well with the Petrarchan lady's role in stimulating her lover to improve himself.[10] It is hard to deny, however, that in a few passages the women abuse the men mostly because they take a perverse joy in doing so. For example, late in the play the Princess asserts that "We are wise girls to mock our lovers so," which is Petrarchan enough, but Rosaline goes on to make a most un-Petrarchan extension:

> They are worse fools to purchase mocking so.
> That same Berowne I'll torture ere I go.
> O that I knew he were but in by th' week!
> How I would make him fawn, and beg, and seek,
> And wait the season, and observe the times,
> And spend his prodigal wits in bootless rhymes,
> And shape his service wholly to my device,
> And make him proud to make me proud that jests!
> So pair-taunt-like would I o'ersway his state
> That he should be my fool and I his fate.
> (5.2.59–68)

Rosaline's concern here is her own joy in the situation; she suggests no possible value in the experience for Berowne, and in fact wants to make him her "fool." This Emasculating view (reminiscent of Andreas's uncourtly refuser of love), like the Ascetic one in Berowne's speech above, would be enough to destroy the play as a comedy if sustained, but as an occasional sidelight it only causes the women to seem less easily understood and more threatening than simple Petrarchan ladies.

Love's Labor's Lost shows itself an early play by not providing much connection between the multiple types used in each relationship. In *As You Like It,* the Ascetic portrayals are usually shown as an act of Rosalind, an accurate commentary on a ludicrous relationship, or a satire of a few excessive actions by an otherwise positive lover; but in *Love's Labor's Lost* no such "explanations" are offered for the Ascetic and Emasculating representations: they are just there, in an uneasy balance with the Petrarchan. Rosaline and Berowne have the most such deviations, which makes them the play's most interesting and complex characters, but the lack of connections between the types ultimately leaves them too chaotic to seem understandable.

Much Ado about Nothing, on the other hand, while presenting a similar situation—a series of deviations from Petrarchism, centered mainly on two characters—provides a much more complete way of making all of the characters seem unified. Actually, even though Beatrice and Benedick are given more of the deviations, the dominant one concerns the play's other lovers,

Hero and Claudio. These two characters are at first represented strictly in terms of the Petrarchan type. Claudio's first words, in fact, are about Hero, and he goes on in the same scene to compare her to a jewel, to call her the most beautiful woman in the world, and to declare that having shown his manhood in war, he has now fallen in love:

> That I love her, I feel. . . .
>   O my lord,
> When you went onward on this ended action,
> I look'd upon her with a soldier's eye,
> That lik'd, but had a rougher task in hand
> Than to drive liking to the name of love.
> But now I am return'd, and that war-thoughts
> Have left their places vacant, in their rooms
> Come thronging soft and delicate desires,
> All prompting me how fair young Hero is,
> Saying I lik'd her ere I went to wars.
>   (1.1.227, 296–305)

Hero, conversely, is so thoroughly discreet and chaste that the only time she works up the courage to declare her love, she does it so softly that only Claudio can hear her (2.1.316–17). Not surprisingly, when Margaret remarks that her heart will "be heavier soon by the weight of a man" (3.4.26), she is embarrassed and thinks Margaret should be ashamed. Even after she has been savagely abused by her fiancé, in church, on her wedding day, she still retains her love, and is perfectly satisfied to marry Claudio after he repents.

Much has been written about how an otherwise positive Claudio could be so vile as to abuse Hero in public, but in terms of the Petrarchan type his actions are quite consistent. Claudio's love for Hero, like all Petrarchan loves, serves for him the same purpose as the recent war where he "better bett'rd expectation": it provides him with honor, makes him more noble. His falling in love with a virtuous and beautiful woman shows his advance from mere military hero, and her acceptance of his love marks a public ratification of his social stature. But when he comes to believe that she is a whore, she ceases to function as a symbol of his nobility and becomes instead a manipulator, drawing him into a corrupt marriage just as she seemed to draw Borachio into her bedroom. Claudio's Hero, then, becomes a Circe figure, that is, a woman whose apparent beauty and virtue are a carefully wrought illusion hiding ugliness and lust. His accusations at the would-be wedding reflect this view:

> There, Leonato, take her back again.
> Give not this rotten orange to your friend,
> She's but the sign and semblance of her honor.

> Behold how like a maid she blushes here!
> O, what authority and show of truth
> Can cunning sin cover itself withal!
> Comes not that blood as modest evidence
> To witness simple virtue? Would you not swear,
> All you that see her, that she were a maid,
> By these exterior shows? But she is none:
> She knows the heat of a luxurious bed;
> Her blush is guiltiness, not modesty....
> Out on thy seeming! I will write against it;
> You seem to me as Dian in her orb,
> As Chaste as is the bud ere it be blown;
> But you are more intemperate in your blood
> Than Venus, or those pamp'red animals
> That rage in savage sensuality.
> (4.1.31–42, 56–61)

The "pamp'red animals" and the exceptionally negative Venus he alludes to are both inhabitants of evil pleasure gardens, and Claudio naturally views himself as in danger of a metaphoric imprisonment in just such a place, with Hero being a Circe figure powerful and evil enough to seem like "Dian in her orb" even as she is accused of the vilest lechery. So, to protect his honor, his virtue, and—ultimately—his manhood, he violently withdraws from the match. And lest we dismiss his accusation out of hand, Shakespeare has Don Pedro—a symbol of moderation and propriety throughout the play—stand by his every word.[11]

Had Hero been portrayed all along as equivalent to Claudio's conception of her, his reactions would not seem so excessive. After all, a sixteenth-century woman bold enough to make love to a ruffian in her father's house on the night before her marriage to a military hero would surely be portrayed as something more dangerous than a simple whore. But we know all along, of course, that Hero is innocent and that the love between her and Claudio is being threatened by Don John; thus we see the relationship in terms of New Comedy, and hence as Petrarchan rather than Emasculating. In other versions of the story, it is this New Comic–Petrarchan view that is given exclusive sway, as in *Orlando Furioso*, where the Claudio figure simply disappears after seeing what he thinks is his fiancé's infidelity. After considerable reflection, he returns to fight his own brother (filling Don Pedro's role) in protection of the woman's honor—which as far as he knows is hopelessly stained. By relieving him of the need to confront the lady, Ariosto allows his hero to express outrage without forfeiting our sympathy. Not all versions portray the hero so positively, but neither do any have such an explicit and painful repudiation scene as *Much Ado*.[12]

Obviously, Shakespeare could have made his version easier to swallow, but instead he plays what is in effect a narrative trick upon his audience. What would be an understandable, if immoderate, denunciation of a witch and whore as part of the exit from an Emasculating relationship seems unforgivable when placed in a New Comic context. As readers or viewers we are therefore asked to conceive of the relationship in terms of two contradictory types, the real Petrarchan view, in which the villain is Don John, and Claudio's false but understandable Emasculating view, in which Hero is a Circe figure about to lead him into a relationship that will destroy both his honor and his self. Ariosto avoids the problems raised by this paradoxical situation by having his deceived lover disappear without saying a word. Rather than sidestep this paradox, as does Ariosto, Shakespeare emphasizes it by making Claudio's denunciation as extreme and unequivocal as possible, while at the same time using Don Pedro's deception as well as other elements in the play to make sure we understand that Claudio is intended to be a positive character.

The story that results is more interesting and complex than Ariosto's, but the ending presents the reader with no obvious way to connect the contradictory types. Such a conclusion may make us see the difficulty in forgiving sin, as R. G. Hunter argues,[13] and it certainly makes us aware of the artificiality of comic structure, much as in *Measure for Measure*, *All's Well That Ends Well*, and to a lesser extext, most of the other comedies. Whatever the interpretation of modern audiences and readers, and whatever Shakespeare's original intention, it is hard to imagine a more forceful combination of two contradictory types in the portrayal of a single figure than the use of Petrarchan and Emasculating in the characterization of Claudio.

The most interesting characters in *Much Ado about Nothing* are Beatrice and Benedick, and they are interesting mostly because the intermixing of the types that define their relationship is more complex than that of Hero and Claudio, if not so obvious. Benedick, like Berowne, plays the Petrarchan role of a disdainer of love who finally falls in love himself, and also like Berowne, his Ascetic disdain is carried farther than is usually the case. He begins as a conventional enough "obstinate heretic in the despite of beauty," who replies to Don Pedro's hope that "I shall see thee, ere I die, look pale with love" by asserting: "With anger, with sickness, or with hunger, my lord, not with love. Prove that ever I lose more blood with love than I will get again with drinking, pick out mine eyes with a ballad-maker's pen, and hang me up at the door of a brothel-house for the sign of blind Cupid" (1.1.249–54). He thanks his mother for conceiving and bringing him up, but otherwise his attitude toward women is that he will "trust none" and hence remain a bachelor, at least until he finds a woman in whom "all graces" reside.[14]

Traditionally, this familiar character type completely reverses form when he falls in love and immediately adopts the mannerisms he previously disdained. Benedick departs from the tradition here, for his falling in love never leads to the changes he so ruefully describes in Claudio (2.2.6–21). Indeed, he seems to fall in love mainly as a response to his friends' criticism of his pride:

Love me? why, it must be requited. I hear how I am censur'd; they say I will bear myself proudly, if I perceive the love come from her; they say too that she will rather die than give any sign of affection. I did never think to marry. I must not seem proud; happy are they that hear their detractions, and can put them to mending. They say the lady is fair; 'tis a truth, I can bear them witness; and virtuous; 'tis so, I cannot reprove it; and wise, but for loving me; by my troth, it is no addition to her wit, nor no great argument of her folly, for I will be horribly in love with her. (2.3.224–35)

In its implicit denial that the lady herself could possibly stimulate a positive relationship, this view suggests the Ascetic, but Benedick later assures us of the Petrarchan basis of his love when he goes against his allegiance, his friendship, and his own inclination to challenge Claudio—all because Beatrice wants him to do so as a proof of his love. So, like Berowne, Benedick is represented in terms of two types, but for the later character Shakespeare suggests the Ascetic not through a denunciation of the lady, thereby making the man's love seem irrational, but through Benedick's more gentle questioning of his pride and its relation to his friends and his ability to love. The result is that whereas the characterization of Berowne seems abrupt and chaotic, that of Benedick seems more realistic—more like a real human struggling to understand his own motivation and place in society.

Beatrice is also portrayed mostly in terms of the Petrarchan type: her beauty attracts her future lover in spite of his resistance (1.1.190–92), she is virtuous and of the upper class, and even though she admits her love for Benedick, she does not yield to him in any real sense until he has worked to avenge the honor of a wronged lady. But woven into this basic Petrarchan cloth is a pattern of Ascetic suggestions that makes her one of Shakespeare's most complex and interesting comic characters.

Throughout most of the first part of the play, Beatrice is represented as the Ascetic counterpart of Benedick: the shrew who refuses to be civil with possible husbands. After her two uncles berate her for being "shrewd of the tongue" and "too curst," she states her aversion to men directly: "Not till God make men of some other mettle than earth. Would it not grieve a woman to be overmaster'd with a piece of valiant dust? to make an account of her life to a clod of wayward marl? No, uncle, I'll none. Adam's sons are my brethren, and truly I hold it a sin to match in my kindred" (2.1.59–65). More succinctly, she tells Benedick that "I had rather hear my dog bark at a crow than a man swear he loves me" (1.1.131–32), to which he responds with an Ascetic portrait of the kind of wife she would be: "God keep your ladyship still in that mind! so some gentleman or other shall scape a predestinate scratch'd face" (1.1.133–35).

And like Shakespeare's other "mixed" women (but unlike Hero), Beatrice is not embarrassed by bawdry and sometimes employs it herself. For example, when Don Pedro tells her that one of her jests at Benedick's expense has "put him down," she answers "So I would not he should do me, my lord, lest I should prove the mother of fools" (2.1.285–86). She is not embarrassed to have Benedick say he wants to "die in thy lap" (5.2.102), and unlike Hero, she is quite able to parley with Margaret, punning on "light-heeled" (unchaste) and barns (bairns) when Margaret wants to dance "light a' love": "Ye light a' love with your heels! then if your husband have stables enough, you'll see he shall lack no barns" (3.4.47–49).[15]

Beatrice is a subplot character, and thus the mixture of types is not as fully developed as it is in Rosalind, but in one important way her portrayal goes beyond that of her *As You Like It* sister: whereas Rosalind eventually returns to a straight, unthreatening Petrarchan representation (dressed in a wedding gown and brought onstage by Hymen himself), Beatrice never really makes this move. Rather than transform her to fit the highly erotic conclusion of the Petrarchan type—the surrender of the previously unassailable lady—Shakespeare stretches the shrew representation almost past recognition when Beatrice proclaims her anger at Claudio: "Is 'a not approv'd in the height a villain, that hath slander'd, scorn'd, dishonor'd my kinswoman? O that I were a man! What, bear her in hand until they come to take hands, and then with public accusation, uncover'd slander, unmitigated rancor—O God, that I were a man! I would eat his heart in the market-place" (4.1.301–7). Shrews are shrews because they disdain the female role, but Beatrice has gone far beyond that point. Partly because her cause is justified—unlike shrews before her, who usually have no cause—and partly because of the masculine connotations of her desire to "eat his heart in the market-place," Beatrice pushes feminine characterization as close to masculine as possible; further identification with masculine types would doubtless leave her completely inexplicable. Rather than let her character disintegrate (in the sense that we would be unable to integrate what we see into the types through which we conceptualize character), Shakespeare backs off, by having Beatrice say that "I cannot be a man with wishing, therefore I will die a woman with grieving" (4.1.322–23) and by having Benedick take up the quarrel for her. Nevertheless, the scene serves as a powerful tool for distancing Beatrice from her basic Petrarchan characterization, a distance that Shakespeare never gives up, even in the conclusion, where Beatrice's explanations to Benedick of why she will marry him take the form of a parody of the Petrarchan rationale for the lady giving in: "I would not deny you, but by this good day, I yield upon great persuasion, and partly to save your life, for I was told you were in a consumption" (5.4.94–97). Beatrice is not Shakespeare's most complete example of mixed types, but she is, in some ways, the most extreme.

The Merchant of Venice, Twelfth Night, All's Well That Ends Well, and *Measure for Measure* also contain women and sexual relationships that are represented in terms of conflicting types, but the comedy that makes the most varied use of types is certainly *A Midsummer Night's Dream.*[16] The play begins with Theseus and Hippolyta set up in terms of a New Comic, Petrarchan relationship: he complains that since they can't be married until the new moon, the old one is an enemy holding him from his love; she soothes that the time will pass quickly enough. Like lovers at the end of a New Comedy, only time now holds them from one another. But as soon as Theseus mentions what the former blocking forces were, we realize that this quiet conclusion hardly fits the beginning and middle:

> Hippolyta, I woo'd thee with my sword,
> And won thy love doing thee injuries;
> But I will wed thee in another key,
> With pomp, with triumph, and with revelling.
> (1.1.16–19)

Military metaphors are common in Petrarchan literature, but in this case Theseus literally had to conquer as his bride the epitome of all women who refuse to accept the physical and social superiority of men. As we learn later (2.1.77–80), Theseus' accustomed procedure with female war prizes is the usual Ascetic one: rape or seduction, then abandonment. But Hippolyta has somehow become a passive and loving fiancé, and there is not the slightest indication of rancor on either side.

The relationship as it is initially presented, then, is contradictory, for a Petrarchan relationship implies a courtship based on service, not injuries, and on metaphoric rather than actual battles. Shakespeare could have provided some sort of bridge between the two, as did Ariosto and Spenser in slightly analogous episodes in *Orlando Furioso* and the *Faerie Queene,*[17] but in this case the only explanation is Theseus' smug conviction that his own military prowess caused Hippolyta to see the light and become a proper woman. This Ascetic fantasy is undercut, however, by the mythic importance of the two lovers, for such a union as theirs implies an end to the eternal war of the sexes, a wonderful and mysterious *discordia concors*. This implied relationship hints at the Etherealized type, where a human sexual union constitutes an ideal state.

The Ascetic view of the relationship, though, is much the stronger in the first speeches, and it becomes stronger the more Theseus and Hippolyta are on stage. Theseus especially contributes to the effect by playing to the hilt the part of a wise king, condescendingly aware of his own legal and intellectual superiority. This wise-king act is apparent later in the first scene when he sternly admonishes Hermia to yield to her father, and it is made quite prominent in the last scene, where he dismisses what the four lovers claim to have experienced (and what we have just seen enacted) as nothing but the product of "seething brains" and as "More than cool reason ever comprehends" (5.1.5, 6). Theseus' condescension toward the lovers, whom he regards as weak and irrational, marks him as strongly tending toward the Ascetic view of love, which might explain why he would prefer to take a wife by military force. In any case, what Shakespeare is doing is solidifying the Ascetic nature of the Theseus-Hippolyta affair by portraying him as absolutely confident—though wrong—and as professing the most conservative possible view of love—and the one the play as a whole most directly contradicts.[18]

But while the Ascetic becomes more and more oppressively apparent once Theseus and Hippolyta return to the stage near the conclusion, Shakespeare uses an interesting technique between the beginning and the end to reevoke the Etherealized type hinted at in the first scene: he creates another Theseus and Hippolyta, but this time as sovereigns of the forest rather than the city. These nighttime reflections and counterparts are linked to the human king and queen by a variety of structural, linguistic, and dramatic parallels, and are sometimes played by the same actor and actress. Oberon and Titania represent the discordia that once prevailed between Theseus and Hippolyta, for the fairy quarrel is also based on the question of whether or not the male should dominate. The result of this otherworldly battle is general disaster on earth, where the seasons have been thrown out of order, and where storms, floods, and infertility have left the world "mazed." As Titania puts it,

> And this same progeny of evils comes
> From our debate, from our dissension;
> We are their parents and original.
> (2.1.115–17)

Oberon and Titania are portrayed as the mysterious forces which, when in unity, produce order and fertility, but working against each other, produce the opposite; they thus serve as a powerful reminder of the special status of the Theseus-Hippolyta marriage.

This view of sexual relationships as mysterious and good calls into question Theseus' Ascetic view of love and sexuality, as do Titania and Oberon's assertion of sexual links between themselves and the two human monarchs. For example, Titania asserts that Hippolyta is sometimes Oberon's "warrior love," but that at other times he has

> in the shape of Corin sat all day,
> Playing on pipes of corn, and versing love,
> To amorous Phillida.
>
> (2.1.66–68)

To this pastoral description (which, if extended, would be either Seduction or Petrarchan, depending on how Oberon's love is represented), Oberon responds with an account of a relationship between Titania and Theseus in which the latter is driven by an overwhelming passion for the former:

> How canst thou thus for shame, Titania,
> Glance at my credit with Hippolyta,
> Knowing I know thy love to Theseus?
> Didst thou not lead him through the glimmering night
> From Perigenia, whom he ravished?
> And made him with fair Aegles break his faith,
> With Ariadne, and Antiopa?
>
> (2.1.74–80)

Even the child they are fighting over is associated with exotic, idealized sexuality:

> His mother was a vot'ress of my order,
> And in the spiced Indian air, by night,
> Full often hath she gossip'd by my side,
> And sat with me on Neptune's yellow sands,
> Marking th' embarked traders on the flood;
> When we have laugh'd to see the sails conceive
> And grow big-bellied with the wanton wind;
> Which she, with pretty and with swimming gait,
> Following (her womb then rich with my young squire)
> Would imitate, and sail upon the land
> To fetch me trifles, and return again,
> As from a voyage, rich with merchandise.
> But she, being mortal, of that boy did die,
> And for her sake do I rear up her boy;
> And for her sake I will not part with him.
>
> (2.1.123–37)

This last passage admirably represents a way to use sexuality to invoke both the ideal and the ordinary worlds. The exotic atmosphere created by the "spiced Indian air" and "Neptune's yellow sands," the Diana-like portrait of women free of men and the ordinary role of their sex (Titania is an Ovidian name for Diana), and the carefree gaiety of the future mother, all combine to make her pregnancy seem somehow uncorrupted and sinless, somehow both sexual and innocent, worldly and ideal. But immediately after this evocative description, the knowledge that the woman died in childbirth—the pain of which is woman's reminder of Eve's sin—brings us back to the ordinary, nonideal world that makes the other seem pleasant and wonderful.

When the fairy king and queen are finally reconciled by her submission to his will (and after her parodic relationship with the ass-eared Bottom), the hinted discordia concors is reinvoked and Oberon's Etherealized blessing of the triple wedding can proceed. But before the marriages, there are the escapades of the nonroyal lovers, who combine and recombine in a dizzying array of separate and often contradictory relationships. This is not the place for a full examination of these relationships, but a few comments will indicate their range and nature, and their difference from the others. The first relationship we see is that of Hermia and Lysander (in 1.1), and since they are portrayed as trueloves held apart by a tyrannical father, their relationship at first seems a clear example of the New Comic (and hence Petrarchan) type. But it soon becomes a parody of the same type as the lovers' analysis of their situation becomes comically extreme:

> *Lys.* Ay me! for aught that I could ever read,
> Could ever hear by tale or history,
> The course of true love never did run smooth;
> But either it was different in blood—
> *Her.* O cross! too high to be enthrall'd to low.
> *Lys.* Or else misgraffed in respect of years—
> *Her.* O spite! too old to be engaged to young.
> *Lys.* Or else it stood upon the choice of friends—
> *Her.* O hell, to choose love by another's eyes!
> (1.1.132–40)

But Lysander follows with what is often quoted as the epitome of statements beautifying—and idealizing—young love (by which is meant Petrarchan love):

> Or if there were sympathy in choice,
> War, death, or sickness did lay siege to it,
> Making it momentany as a sound,
> Swift as a shadow, short as any dream,
> Brief as the lightning in the collied night,
> That, in a spleen, unfolds both heaven and earth;
> And ere a man hath power to say "Behold!"
> The jaws of darkness do devour it up:
> So quick bright things come to confusion.
> (1.1.141–49)

In addition to the Petrarchan, the Etherealized is suggested here by paradoxically linking it to mysterious aspects of nature and to extreme brevity—the latter because nothing ideal can be imaged as existing long on the corrupt

68 / *The Structure of Love*

earth (hence the frequent use of flowers as symbols of the ideal). But immediately after this passage, the excessiveness of the lovers becomes quite apparent again, as in Hermia's long, ridiculous promise to meet Lysander in the woods, which concludes:

> And by that fire which burn'd the Carthage queen
> When the false Troyan under sail was seen,
> By all the vows that ever men have broke
> (In number more than ever women spoke),
> In that same place thou has appointed me
> To-morrow truly will I meet with thee.
> (1.1.173–78)

Once in the forest the relationship changes, first to a lighthearted Seduction-based parody of Petrarchism in which Hermia refuses Lysander's suggestion that "by your side no bed-room me deny" (2.2.51), then to another serious portrayal of Petrarchism.[19] This regained seriousness is indicated by Hermia's depth of feeling and by her allusion to a threatening outside force upon finding Lysander vanished into the night (but not, we know, of his free will):

> Help me, Lysander, help me! do thy best
> To pluck this crawling serpent from my breast!
> Ay me, for pity! what a dream was here!
> Lysander, look how I do quake with fear.
> Methought a serpent eat my heart away,
> And you sate smiling at his cruel prey.
> Lysander! what, remov'd? Lysander! lord!
> (2.2.145–51)

Helena's tribulations also begin in seriousness but quickly change to parody. Her chasing of Demetrius reverses the usual sexual roles of the Petrarchan type and creates parody as a result, because the traditional images of servitude she uses cannot remain serious (unless completely perverse) once stripped of their conventional gender context:

> You draw me, you hard-hearted adamant;
> But yet you draw not iron, for my heart
> Is true as steel. Leave you your power to draw,
> And I shall have no power to follow you. . . .
> I am your spaniel; and, Demetrius,
> The more you beat me, I will fawn on you.
> Use me but as your spaniel; spurn me, strike me,
> Neglect me, lose me; only give me leave,
> Unworthy as I am, to follow you.
> What worser place can I beg in your love

> (And yet a place of high respect with me)
> Than to be used as you use your dog?
>
> (2.1.195–98, 203–10)

If serious, this would have to be regarded as an Emasculating relationship with Demetrius filling the role of the lady who refuses to love, but nothing the lovers do in the forest seems serious enough to be evil.

Later, Helena is able to take the usual female role in a Petrarchan relationship, but it is made parodic nonetheless by our knowledge that both suitors are under a spell, and by Helena's constant assertion that she is being joked with; both of these again help strip away the normal context and let the natural excessiveness of such Petrarchan rhetoric as this shine through:

> O Helen, goddess, nymph, perfect, divine!
> To what, my love, shall I compare thine eyne?
> Crystal is muddy. O, how ripe in show
> Thy lips, those kissing cherries, tempting grow!
> That pure congealed white, high Taurus' snow,
> Fann'd with the eastern wind, turns to a crow
> When thou hold'st up thy hand. O, let me kiss
> This princess of pure white, this seal of bliss!
>
> (3.2.137–44)

So, while the royal lovers and the play's beginning and end oppose the Ascetic and the Etherealized, these nonroyal, middle relationships oppose the Petrarchan to itself, giving us a radical view of characters who are at once serious and parodic, sympathetic and ludicrous.

The conclusion of a *Midsummer Night's Dream* is, again, a study in contrasts. First comes Theseus' smug Ascetic deprecation of love and lovers, then the Mechanicals' "Pyramus and Thisbe," a ludicrous parody of a New Comic relationship (but one where the blocking force wins), punctuated by insults from the three pairs of newlyweds. The Hermia-Lysander and Helena-Demetrius relationships, it might be added, have now become quite as staid and Ascetic as Theseus and Hippolyta's, the blocking forces that made them special and Petrarchan having evaporated with the dawn.[20] But after the now ordinary humans exit at midnight, they are replaced by the fairies, who are definitely not ordinary and who remind us that the lovers are not to be seen as quite so ordinary as they act. The fairies have come to bless the lovers, or more particularly, to bless their beds:

> Now, until the break of day,
> Through this house each fairy stray.
> To the best bride-bed will we,
> Which by us shall blessed be;
> And the issue, there create,

> Ever shall be fortunate.
> So shall all the couples three
> Ever true in loving be;
> And the blots of Nature's hand
> Shall not in their issue stand;
> Never mole, hare-lip, nor scar,
> Nor mark prodigious, such as are
> Despised in nativity,
> Shall upon their children be.
>
> (5.1.401–14)

This connection of the supernatural to the sex act is clearly Etherealized, suggesting as it does that what is going on upstairs has a significance far greater than its importance to those involved—and certainly far greater than is suggested by the Ascetic Theseus, whose main worry seems to be that he is going to bed so late that he might "outsleep the coming morn." What is worthy of supernatural blessing to the fairies is not to him worth sleeping late for.

The result of this melange of types is clearly not, as in the other plays discussed, the creation of complex characters, for in *A Midsummer Night's Dream* the nonroyal lovers are so undifferentiated as to be interchangeable, and all of the others except Bottom (who has little relation to love types) are on stage too little for much development. Rather, the result is exactly what Puck tells us in the epilogue, to create the sensation of a dream:

> If we shadows have offended,
> Think but this, and all is mended,
> That you have but slumb'red here
> While these visions did appear.
> And this weak and idle theme,
> No more yielding but a dream,
> Gentles, do not reprehend.
>
> (5.1.423–29)

What *A Midsummer Night's Dream* gives us is a series of contradictory characterizations, each of which in isolation seems a straightforward recreation of the type it is taken from. Taken alone, each is quite understandable. Most of us easily understand the signs telling us that lovers are to be understood as serious and worthy of identification and sympathy; likewise we know when to take an Ascetic or Seduction perspective and view lovers as silly and excessive. And, given our experience with Shakespeare and his successors, we know now how to understand lovers who are both serious and silly, Petrarchan and Ascetic, provided we are given a context to work with—such as that the love itself is true, but the lovers are to be seen as temporarily silly while they and their relationship mature. In *A Midsummer*

Night's Dream, however, no such connections are provided, and in fact Shakespeare goes out of his way to make the oppositions in the portrayals of relationships as absolute and unbridgeable as possible. The result is to give us a sense of security in our identification of the types, but then radically to undermine that security by giving us type combinations we cannot identify. Thus the familiar and the strange, the ordered and the chaotic are presented to us, not just in the same play, but in the same representations—each of which seems real by itself, but unreal in combination with another type.

Such a sense—the strange made out of the very stuff of the familiar—is similar to the perception of a dream, where bizarre and impossible events often seem perfectly normal and in keeping with the realistic world. Finally then, the use of love types in *A Midsummer Night's Dream* is only partly concerned with representing love; the opposition of the types also aids in an entirely unrelated purpose—to give the play some of the same sense as a dream. Such a sophisticated use of types is not the norm in the comedies, but it is in some of the tragedies. And so with the types themselves and their use in the comedies as background, we can begin to examine the way in which types contribute to the process of perception in four tragedies.

4

The Paradise of Flesh:

Romeo and Juliet

Romeo and Juliet is not a profound play. Unlike the mature tragedies, which explore the nature of men, the workings of the gods, and similarly weighty subjects, it is content with showing that feuds are evil and that young love can be thwarted in the most pathetic ways. There are a few allusions to inexorable fate here and there, but as has been forcefully shown, they are inconsistently and somewhat unenthusiastically incorporated into the fabric of the play.[1] And while Romeo and Juliet do mature as the action progresses, they are hardly Hamlet or Cleopatra.[2] The play does have splendid poetry, but I do not think that the poetry alone can account for the popularity *Romeo and Juliet* has enjoyed for nearly four hundred years. The poetry certainly helps, but behind it is what may be Shakespeare's most carefully wrought and systematically developed plot.

The basis of this plot is our New Comic sympathy with the young lovers in their struggle against bad fortune and a hostile world. There are, however, at least a couple of major deviations from the usual. First, of course, most New Comedies end with the lovers victorious and the society cleansed and regenerated. Less obvious, *Romeo and Juliet* breaks from the mold by having its blocking character not a character at all, but rather a disembodied force: the feud. Using the feud as the blocking force has an important advantage over an actual character in serving its structural function: because it can be represented onstage by more than one character, it can be associated with the numerous and sometimes contradictory qualities of a series of personalities. So, unlike an ordinary character, which must be at least somewhat psycho-

The Paradise of Flesh: Romeo and Juliet / 73

logically consistent, the feud as interior system is limited only by the necessity that it oppose the lovers and seem repellent in comparison with them.

This freedom is important because the two most common ways in which one character is made to seem less attractive than another are directly contradictory. One way, of course, is to associate the repellent character with qualities that connote evil of one kind or another, as the prologue does by describing the feud through images of hate, broken order, and irrationality. The other way is to associate the repellent character with weakness or physical repulsiveness; it is through this method that ugly women, impotent or cowardly men, and deformed or socially deficient people of both sexes are made the butts of jokes in fabliaux, Greek and Roman comedy, and other literary forms. These two methods are contradictory because it is almost impossible for a thoroughly weak character to seem threateningly evil. For example, we have seen that repellent women could be portrayed in the sixteenth century as either weak and childlike (Ascetic) or powerful and intentionally perverse (Emasculating), but not both.

Obviously, the main opponent for any positive character must be portrayed as strong—that is, as evil instead of weak—for otherwise there could be no significant conflict between them. Thus the victim of an Ascetic woman must be portrayed as a weak individual, fit only for our laughter and scorn, while Circe figures commonly struggle with and defeat our most admired heroes. A New Comic narrative, as a result, must present its blocking force as evil rather than weak or its lovers will inevitably seem foolish and insignificant.

The prologue to *Romeo and Juliet* clearly portrays the feud as such a strong and evil force. The feud, we hear, has already caused mutiny within the state and led to the dissolution of normal civilities, and it will soon lead to the destruction of the "star-cross'd lovers," whose "misadventur'd piteous overthrows" are the direct result of the "continuance of their parents' rage." We are led to expect a conflict between two serious, capable adversaries who are fully capable of destroying both themselves and their children. There is not the slightest hint that either the feud or the lovers are to be understood with less than complete seriousness.

Scene one eventually provides a dangerous brawl covering both the stage and the social strata with "purple fountains" and "bloody hands." The exchanges leading to this conflagration, however, are surprisingly comic, and suggest weakness and impotence instead of strength. Our first two representatives of the feud are the clownlike servants Sampson and Gregory. The former is full of bluster toward Montague servants, especially the women, whom he would "thrust . . . to the wall" and make "feel while I am able to stand." Continuing the association of sexual and physical potency, he de-

74 / *The Structure of Love*

clares that "My naked weapon is out" when Abram and Balthasar appear. But Sampson's name is thoroughly ironic, for Gregory tells us that the "tool" in question is actually much like a dried fish, then has to prevent his partner from running away from the Montague servants.

After a silly exchange of legalisms, the four antagonists begin a swordfight so incompetent that Benvolio is appalled: "Part, fools! / Put up your swords, you know not what you do" (1.1.64–65). And Tybalt, crueler yet, calls the servants "heartless hinds" (1.1.66), a pun that not only compares the servants to females, but also asserts the same relationship of Tybalt to the servants that Sampson claimed he has to Montague's maids: male to female, strength to weakness, potency to impotence. But Tybalt is evidently not much of a swordsman either. He is able to kill Mercutio (in 3.1) only when Romeo holds his friend back, and in this scene is, according to Benvolio, blustery but ineffectual:

> In the instant came
> The fiery Tybalt, with his sword prepar'd
> Which, as he breath'd defiance to my ears,
> He swung about his head and cut the winds,
> Who, nothing hurt withal, hiss'd him in scorn.
> (1.1.108–12)

Tybalt cannot even hurt the wind, and as a result he, like Sampson, manages to associate himself with the weakness and impotence which he tries to ascribe to others.

The first Montague-Capulet altercation begins with servants and moves on to members of the families, Benvolio and Tybalt. From there it logically progresses to the two family patriarchs who originally started the feud and who should naturally be expected to demonstrate its seriousness and strength. But the two old men enter in their bedclothes instead of their armor, and rather than fight each other, they have more than enough trouble controlling their wives:

> *Cap.* What noise is this? Give me my long sword
>   ho!
> *La. Cap.* A crutch, a crutch! why call you for a
>   sword?
> *Cap.* My sword, I say! Old Montague is come,
> And flourishes his blade in spite of me.
> *Mon.* Thou villain Capulet!—Hold me not, let me go.
> *La. Mon.* Thou shall not stir one foot to seek a
>   foe.
> (1.1.75–80)

Old men dominated by their wives are a stock fixture of fabliaux and many other forms, and such characters are always associated with weakness and

The Paradise of Flesh: Romeo and Juliet / 75

impotence. As a result, the suggestions of these qualities are even stronger for Montague and Capulet than for Sampson and Tybalt, and where we expect the chief warriors of a dangerous little war, we get instead a careful evocation of one of literature's most laughable types.³

There is a serious risk in associating those representing the feud with impotence and domination by women: if the feud is entirely represented by fools we may not be able to take either it or the lovers seriously, the result of which would be the destruction of the New Comic plot and the reduction of the whole drama to either triviality or parody. Such might well have happened if Shakespeare had ended the scene with the wives henpecking the two patriarchs while Tybalt hacked away at the air. But instead the onstage brawl becomes serious enough to merit Escalus' description, the stern tone of which quickly reestablishes the sense of threat so apparent in the prologue. When Escalus and most of the others then quickly leave the stage only 103 lines into the play, Shakespeare has accomplished the seemingly impossible task of associating the feud with directly contradictory values: the strength to destroy the lovers on the one hand, but weakness, impotence, and even femaleness on the other.⁴

These 103 lines, plus the fourteen where Benvolio tells Montague and Lady Montague what happened, mark the first half of the scene. With the fourteen of the prologue, we have a unit parallel with the concluding 121 lines of scene 1.⁵ But this time Romeo's self-destructive love for Rosaline is the subject. Again, the initial description is in terms of genuine threat, for Benvolio and Montague describe Romeo's recent actions as a dangerous case of love melancholy. Romeo has been shunning his friends, staying up all night crying and wandering about, and spending the days locked in a shuttered room. His father is understandably worried about a son who seems to be slipping into a permanent "artificial night": "Black and portendous must this humor prove, / Unless good counsel may the cause remove" (1.1.141–42). Sampson's assertion that rape is an appropriate way to keep women in line and—especially—the wives attempting to overpower the patriarchs both suggest the Ascetic, but this description of Romeo's love as a serious disease is a far more straightforward evocation of the type. From this perspective, Romeo's love has made him a dangerously and perhaps fatally ill man, and strong corrective action is clearly warranted.⁶

But when Romeo appears, we get a very different picture. Like the clowns who follow the somber prologue, the Romeo who enters after Montague's speech seems to parody the seriousness that has preceded him. This comic instead of serious mood is established as soon as Romeo enters, for his deliberately confusing manipulation of Benvolio's questions, followed by a ludicrous subject change, is reminiscent both of numerous Shakespearean clowns and of comedy in general:

> *Ben.* What sadness lengthens Romeo's hours?
> *Rom.* Not having that which, having, makes them short.
> *Ben.* In love?
> *Rom.* Out—
> *Ben.* Of love?
> *Rom.* Out of her favor where I am in love.
> *Ben.* Alas that love, so gentle in his view,
> Should be so tyrannous and rough in proof.
> *Rom.* Alas that love, whose view is muffled still,
> Should, without eyes, see pathways to his will!
> Where shall we dine?
>
> (1.1.163–73)

No less ridiculous are the wild oxymorons immediately following:

> O me! what fray was here?
> Yet tell me not, for I have heard it all:
> Here's much to do with hate, but more with love.
> Why then, O brawling love! O loving hate!
> O any thing, of nothing first create!
> O heavy lightness, serious vanity,
> Misshapen chaos of well-seeming forms,
> Feather of lead, bright smoke, cold fire, sick health,
> Still-waking sleep, that is not what it is!
> This love feel I, that feel no love in this.
> Dost thou not laugh?
>
> (1.1.173–83)

Benvolio might well laugh, for Romeo's excessiveness is genuinely funny. Thus whatever danger that Elizabethans could see in melancholia in certain contexts, Romeo's affection is very difficult to take seriously, and what we get is, again, parody. Just as the feud is introduced as a serious, powerful negative force in the prologue, Montague's description makes Romeo's love-sickness serious and dangerous. But both are followed immediately by parodies of the supposedly dangerous forces: where we expect villains, fools appear instead.

Romeo's lovesickness is an obvious parody of a Petrarchan relationship, and as is usually the case, the Ascetic is the point of view, though not an Ascetic as ominous as that presented earlier in the scene. So while Romeo fails to justify for us his father's fear of impending death, he does justify the distrust of love melancholy implied by that fear. The question is one of action versus impotence, strength versus weakness, but in either case the point of view is the Ascetic distaste for men who are controlled by love.

At the end of the scene, the tone becomes more serious again, but this time the imaging of the relationship is in terms of a different type. The first hint comes when Benvolio asks Romeo why he does not simply seduce Rosaline. Romeo replies that

> she'll not be hit
> With Cupid's arrow, she hath Dian's wit;
> And in strong proof of chastity well arm'd,
> From Love's weak childish bow she lives uncharm'd.
> She will not stay the siege of loving terms,
> Nor bide th' encounter of assailing eyes,
> Nor ope her lap to saint-seducing gold.
> O, she is rich in beauty, only poor
> That when she dies, with beauty dies her store.
> (1.1.208–16)

And when Benvolio asks if Rosaline has gone so far as to swear eternal chastity, Romeo continues:

> She hath, and in that sparing makes huge waste;
> For beauty starv'd with her severity
> Cuts beauty off from all posterity.
> She is too fair, too wise, wisely too fair,
> To merit bliss by making me despair.
> She hath forsworn to love, and in that vow
> Do I live dead that live to tell it now.
> (1.1.218–24)

These passages represent an attitude toward love that is obviously more complex than mere parody, reminiscent as they are of the first seventeen of Shakespeare's sonnets, which also assert that eternal chastity is a crime against nature. But the Emasculating association is much more insistent here, since Romeo accuses his lady of deliberately refusing to play her part. Like the Dark Lady in sonnet 131 or the witchlike representation of Stella in Sidney's song five, this woman is destroying her man by frustrating his attempt to love her in the only way that can produce honor: Petrarchan service. According to his description of the relationship, her refusal to offer him a suitable reward for his devotion is unnatural and leaves him in "despair" and "dead," both terms indicating the frustrating and unmanning nature of such Emasculating relationships.

The Ascetic and Emasculating types are compatible in this instance because they both paint Romeo's lovesickness as wrong and a sign of weakness, but more importantly, the Emasculating view of the Romeo-Rosaline relationship helps to connect it to the feud. On the most obvious level, Rosaline dominates the second half of the scene in the same way that the feud dominates the first half: neither is physically embodied, but each still manages to dominate the attention of the participants in its half scene. And despite this attention, nothing is resolved in either half, both the feud and the love relationship preventing any kind of natural conclusion. But more significantly, the love relationship is like the feud in that both are unnatural, frustrating, destructive, and emasculating. Rosaline's rebellion against her proper role in society and in the love game reminds us that the feud as a "mutiny" is also a rebellion against the natural order, and Romeo's inability to force his lady to submit to his will reminds us that Sampson and Tybalt also defined strength and potency in terms that they were unable to meet.

The Emasculating representation of the Romeo-Rosaline relationship, then, makes a significant contribution to the developing value structure of the play by making clear what was already implicit in the swordfight scene: even if seemingly innocent and even silly, the feud is nonetheless dangerous in that it saps the masculinity of those involved and prevents the proper development of society. From this point of view, the feud holds the same relationship to society as a Circe figure holds to her emasculated lover, and we can see that the prologue, Montague's warning, and Romeo's echo of the sonnets all serve the same purpose of assuring us that behind the silliness lies an ominous Ascetic nightmare of collapsed degree, unchecked mutiny, and unnatural disorder.

Romeo's Emasculating relationship with Rosaline also resembles the feud in that both represent the tyrannical and impotent old society that is traditionally replaced by a liberated new one in a New Comedy. The difference between these two societies in *Romeo and Juliet* is made especially vivid by the transition from the Romeo-Rosaline to the Romeo-Juliet relationship, the unnaturalness, tyranny, and impotence of the former set in bold relief to the freedom and potency of the latter. Indeed, the main reason the Romeo-Juliet relationship seems so immediately vibrant and attractive is that our perception of it develops in sharp contrast with the earlier affair and in general with the world of the feud.

One of the reasons *Romeo and Juliet* often is less satisfactory on stage than its brilliant poetry and almost universally familiar plot would suggest is that directors oversimplify the nature of this contrast. In every production I have seen, the low comedy in scene one has been underplayed or cut so as to make the feud seem more dangerous (and to show off the skills of the fencing choreographer). At the same time, the passages making clear the danger of Romeo's lovesickness—both the Ascetic and Emasculating ones—are frequently cut severely, and the Rosaline-Romeo relationship evidently is always played as innocent, lighthearted, and a good excuse for bawdry. It is all of these, just as the feud is dangerous. But reducing the threat of the one and silliness of the other, and hence eliminating the powerful images of impotence and frustration produced by both, seriously reduces the ability of the play to make the title relationship powerful.

No matter how the first scene is played, the Romeo-Juliet relationship will seem attractive and the participants' love real: the New Comic opposition of the relationship to the feud ensures such a reaction. But for the balcony scenes and especially the last act to work as well as I think they can, we must see the relationship as more than just true and preferable to the feud. We must see it as mysterious and not of the earth, in much the same sense that Donne (and dozens of other Renaissance poets) defines love. And we must see it as heroic and as making the two young lovers heroic as well. If instead we see the central relationship as authentic but nevertheless the usual kind of teenage passion, not only will the balcony scenes lose much of their magic, but the conclusion of the play will fall flat (as it often does), seeming mostly pathetic, sentimental, and histrionic. *Romeo and Juliet* does not have a weighty enough use of themes and complex characterization to allow for the kind of cut-and-paste approach that works (sometimes) for some other tragedies; like its close cousin *A Midsummer Night's Dream*, all of the parts have to work together for the overall effect to be produced.

With the way prepared for it by the first scene, the central relationship makes its first appearance in the banquet scene ending the first act. The Romeo at the beginning of this scene (split into 1.4 and 1.5 by modern editors) is just as dominated by his love for Rosaline as in the first scene, and his imagery reflects the same despair and rejection of life. He refuses to dance because he is "heavy":

> a soul of lead
> So stakes me to the ground I cannot move....
> I cannot bound a pitch above dull woe;
> Under love's heavy burthen do I sink.
> (1.4.15–16, 21–22)

At the same time his friend Mercutio reminds us of Sampson in his Ascetic belief that unrequited love should be corrected by force: "If love be rough with you, be rough with love; / Prick love for pricking, and you beat love down" (1.4.27–28).

Romeo's assertion that he cannot dance is indicative of his Emasculated state, and it becomes more significant when Capulet and his guests enter, and the host immediately calls for a dance:

> Welcome, gentlemen! Ladies that have their toes
> Unplagu'd with corns will walk a bout with you.
> Ah, my mistresses, which of you all
> Will now deny to dance? She that makes dainty,
> She I'll swear hath corns. Am I come near ye now?
> Welcome, gentlemen!
> (1.5.16–21)

Dances are always emblematic of fertility and antithetical to impotence, so it is appropriate that Capulet himself immediately retires to a part of the stage away from the dance to reminisce with an old friend.

> *Cap.* Nay, sit, nay, sit good cousin Capulet,
> For you and I are past our dancing days.
> How long is't now since last yourself and I
> Were in a mask?
>   2. *Cap.*   By'r lady, thirty years.
>   *Cap.* What, man? 'tis not so much, 'tis not so much:
> 'Tis since the nuptial of Lucentio,
> Come Pentecost as quickly as it will,
> Some five and twenty years, and then we mask'd
>   2. *Cap.* 'Tis more, 'tis more. His son is elder,
>   sir;
> His son is thirty.
>   *Cap.*   Will you tell me that?
> His son was but a ward two years ago.
>
>   (1.5.30–40)

The two old men sit on one side of the stage and discuss their lost youth, now thirty years in the past, while the current youth dance across stage from them. The result is a sort of stage metaphor, a dramatization of the play's two dominant principles, impotence and fertility, neatly arranged in spatial as well as ideological and narratological opposition.

It is in this context that Romeo first tells us of his sudden love for Juliet:

> O, she doth teach the torches to burn bright!
> It seems she hangs upon the cheek of night
> As a rich jewel in an Ethiop's ear—
> Beauty too rich for use, for earth too dear!
> So shows a snowy dove trooping with crows,
> As yonder lady o'er her fellows shows.
> The measure done, I'll watch her place of stand,
> And touching hers, make blessed my rude hand.
> Did my heart love till now? Forswear it, sight!
> For I ne'er saw true beauty till this night.
>
>   (1.5.44–53)

The Petrarchan imagery of light, jewels, doves, and crows is really not very different from that in his declaration of love for Rosaline; why then does this declaration seem so much more serious and attractive, that is to say, more genuinely Petrarchan?

Part of the reason is that we expect the imminent establishment of such a relationship. Part also is the optimistic tone of this speech, compared to the pessimism of all his discussions of Rosaline. All of his speeches concerning her have addressed themselves to the sole subject of how terrible it is to be in love and unable to do anything about it, but this speech combines Romeo's first unequivocal compliment with a statement indicating that this time, fulfillment will be achieved. Romeo up until this point has refused to dance, that is, refused to join in the fertility ritual proceeding on one side of the stage. Perhaps he even stands near the seated old men, thereby indicating his position in the fertility-impotence tableau. But his declaration of love for Juliet marks his return to the dance, for he declares that he will walk across stage and touch her hand, hardly a seduction, but definitely a rejection of his previous despair at the possibility of successful action. Since both the feud and the Romeo-Rosaline relationship have already been associated with frustration and impotence, the images of completion and fertility here are immediately attractive and make the new relationship seem different and better.

Furthermore, while the earlier speeches concerning Rosaline are also full of conventional Petrarchan imagery, in them the references to perversity and unnaturalness induce us to see the relationship as Emasculating, just as Montague's imagery of disease causes us to see the otherwise Petrarchan sighs and melancholy as satiric. This initial description of the Romeo-Juliet relationship, on the other hand, contains no such dominant, qualifying images, and thus we immediately see it as Petrarchan and hence positive.

This attractiveness is immediately reinforced when Tybalt, who certainly does stand both physically and symbolically with the old men, tries to start a new brawl:

> This, by his voice, should be a Montague.
> Fetch me my rapier, boy. What dares the slave
> Come hither, cover'd with an antic face,
> To fleer and scorn at our solemnity?
> Now, by the stock and honor of my kin,
> To strike him dead I hold it not a sin.
>   (1.5.54–59)

In the first scene, Tybalt clearly represents the feud and everything that is negative in the play, and Benvolio automatically seems positive for opposing him. The same thing is true here: when Tybalt spouts fire and hate just after Romeo's declaration of love, Romeo immediately seems more positive and more identified with the positive values of the play. And as if to emphasize just what the most important of these positive and negative values are, Tybalt's attempt to defeat Romeo is defeated, not by his adversary, but by old Capulet himself, who calls him a "saucy boy" and virtually runs him off stage (1.5.72–88). The old man can hardly get his words out, but when he does they are more than enough to make the potential interrupter of his party seem weak and insignificant. The effect, of course, is once again to associate this representative of the feud with impotence, and thus anyone who opposes him with fertility.

We can see, then, that the frame for the Romeo-Juliet relationship is carefully prepared before the lovers even meet. And when they do meet, in the well-known sonnet dialogue immediately following Capulet's denunciation of his nephew, it is not surprising that the values and relationships established in earlier scenes continue to be exploited. The Romeo-Rosaline relationship presented a lover dominated by a lady whose unnatural chastity denied both of them fulfillment. Similarly, the sonnet dialogue begins with a submissive lover, worried lest he "profane with my unworthiest hand / This holy shrine" (1.5.93–94). This time, however, there is no suggestion that this submissiveness will unnaturally be turned to emasculation; in fact, Juliet is immediately cooperative, soothing Romeo's nervousness and assuring him that "you do wrong your hand too much." Frustration is generally an important part of the Petrarchan type, but in *Romeo and Juliet* Shakespeare is careful to associate it with Rosaline and the feud, so that the Romeo-Juliet relationship can be immediately associated with fulfillment (usually only introduced at the completion of a Petrarchan narrative), and the lovers can move immediately to seal their affection with a kiss. Juliet's quick yielding could be made negative in another context, but by making negative the conventional resisting lady in the context of this play, Shakespeare makes Juliet's quick kiss both acceptable and doubly appealing: it connotes the reverse of everything associated with Rosaline and the feud, and it represents the sexual union that is the goal and conclusion of New Comic Petrarchan narratives. Juliet, we might say, creates the relationship type promised in the prologue. Whereas before her responsiveness love was portrayed in terms of the Ascetic or Emasculating types, it is now unquestionably Petrarchan New Comic, for the lovers have fully accepted each other and can only be thwarted by an outside force.

We respond to the Romeo-Juliet relationship, then, partially because we always respond to the threatened lovers in a New Comedy but also because the mutuality of affection inherent in New Comedy is in this play a particularly positive value. In fact, one way to look at the first scene is as a prolonged conflict pitting men who want to dominate women against either a dominating woman or a dominating feud that is closely associated with women. This being the case, the Romeo-Juliet relationship seems attractive in some measure because we respond to the cessation of this particularly destructive battle of the sexes. In one sense, the lovers temporarily defeat the feud by declaring their love in spite of it; in another, the mutuality of their love represents the defeat of relationship types which, like the feud, insist on continual warfare between the parties involved.[7]

The Paradise of Flesh: Romeo and Juliet / 83

This same opposition between the old and new relationship types is repeated to some extent in all of the love scenes that occur before Romeo leaves Verona, but nowhere more emphatically than in the longest and best-known of them, the balcony scene (again split into two by modern editors) beginning the second act. It begins with Romeo once more declaring his new love, then withdrawing to some part of the stage that represents the inside of Juliet's garden. At this point Benvolio and Mercutio appear and pointedly remind us of Romeo's former relationship:

> *Ben.* He ran this way and lept this orchard wall.
> Call, good Mercutio.
> *Mer.*   Nay, I'll conjure too.
> Romeo! humors! madman! passion! lover!
> Appear thou in the likeness of a sigh!
> Speak but one rhyme and I am satisfied. . . .
> He heareth not, he stirreth not, he moveth not,
> The ape is dead, and I must conjure him.
> I conjure thee by Rosaline's bright eyes,
> By her high forehead and her scarlet lip,
> By her fine foot, straight leg, and quivering thigh,
> And the demesnes that there adjacent lie,
> That in thy likeness thou appear to us!
>   (2.1.5–9, 15–21)

Mercutio here neatly sums up the two ways in which the Romeo-Rosaline relationship has been portrayed in previous scenes. His parody of Romeo's Petrarchism reminds us that the Emasculated Romeo was indeed little more than a personified sigh, while his obscene conjuration is just one of many examples of the Ascetic understanding of sexual relationships. But even as Mercutio speaks, we know that Romeo has given over Rosaline and is beginning a relationship in which he neither dominates nor is dominated. And since Romeo remains onstage while his friends talk, we again see an important opposition personified: Mercutio represents the Ascetic and Emasculating types, Romeo the New Comic.

Once Benvolio and Mercutio leave the stage and Juliet appears at the balcony, this love scene too moves joyously toward its own special kind of New Comic triumph. Full of beautiful and generally quite conventional Petrarchan poetry, the scene (which has been thoroughly analyzed elsewhere) is straightforwardly Petrarchan without a hint of irony. Without the preparation of the earlier scenes it might seem a little much, but within the context Shakespeare has prepared it obviously works very well indeed.

In addition to the poetry, the scene also presents its own miniature New Comic narrative, though one in which the obstacles are overcome very quickly. Like the kiss in the sonnet dialogue, the exchange of vows represents the victory of love over the constantly threatening feud: it is the surrogate for the customary New Comic concluding marriage. In each of the other two love scenes before Romeo leaves Verona, there is a similar concluding symbol of triumph: in act 2 scene 6 it is Friar Laurence's taking the lovers to their marriage ceremony; and in act 3 scene 5, where Romeo must head for Mantua at the break of day, the reward is the actual sexual union that has just taken place. In each of the love scenes, Romeo and Juliet are defiant in their rejection of conflict either in love or in family politics, and they are temporarily victorious over the feud, which always lurks ominously in the background, ever threatening to break them apart. In their New Comic triumphs and in their selection of peace and fertility over war and impotence the lovers replay patterns that people have responded to for many centuries. It is thus not surprising that we are as emotionally drawn to them and the love scenes as to any Shakespeare produced.

The movement early in *Romeo and Juliet* from the Ascetic and Emasculating types to the Petrarchan is mainly developed in terms of three oppositions: mutuality-conflict, fertility-impotence, and freedom-constriction. The first two of these are probably the most important to the initial establishment of the central relationship, but it is the last, freedom-constriction, that may be of more significance to the play as a whole. In fact, one way of reading the development of the lovers through the course of the play is as a constant movement away from the values and rules of the feud-dominated world of the play and toward a virtual isolation in which the love relationship exists only in its own terms. Viewed in this way, the play steadily progresses from the constrictive Ascetic insistence on eternal sexual conflict, through the lovers' Petrarchan fulfillment, and into a final Etherealized phase. There the love relationship is completely severed from and made superior to what the play presents as the ordinary world.

An Etherealized portrait of the lovers is useful in this play because it provides a way of making them seem significant despite their lack of political, military, or intellectual distinction. All of the Etherealized relationships discussed in the first chapter are made with similarly undistinguished lovers: Amoret and Scudamour are both generally portrayed as helpless characters who must be saved from their troubles by Britomart and others, and Donne's lovers are never given any mark of importance or superiority other than their relationship itself. In each of these cases the relationship seems significant because it is given an aura of otherworldliness, of closeness to mysterious and powerful forces beyond human comprehension. The essential component of the Etherealized type is this sense of idealism and magic, thereby making it imperative that Etherealized relationships be radically dissociated from whatever is portrayed as the ordinary world. Spenser creates this dissociation through the use of paradox and classical allusion while Donne uses both of these in addition to religious imagery. While effective in lyric poetry, these devices would not be effective in a play, where the physical presence of the lovers renders their dissociation from other characters much more difficult. Thus several techniques and a substantial portion of the text of *Romeo and Juliet* are devoted to the establishment of an Etherealized representation of the central relationship. The first and most persistent such technique is the use of imagery.

The most important images for dissociating the love relationship from the ordinary world are of light and dark and of day and night.[8] The first significant use of these images occurs in the first scene, in the dialogue between Benvolio and Montague partially quoted earlier. In it we find that the brawl just completed happened in the daytime, but that Romeo prefers to go out at night or to create an "artificial night" by shutting himself in his chamber. Because he avoids the "all-cheering sun," Romeo is suffering from a "Black and portendous" humor. This imagery begins what will soon become an almost omnipresent association of the feud with daytime and the lovers with night, but also light with life and darkness with death. Such a chain of associations is not at all what one would expect, since light and daytime are usually associated, and death and love usually are not. But there is, as we shall see, a rationale behind the choice.

First of all, Shakespeare avoids the problem of light's representing the feud by emphasizing the day's heat instead of its light. Daytime in this play is almost always associated with heat and the feud; light is almost never mentioned. Thus we find that the first two swordfight scenes both occur in the heat of the midsummer day (for the date, see 1.3.14–15), the first beginning with a pun on coals and choler and the second with Benvolio's advice that since "The day is hot" and it is the "hot days" that keep the "mad blood stirring," he and Mercutio should retire (1.1.1–3, 3.1.2–4). Doubtless Benvolio is thinking of the "fiery Tybalt" (1.1.109), who does indeed provoke two fights, first with the "all as hot" Mercutio (3.2.160), then with the "fire-ey'd fury" that Romeo becomes (3.1.124). Earlier the Prince enjoined the patriarchs to "quench the fire of your pernicious rage" (1.1.84). Friar Laurence does not come in contact with any fiery combatants, but he does worry about completing his work before "Titan's fiery wheels" and the "burning eye" of the sun make reasonable activity impossible. Similarly, Juliet thinks of day in terms of Phaeton's "fiery-footed steeds," which are always being whipped toward the west (3.2.1–3).

And with the feud so closely linked to fire and heat, it is not surprising that Romeo images his love for Rosaline in similar terms, declaring that "Love is a smoke made with the fume of sighs" and a "fire sparkling in lovers' eyes" (1.1.190–91). Benvolio suggests that a new love will cure the old because "one fire burns out another's burning" (1.2.45), but Romeo asserts that should his eyes wander, his tears should turn to fire, thereby causing his eyes to be "burnt for liars" (1.2.91). Thus not only the feud but the Romeo-Rosaline relationship is linked to fire and heat, which are in turn repeatedly linked to daytime. Light, however, is seldom mentioned in connection with the day, thereby avoiding the problem of how light could be associated with the play's negative values and characters and allowing its use in a different context.

Shakespeare keeps the ideological categories straight by using many images of light within darkness, often as a brilliant but quickly extinguished flash. Capulet begins this chain of images with his assertion that the "earth-treading stars" of his party will "make dark heaven bright" (1.2.25), but almost all of the rest are directly associated with the lovers. Juliet, as we all know, teaches the torches to burn bright, and, as the light in yonder window, kills the envious moon. In addition, Romeo exclaims that

> The brightness of her cheek would shame those stars,
> As daylight doth a lamp; her eyes in heaven
> Would through the airy region stream so bright
> The birds would sing and think it were not night.
> (2.2.19–22)

Later, Juliet reverses the tables and images Romeo as a future constellation that

> will make the face of heaven so fine
> That all the world will be in love with night,
> An pay no worship to the garish sun.
> (3.2.23–25)

The lovers as a pair are compared to a comet in the prologue; their love is likened to a flash of gunpowder by Friar Laurence (2.6.9–11), and as "the lightning, which doth cease to be / Ere one can say it lightens" (2.2.119–120) by Juliet. And finally, Romeo tells us that Juliet's body makes the Capulet tomb, otherwise a "palace of dim night," a "feasting presence full of light" (5.3.86, 107).

Love as the light punctuating the darkness is a common Petrarchan image, but it quickly becomes apparent in *Romeo and Juliet* that the night itself, along with its inevitable imagistic companion, death, is also closely associated with the lovers. In the first balcony scene Juliet may be the sun, but she also has the "mask of night" upon her face (2.2.85), much the same as Romeo is hidden by "night's cloak" and the whole relationship has been "discovered" by "dark night" (2.2.75, 106). Romeo's "O blessed, blessed night!" (2.2.139) in the same scene is balanced by Juliet's passionate prayer for the coming of "love-performing night" (3.2.5) in the next act.

There are even some instances where the love relationship is directly associated with death, especially in connection with the sexual double meaning of "die." The prologue tells us to expect a "death-mark'd love," and balancing Juliet's wish that Romeo be made into a constellation "when I shall die" (3.2.21), is Romeo's concluding desire to "die and lie with Juliet" (5.3.290). Even Juliet's garden, certainly associated with love, is, as Juliet reminds Romeo, also a place of death: "The orchard walls are high and hard to climb, / And the place death, considering who thou art" (2.2.63–64). Later, when she looks down at her lover as he is about to leave that same garden for Mantua, he seems "As one dead in the bottom of a tomb" (3.5.56).

One way to look at these images is in terms of an *amour passion* driving the lovers to death as much as love,[9] but whatever the applicability of this particular pattern, the night and death images serve the structural purpose of dissociating the love relationship from the feud. From the prologue onward the relationship is portrayed as unable to survive in the daytime world; like a comet or a meteor it is wonderful to behold but marked for certain and quick extinction. Even at the lovers' most triumphant moment, the balcony scene beginning the second act, we are made cognizant of their vulnerability and ephemerality. The result is to make the lovers and their relationship seem ill-adapted to existence in the ordinary world, hence implying that they are more suited to another. The painting of the lovers and their relationship in terms of vulnerability and ephemerality is reminiscent of conventional descriptions of flowers or visions, and like them the result is a sense of idealism, otherworldliness, and mystery.

In addition to its imagery, the love relationship is dissociated from all other aspects of the world of the play by the gradual portrayal of every major character either as connected with some form of the New Comic blocking force or as impotent to control or even to understand the rush of events. Thus Capulet, though he ceases to support the feud overtly after the first scene, is nevertheless associated with the blocking force through his championing of the forced marriage of his daughter to Paris, the same avenue through which Lady Capulet and Paris himself are opposed to the lovers. Mercutio and the Nurse are attractive, comic characters through most of their tenure on stage, but the former eventually becomes as intent on continuing the feud as Tybalt, while the latter loses our sympathy as well as Juliet's when she calls Romeo a "dishclout" (3.5.219) and advises her charge to marry Paris after all.

Friar Laurence, on the other hand, is separated from the lovers not by support of the feud or the forced marriage but by his increasing inability to aid them in their struggle against the various threatening forces. At first, he helps the lovers to marry and then to spend their one night together, but his continual insistence on moderation and deliberation is out of touch with the reality of both the world around him and the lovers he wants to help. He advises them to go "Wisely and slow, they stumble that run fast" (2.3.84), but all around him events, including his own stratagems, move too fast and too precipitously for him to control or even to understand. In the end, his overmoderation in communicating with Romeo contributes to the lovers' destruction, and he is left confused, frightened, and anxious to flee the evidence of his own failure. The Prince also unintentionally contributes to the breaking apart of the lovers when he banishes Romeo, and like Friar Laurence and Benvolio to some extent, our growing awareness of his impotence to effect anything positive contributes to making him seem completely unconnected to the lovers or the values their relationship represents.

Even the lovers are not immune from being temporarily isolated from their own affair, for in the pivotal first three scenes of the third act they too are associated for a moment with support of the feud. The first of these, the scene in which Mercutio and Tybalt are killed, closely parallels the swordfight scene at the beginning of the play. Like the initial scene, act 3 scene 1 opens with just over thirty lines of mostly idle conversation about the feud by two characters connected with the house of Montague, Mercutio playing Sampson's role of chief fool, with Benvolio, like Gregory, his straight man. Two Capulets enter at about the same place in both scenes (1.1.33 and 3.1.34) and promptly begin to squabble with the Montagues. About twenty lines later (1.1.59 and 3.1.56) a third Montague enters and attempts to break up the fight (Benvolio, Romeo), only to be embroiled in it himself. Like Benvolio in the first swordfight scene, Romeo in the second attempts to contradict the values of the feud and serve as peacemaker. Responding to Tybalt's challenge, he asserts "I do protest I never injured thee, / But love thee better than thou canst devise" (3.1.68–69). Romeo is attempting to move away from the feud, which constricts everyone else in the scene to a narrow world of absolute familial allegiances, and toward a world where he can love his former enemy Tybalt as freely as he does his former enemy Juliet. In the process he dramatizes for us the constriction, conflict, and impotence of the world of the feud with the free, Edenic world of reconciled and unified opposites suggested by the central relationship.

The others present, however, are still living in the Ascetic world of the feud, and thus misunderstand Romeo's words as evidence of cowardice and effeminacy. Mercutio calls what he has seen and heard a "dishonorable, vile submission" (3.1.73) and attempts to fight in Romeo's stead, only to be killed under his friend's arm. This accident brings Romeo face to face with the inapplicability of his newfound values to the outside world; they function, he finds, in Juliet's garden and nowhere else. As a result, he find himself caught between two irreconcilable worlds, wanting to maintain the values he has so recently sworn himself to, but at the same time needing to communicate with and maintain his position in the ordinary world. He chooses the latter:

> This gentleman, the Prince's near ally,
> My very friend, hath got his mortal hurt
> In my behalf; my reputation stain'd
> With Tybalt's slander—Tybalt, that an hour
> Hath been my cousin! O sweet Juliet,
> Thy beauty hath made me effeminate,
> And in my temper soft'ned valor's steel!
> (3.1.109–15)

The idea that love makes a man effeminate is straight out of the Ascetic tradition, and his "soft'ned valor's steel" is reminiscent of the phallic swords of the first scene. This association of Romeo with the feud leads immediately to the fatal duel with Tybalt and eventually to both lovers' deaths.[10] Almost as important as this crucial turn in the plot, however, is the clarity with which the scene establishes the opposition of the feud and the central relationship, for with the defection of Romeo, we begin to see love, like the feud, as an entity independent of the characters who represent it.

Juliet's turn to defect comes in the next scene, when after the passionate calling for night and Romeo, the Nurse brings the news of Tybalt's death. Suddenly Juliet, like Romeo himself in the previous scene, is presented with a paradox concerning Romeo's true identity: how could he be both her lover and her cousin's killer? Again, like Romeo, her response is to interpret the conflicting views of reality in favor of the feud:

> O serpent heart, hid with flow'ring face!
> Did ever dragon keep so fair a cave?
> Beautiful tyrant! fiend angelical!
> Dove-feather'd raven! wolfish ravening lamb!
> Despised substance of divinest show!
> Just opposite to what thou justly seem'st,
> A damned saint, an honorable villain!
> O nature, what hadst thou to do in hell
> When thou didst bower the spirit of a fiend
> In mortal paradise of such sweet flesh?
> Was ever book containing such vile matter
> So fairly bound? O that deceit should dwell
> In such a gorgeous palace!
> (3.2.73–85)

These thirteen lines of bizarre paradoxes reflect the disorder in Juliet's mind, and remind us of the Romeo (of 1.1) whose wild oxymorons also indicated an inability to interpret reality properly.[11] And just as Romeo's inflated rhetoric helped link him temporarily with the feud, so Juliet's, along with her overt rejection of her lover, makes the same uncomfortable association. But when the Nurse takes the hint and hopes that "shame come to Romeo" (3.2.90), Juliet quickly returns to opposition to the feud:

> Blistered be thy tongue
> For such a wish! he was not born to shame. . . .
> O, what a beast was I to chide at him. . . .
> Shall I speak ill of him that is my husband?
> Ah, poor my lord, what tongue shall smooth thy name,
> When I, thy three-hours wife, have mangled it?
> (3.2.90–91, 95, 97–99)

Like Romeo in the previous scene, Juliet moves from opposition to support of the feud, but her recovery is almost immediate. Romeo does not recover until the next scene, and then not until the Nurse and Friar both advise him to stop "weeping and blubb'ring" and "rise and stand" like a man (3.3.87–89). Caught between two completely antithetical worlds and infected with the frustration and impotence of all who participate in the world of the feud, Romeo is initially reduced to a complete inability to act. But the Nurse's chiding, Friar Laurence's consolation, and—especially—the knowledge that Juliet still loves him all combine to restore Romeo to his position as a supporter of the love relationship and the values it represents.

Juliet's alienation from and return to love are encased by Romeo's, thereby providing a nice sense of parallelism, but more importantly demonstrating that the lovers are not always to be identified with love. The lovers, like everyone else in the play, are in these three scenes portrayed as irrational, changeable people; it is only their relationship that makes them special. So although the lovers never again demonstrate infidelity to their relationship, these scenes help establish what most who see or read the play surely feel: that it is love that makes the lovers significant, not the reverse. Romeo and Juliet are portrayed as extraordinary only when under the influence of their love, unlike, for example Rosalind and Orlando in *As You Like It,* or the central characters in most of the other comedies. It is love itself—represented through the Petrarchan or Etherealized types—that is extraordinary and produces the play's positive values.

Petrarchan representations of the relationship are present from the prologue onwards, but Etherealized ones start to appear only in the middle scenes. They are made possible by the careful dissociation of the love relationship from the world of the play, thereby allowing it to seem ephemeral and potentially extraordinary. Eventually, this will allow the creation of an ideal world of eternal love, where the lovers, like their predecessors in Brooke's *Tragicall Historye of Romeus and Juliet,* "In place of endlesse light and blisse, may ever live yfere."¹² But before such an ideal is possible, at least within an Etherealized representation, the lovers' sexuality has to be given some sort of special significance. Hence the sexual part of the relationship is increasingly idealized and mystified as the play builds towards its conclusion.

The first such imaging is in the lovers' first conversation, where Romeo's kiss is compared to a pilgrim's devotion. Much more insistent is the balcony scene, which begins with Romeo vaulting over the wall and into Juliet's previously inviolate orchard. As Roselie Colie has noted, this action is immediately suggestive of the virgin garden, that medieval setpiece in which movement toward the garden's center is equivalent to movement toward sexual consummation.¹³ But even without specific knowledge of this tradition, surely most readers would interpret the situation and the lovers' comments in much the same terms:

> *Jul.* How camest thou hither, tell me, and wherefore?
> The orchard walls are high and hard to climb,
> And the place death, considering who thou art,
> If any of my kinsmen find thee here.
> *Rom.* With love's light wings did I o'erperch these walls,
> For stony limits cannot hold love out,
> And what love can do, there dares love attempt;
> Therefore thy kinsmen are no stop to me.
> (2.2.62–69)

Romeo is able to get into the garden because he has "love's light wings," but like the lover in the *Romance of the Rose,* love only gets him into the garden. The denial of the final goal is symbolized by a second physical barrier, in this case a balcony rather than a hedge of thorns.

This barrier is finally breached in act 3 scene 5, where both lovers appear on the balcony after their one night together. There the lovers refer to "yond pomegranate tree" and the "misty mountain tops" in the distance, in addition to the nightingales and larks (3.5.1–36), before Romeo climbs down from the balcony in full view of the audience. As the imagery and stage action make clear, the balcony is still the inner sanctum of Juliet's garden. It is, however, no longer a virgin garden but a garden of love, for it is now the place where the lovers can frankly enjoy their sexuality. So rather than a rose surrounded by thorns, the balcony is now more like the "pleasant arbour" in the "thickest couert of that shade" of the Garden of Adonis, where Venus and Adonis engage in celestial and continuous copulation (*Faerie Queene,* 3.6.44–49).

A few scenes before this famous aubade, Juliet's amazing exhortation to Night to bring her Romeo and the consummation of her marriage provides an even stronger mystification of the lovers' sexuality. She begins by demanding that "love-performing night" cause Romeo to "Leap into these arms untalk'd of and unseen" (3.2.5, 7), and goes on to demand:

> Come, night, come, Romeo, come, thou day in night,
> For thou wilt lie upon the wings of night,
> Whiter than new snow upon a raven's back.
> Come, gentle night, come, loving, black-brow'd night,
> Give me my Romeo, and, when I shall die,
> Take him and cut him out in little stars,
> And he will make the face of heaven so fine
> That all the world will be in love with night,
> And pay no worship to the garish sun.
> (3.2.17–25)

Juliet's love for Romeo may be the origin of her desire, but in this speech love is not mentioned. She desires him as if he were an inanimate object useful only for the sexual fulfillment that he can provide. Again, this passage is reminiscent of the Garden of Adonis, where Venus does what Juliet wishes for: brings a male into her inner sanctum and "Possesseth him, and of his sweetness takes her fill" (F.Q. 3.6.46).

One might argue that the seeming selfishness of Juliet's desire runs contrary to the mutuality emphasized previously, but her conclusion sets the passage in a better context:

> O, I have bought the mansion of a love,
> But not possess'd it, and though I am sold,
> Not yet enjoy'd.
> (3.2.26–28)

The first of these metaphors again makes Romeo into Juliet's personal, inanimate property, but in the second Juliet seems to revel in the weakest and most dominated of traditional female roles: a chattel purchased for the sexual enjoyment of a male. Juliet is obviously just as content to be Romeo's sexual object as she is to have him hers. Just as Adonis "liueth in eternall blis, / joying his goddess, and of her enjoyed" (F.Q. 3.6.48), so Romeo will frankly and unashamedly take his pleasure of Juliet at the same time that she takes her pleasure of him.[14]

The key word in the last sentence is "unashamed," for Juliet seems intent throughout her speech in overcoming her "strange love," that is, the modesty and denial of passion which her society has taught her is proper maidenly demeanor (see 2.2.98–107). She wants to replace the constriction of this Ascetic distaste for sexuality with the freedom of Venus' garden of love, where

> all plentie, and all pleasure flowes,
> And sweet loue gentle fits emongst them throwes,
> Without fell rancor, or fond gealosie;
> Frankly each paramour his leman knowes,
> Each bird his mate, ne any does enuie
> Their goodly meriment, and gay felicitie.
> (F.Q. 3.6.41)

This view of sexuality is, of course, Etherealized, and Juliet's speech works toward the same effect of placing the relationship outside of the bounds of ordinary moderation and morality. Instead of the demure maiden and obedient daughter (of 1.2), this Juliet (of 3.2) is a defiantly unrestrained woman—indeed more than a woman as that gender is defined in the play—for she rejects the Ascetic view of the ordinary world of this play that female sexuality should be suppressed and women should be subservient to men. As a result, this speech helps define the Romeo-Juliet relationship in terms totally foreign to the rest of the play. The relationship is therefore neither moral nor immoral; like the speaker of "The Canonization" and his lady, Romeo and Juliet are simply "Mysterious by this love."

The mystery and idealization of the central relationship is most unabashedly developed in Juliet's speech, but it also comes to function in the basic New Comic narrative that holds the play together. Throughout the first part of the play, the blocking force is clearly the feud, and the feud remains an important threat until the end. But after Juliet's Etherealized speech and her temporary turning away from Romeo, a new blocking force in introduced. The Nurse has just told Juliet that her parents are "Weeping and wailing over Tybalt's corpse"; Juliet replies:

> Wash they his wounds with tears? Mine shall be spent,
> When theirs are dry, for Romeo's banishment.
> Take up those cords. Poor ropes, you are beguil'd,
> Both you and I, for Romeo is exil'd.
> He made you for a highway to my bed,
> But I, a maid, die maiden-widowed.
> Come, cords, come, Nurse, I'll to my wedding-bed,
> And death, not Romeo, take my maidenhead!
> (3.2.130–37)

We might regard Juliet's words as mere verbal exuberance, but the image of Death as her husband or ravisher becomes insistent as the play progresses. In act 3 scene 5, for example, Lady Capulet declares that "I would the fool were married to her grave" (140) when Juliet refuses to marry Paris, and Juliet responds to her parents' pressure by pleading

> Is there no pity sitting in the clouds,
> That sees into the bottom of my grief?

> O sweet my mother, cast me not away!
> Delay this marriage for a month, a week,
> Or if you do not, make the bridal bed
> In that dim monument where Tybalt lies.
>   (3.5.196–201)

In the next scene, Friar Laurence uses a similar image when he asks Juliet if she would rather contend with Death than marry Paris:

> If rather than to marry County Paris,
> Thou hast the strength of will to slay thyself,
> Then is it likely thou wilt undertake
> A thing like death to chide away this shame,
> That cop'st with Death himself to scape from it;
> And if thou darest, I'll give thee remedy.
>   (4.1.71–76)

And when Capulet tells Paris about his daughter's apparent death, the image reappears in its most elaborate form yet:

> O son, the night before thy wedding day
> Has Death lain with thy wife. There she lies,
> Flower as she was, deflowered by him.
> Death is my son-in-law, Death is my heir,
> My daughter he hath wedded. I will die,
> And leave him all; life, living, all is Death's.
>   (4.5.35–40)

Capulet sees the conflict as between Paris and Death and as concluded in Death's favor. For us and for the lovers, however, Paris is never really in the picture; the battle in the last three acts is between Death and Romeo exclusively. Juliet says as much in her soliloquy before she drinks the sleeping potion:

> How if, when I am laid in the tomb,
> I wake before the time that Romeo
> Come to redeem me? there's a fearful point!
> Shall I not then be stifled in the vault,
> To whose foul mouth no healthsome air breathes in,
> And there die strangled ere my Romeo comes?
>   (4.3.30–35)

By drinking the potion, Juliet declines to return to the ordinary world. Instead, she stakes her future on Romeo's ability to wrest her from Death and return with her to the garden of love. If he does not come, she will remain forever a prisoner in the tomb, which like the garden lies beyond ordinary rationality and morality. As Juliet goes on to tell us, the tomb is a place of strange smells, ghosts, and "shrieks like 'mandrakes' torn out of the earth" that cause any living person to go instantly mad. Horribly opposed as they are, the garden and tomb are linked by their mutual difference from the ordinary world, and the narrative structure in effect renders the ordinary irrelevant, shifting gradually to a heroic, mysterious, and highly idealized realm where a lover can battle death itself for possession of his lady.

As the play moves toward its conclusion, it soon becomes evident that Romeo perceives the situation in much the same terms as Juliet, even though he thinks that she really is dead. His first comment upon hearing the news—"Well, Juliet, I will lie with thee to-night" (5.1.34)—reflects in the ambiguity of "lie" his refusal to accept her death as final or as a defeat. When he arrives at the Capulet tomb, he first asserts that he is not to be perceived as ordinary or as constrained by ordinary rules:

> The time and my intents are savage-wild,
> More fierce and more inexorable far
> Than empty tigers or the roaring sea.
> (5.3.37–39)

Romeo then states directly the terms of his conflict:

> Thou detestable maw, thou womb of death,
> Gorg'd with the dearest morsel of the earth,
> Thus I enforce thy rotten jaws to open,
> And in despite I'll cram thee with more food.
> (5.3.45–48)

Romeo has, of course, come with the intention of committing suicide, not resurrecting Juliet, and his comments indicate this desire. But at the same time, his description of the tomb and his use of terms such as "enforce," "despite," and "cram" indicate his sense of personal conflict with Death, as does his impatience with the "boy" Paris. Paris wants to fight the man he believes is desecrating his lady's grave, thus setting up a concluding struggle between a representative of the feud and one of the lovers. Romeo, however, no longer perceives Paris or the threatening force he represents as either significant or his true adversary. His enemy is inside the tomb, and he kills Paris only because he will not step aside.

Having done so, he drags the body into the tomb and there describes a most unusual scene:

> I'll bury thee in a triumphant grave.
> A grave? O no, a lanthorn, slaught'red youth;
> For here lies Juliet, and her beauty makes
> This vault a feasting presence full of light. . . .
>   O my love, my wife,

96 / *The Structure of Love*

> Death, that hath suck'd the honey of thy breath,
> Hath no power yet upon thy beauty:
> Thou are not conquer'd, beauty's ensign yet
> Is crimson in thy lips and in thy cheeks,
> And death's pale flag is not advanced there.
>
> (5.3.83–86, 91–96)

Juliet feared what the tomb would do to her, but in Romeo's description it is the tomb that has been altered: her presence has transformed the death and darkness of the grave to the light and life of a feast. Thus her grave is triumphant because she has prevented Death's attempt to enclose her in darkness. But as Romeo's military imagery indicates, the battle is not finished, for though "beauty's ensign" has held off "death's pale flag," the "yet" suggests the continuation of the struggle. It is at this point that Romeo elects to step in and defeat his rival permanently and completely:

> Ah, dear Juliet,
> Why are thou yet so fair? Shall I believe
> That unsubstantial Death is amorous,
> And that the lean abhorred monster keeps
> Thee here in dark to be his paramour?
> For fear of that, I still will stay with thee,
> And never from this palace of dim night
> Depart again.
>
> (5.3.101–8)

Romeo sees Death as a monster attempting to make Juliet his unwilling mistress and himself as her only protector. Or, put in different terms, Death wants to place Juliet in a perverse garden of love, one built on coercion, sexual conflict, and the barrenness of the tomb, while Romeo wants to return her to a relationship based on freedom, mutuality, and the unending fertility of a genuine garden. So just as he saved her once from marriage to Paris, Romeo will now save her from Death, which he accomplishes by using a last "righteous kiss" to seal "A dateless bargain to engrossing death" (5.3.114–15). Death may be "engrossing" in its permanence, but Romeo will force from it a "dateless bargain" to allow himself and Juliet to remain forever united. Like a knight in shining armor, Romeo has arrived and defeated the villain just when the heroine's violation seemed inevitable, but unlike the lovers in a western, he and Juliet have an undisturbed place where they can eternally reside: the paradox of a world that is tomb and garden at the same time.

When Juliet awakes, she repeats much the same sentiment, wishing to use Romeo's poison to "die with a restorative" (5.3.166). And when she quickly follows Romeo into their paradoxical world of death-like, we naturally expect a quick conclusion. We get instead another 140 lines of dialogue, dominated by the Friar's long and tedious recapitulation of the plot. Most modern productions cut large portions of this conclusion, but I think that in one way its length is a virtue: its long and largely mundane speeches bring us back to the world of the play and through it to our own world. In the process we are reminded that the lovers—or more properly the love that animated them—was as exciting as the patriarchs and Friar are dull, as unconstrained as the Prince and patriarchs are pompous and formal, and as ethereal and mysterious as everything onstage (or in the audience) is constant and ordinary. Though nothing of much importance is said, the conclusion is thus effective nonetheless because it makes us feel the wonder and perfection of the world we have seen, while at the same time reminding us how little it resembles our own.

5

Magic in the Structure:

Othello

A recent essay argues that Othello suffers from an "immature ego," a malady that accounts for his social naiveté, rashness, and generally excessive behavior, all of which combine to force *Othello* "into the genre of melodrama, in spite of our frequent critical efforts to maintain its position in the small circle of high tragedies."[1] This particular psychoanalytic approach may be new, but the belief that the quality of the play can be determined by the quality of the main character is not. Shaw and Eliot both argued that Othello is more a fool than a hero and hence the play not among Shakespeare's best, and various others have followed their lead, at least to some extent.[2] Even those who defend the quality of the play usually betray the same uneasiness with the central character by focusing their analyses on Iago, giving the Moor scarcely more emphasis than Claudius is usually afforded in essays on *Hamlet*.[3]

The uneasiness of even the play's defenders is quite understandable, since the characterization of Othello differs substantially from that of other tragic heroes, in Shakespeare's works or elsewhere. Most of the descriptions of him as heroic are provided by the character himself, and his most heroic action within the play is killing himself, an action which, given the circumstances, does not work unambiguously to his credit. Whatever evanescent heroism he achieves elsewhere (such as his breaking up the swordfight between his and Brabantio's supporters) hardly balances his failure to make any significant correct decisions (except killing himself) and his astonishing gullibility, greater even than Roderigo's. After all, he does not require a shred of evidence or even a scene change to move from professed total love to calling his wife a whore whom he will now "loathe." Iago, whom one would expect to be secondary to the tragic hero, in fact has in excess of two hundred more lines than Othello (fully a third of those in the entire play), and uses many of them to berate Othello and call his motivations into question. Shakespeare's other major tragic heroes also have faults, make mistakes, and succumb at least partially to antagonists, but they always have several counterbalancing heroic actions, and usually more completely dominate their play.[4] Othello alone appears unworthy of heroic status.

Experience and basic tragic theory, however, tell us that this view is wrong, for the play could not have remained popular if the central character were viewed as a gull. If readers generally perceived Othello as the irrational, posturing dolt he appears in isolation, the play could not seem serious and tragic, and would instead probably seem a bleak and farcical comedy, rather like *Troilus and Cressida*. That we do not respond in this way suggests that we somehow perceive Othello as heroic, even though his character, viewed as a whole, does not suggest such a response. Even if there seems no retrospective reason for it, we somehow view Othello as a tragic hero, and hence view the central relationship as of especial value. In effect, we make *Othello* into a heroic tragedy in defiance of the facts; why we do so reflects the power and tenacity for us of both the tragic form and the Petrarchan type. That response is the subject of this chapter.

The play begins with Iago proposing a thoroughly Ascetic view of Othello and Desdemona's marriage. For him, the relationship is grossly physical, even to the point of bestiality; he tells Brabantio that "now, now, very now, an old black ram / Is tupping your white ewe" and "your daughter and the Moor are now making the beast with two backs" (1.1.88–89, 115–17). A little later he tells Roderigo and us why we should regard the lovers as beasts. Responding to his gull's drunken assertion that he would rather die than lose Desdemona, Iago declares, "If the beam of our lives had not one scale of reason to poise another of sensuality, the blood and baseness of our natures would conduct us to most prepost'rous conclusions. But we have reason to cool our raging motions, our carnal stings, our unbitted lusts; whereof I take this that you call love to be a sect or scion" (1.3.326–32).[6] For him, all sexual relationships are based on lust, and love is merely glamorization of "carnal stings." Given this definition of their relationship, Iago has no trouble explaining the "erring barbarian" and "super-subtle Venetian": "These Moors are changeable in their wills—fill thy purse with money. The food that to him now is as lucious as locusts, shall be to him shortly as acerb as the coloquintida. She must change for youth; when she is sated with his body, she will find the error of her choice" (1.3.346–51).

Iago's exuberant Ascetic representations surround the Petrarchan portrayal almost all readers immediately accept as true. It begins with the entrance of the enraged Brabantio, who after an abortive attempt to capture Othello by force, retreats into insults, asserting that the Moor has "enchanted" his daughter, that only "chains of magic" could cause her to "incur a general mock" and "Run from her guardage to the sooty bosom / Of such a thing as thou" (1.2.63–71).[5] This *senex iratus* representation leads us to distrust Brabantio and thus to believe Othello when he recounts how telling the story of his heroic life caused Desdemona to fall in love with him and make the advances which led him to propose:

> Upon this hint I spake:
> She lov'd me for the dangers I had pass'd,
> And I lov'd her that she did pity them.
> This only is the witchcraft I have us'd.
> Here comes the lady; let her witness it.
> (1.3.166–70)

Even though Othello's adventures were not stimulated by Desdemona—and thus do not quite fit the pattern of Petrarchan-influenced romances—they do at least prove him noble and worthy of his lady's love. And if we miss the point, the Duke immediately supports Othello's view by quieting Brabantio and noting that "I think this tale would win my daughter too."

Desdemona, for her part, is calm and rational in answering her father's question of where her allegiance lies, explaining that while she respects and honors her father, she gives precedence to her husband, following the example of her mother. Just as Othello's earlier comments prove his worthiness as a lover, Desdemona's answer to her father makes her seem just as positive by demonstrating both her intelligence and her loyalty to the people she loves. A few lines later she shifts into a straightforward Petrarchan idiom, but one that also carries overtones of the overt sexuality more associated with the Ascetic:

> That I did love the Moor to live with him,
> My downright violence, and storm of fortunes,
> May trumpet to the world. My heart's subdu'd
> Even to the very quality of my lord.
> I saw Othello's visage in his mind,
> And to his honors and his valiant parts
> Did I my soul and fortunes consecrate.
> So that, dear lords, if I be left behind,
> A moth of peace, and he go to the war,
> The rites for why I love him are bereft me,
> And I a heavy interim shall support
> By his dear absence. Let me go with him.
> (1.3.248–59)

Othello has proved himself noble to her, and her response is eternal love. But she also fully intends to have her sexual "rites."

Hearing this assertion of love and sexual desire from his daughter, Brabantio drops his claim of enchantment and adopts a more overtly Ascetic interpretation, warning Othello, "Look to her, Moor, if thou has eyes to see; / She has deceiv'd her father, and may thee" (1.3.292–93). He knows that she has not always shown the fealty she claimed in the one speech, and from the other he ignores the Petrarchan rhetoric and emphasizes instead the sexuality that he thinks attracted her to the Moor in the first place.

Brabantio's warning and to some extent the actions and words of Desdemona on which they are based are suggestive of an Ascetic relationship, but Othello's response is so powerfully suggestive of the Petrarchan that it prevents any question of our seeing the true relationship in terms of the opposite type: "My life upon her faith!" For Othello, a person's love is indivisible from his soul, and it is no more possible for him to conceive of the rebellion of the one than the other. Othello's love is complete and without reservation, and his certainty helps overwhelm any doubts that we might otherwise have.[6]

This ringing affirmation of love fits nicely into the overall structure of the first act: Iago's two excessive denunciations of the Othello-Desdemona relationship as mere lust surround a central section in which two more subtle Ascetic accounts are each answered forcefully with a Petrarchan one. This opposition of the Petrarchan and the Ascetic forces us to see the relationship as one or the other (rather than as a combination), not a difficult choice given the necessity that the central character in a tragedy be noble (and hence in love rather than in lust) and given that we, like Othello himself, build our world on the assumption that lust cannot be the only motivation for relationships. And because Iago is personally vile and offers such a debased view of sexual attraction, our choice is also strongly dictated by our desire to find an alternative, just as the representation of Brabantio as a *senex iratus* leads us to sympathize with the pair he is trying to separate. Ironically, if Iago's view of the lovers were less revolting, or if Brabantio supported their relationship, we would be less attracted to them. Just as in *Romeo and Juliet*, the opposition is at least as responsible for our attraction to the central relationship as are the lovers themselves.

In fact, the relationship itself is not represented as completely positive, for threatening our wish to identify with it is the troubling portrait of a love more violent and less rational than the words of the lovers suggest—a love that involves eloping in the middle of the night and exposing an old man to public ridicule even at the moment when the love is consummated. Brabantio may fill the *senex iratus* role briefly, but he is no Iago, and the comparison works to the disadvantage of the Petrarchan view of the relationship. Act 1 begins and ends with debased reductions that make us want to uphold the Petrarchan vision at all costs, but at the center of the scene, where that vision should be strongest, Shakespeare has given us a more equivocal portrait than he might have. The result is to suggest the frailty of love even as we, like Othello, unwisely wish to rely absolutely on its strength.

This frailty results mainly from the characterization of Desdemona. Her actions are the ones that have hurt her father, and it is her integrity that his ominous final comment questions. Iago's savagery is mostly directed at her, and she is the one who subverts Othello's idealized, chaste view of their relationship with a suggestion of sexuality. Thus the representation of the lovers at this point in the play is slightly skewed: Othello is wholly heroic and wholly within the Petrarchan tradition, but Desdemona is not; her violation of filial duty and her suggestion of sexual desire add a hint of the Ascetic.[7]

This slightly contradictory portrayal of the central relationship is reinforced in act 2, which begins with Desdemona and Emilia engaging in a sexually suggestive repartee with Iago—but one in which he makes most of the sexual allusions. For example, to his claim that wives are "Players in your huswifery, and huswives in your beds," Desdemona replies "O, fie upon thee, slanderer!" After another fifty lines of similarly light bawdry, she indicates her pleasure at listening to, but not materially contributing to such a subject: "O most lame and impotent conclusion! Do not learn of him, Emilia, though he be thy husband. How say you, Cassio? is he not a most profane and liberal counsellor?" (2.1.161–64). Desdemona's use of "impotent" hardly qualifies as bawdry, but it is not within the Petrarchan idiom either.[8] So when Othello enters with a compliment that is the epitome of Petrarchan rhetoric, the description does not quite fit the Desdemona we have been watching:

> O my soul's joy!
> If after every tempest come such calms,
> May the winds blow till they have waken'd death!
> And let the laboring bark climb hills of seas
> Olympus-high, and duck again as low
> As hell's from heaven! If it were now to die,
> 'Twere now to be most happy; for I fear
> My soul hath her content so absolute
> That not another comfort like to this
> Succeeds in unknown fate.
>
> (2.1.184–93)

For Othello, the recent sea storm was a heroic battle he fought largely to be rewarded with the mere sight of his lady, who is the very center of his soul. The Desdemona we have seen is certainly no whore, but neither does such heroic idealization seem appropriate.

But lest we feel too strongly the difference between our Desdemona and Othello's, Iago again comes to the rescue by overstating the case for the Ascetic, spending almost forty lines trying to convince Roderigo that Desdemona is whorish, already tired of Othello and panting for Cassio. Her courteous taking of Cassio's hand when he came ashore is "Lechery, ... an index and obscure prologue to the history of lust and foul thoughts," which is not surprising considering the inevitability that her "eye"—with a play on the vaginal double sense of the word—⁹ will demand more than just the Moor: "Her eye must be fed; and what delight shall she have to look on the devil? When the blood is made dull with the act of sport, there should be, again to inflame it and to give satiety a fresh appetite, loveliness in favor, sympathy in years, manners, and beauties—all which the Moor is defective in" (2.1.225–31). These excessive comments cause us to sympathize with the lovers—or rather with the Petrarchan view of their relationship—for several reasons. First, they so thoroughly fly against the view we have formed by watching the lovers themselves, which even at its most negative implied nothing like Iago's image of an insatiable Desdemona, that we are drawn back toward the Petrarchan interpretation, just as any excessive statement implies the validity of the opposite. Second, Iago's representation of Othello and Desdemona as fool and whore is untenable for us, since to accept it would reduce the play to the status of farce; viewing the destruction of a noble man has a long narrative history, but we have no mechanism for understanding a narrative in which the protagonist is somehow to seem completely debased and yet worthy of our concern. And last, accepting Iago's view puts us in the equally untenable position of swallowing the same information as an obvious fool; almost anything Roderigo believes we will naturally react against. Iago's excessiveness, again, is very important, for without it our inclination toward the Petrarchan interpretation would not be felt so strongly; the lack of a clearly wrong view would lead us to give more weight to the many understated Ascetic suggestions hovering about the Petrarchan center of the relationship.[10]

Having forced us to commit ourselves to a view that is everywhere surrounded with signs of its opposite, Shakespeare then moves on to make us squirm with our decision. Iago now begins to speak directly to us, rather than to his gull, and his comments become much more moderate, even to the point of directly contradicting the previous ones. First, he admits the honor of both lovers and suggests that his reason for attacking them is purely selfish:

> That Cassio loves her, I do well believe't;
> That she loves him, 'tis apt and of great credit.
> The Moor (howbeit that I endure him not)

> Is of a constant, loving, noble nature,
> And I dare think he'll prove to Desdemona
> A most dear husband.
>
> (2.1.286–91)

On the surface, this admission might seem to reinforce the Petrarchan view, but actually it undermines it by shifting attention away from Desdemona, whom we have all along seen as weak but not the animal of Iago's diatribes, and toward Othello, who has always before seemed unshakably within a Petrarchan representation. Rather than vilify Othello as he previously had Desdemona, Iago now portrays him as positive, but positive in a traditionally patriarchal way: as a good husband who intends to fulfill his hierarchial position as his wife's protector and leader. This view is closer than it seems to Iago's earlier description of the relationship as lust, since male-dominated, nonpassionate relationships are the ideal that the Ascetic type sets up as its model; Iago's new Othello is what his old one deviates from—a different face of the same type. Having given us its most positive, Iago immediately begins to move back toward the negative:

> Now I do love her too,
> Not out of absolute lust (though peradventure
> I stand accomptant for as great a sin),
> But partly led to diet my revenge,
> For that I do suspect the lusty Moor
> Hath leap'd into my seat.
>
> (2.1.291–96)

The Othello who was once a lust-driven barbarian and then a traditional husband is now a fabliaulike antagonist in a cuckolding contest, and the view Iago gives in his next soliloquy, in which he explains his plot to us, is even more threatening to the view we prefer to have of the Moor and the central relationship:

> His soul is so enfetter'd to her love,
> That she may make, unmake, do what she list,
> Even as her appetite shall play the god
> With his weak function.
>
> (2.3.345–48)

Instead of a good husband, Othello is now a prime example of a bad one: a man whose affection for his wife has led him to unreasonably forsake his natural hierarchical position and place himself beneath an "inclining" woman. There is no mention here of trust or honor or anything else that would redeem the description for the Petrarchan view, nor is there any substantial excessiveness—such as an assertion that Othello could never love under any circumstances. There is only a rather straightforward description of the Moor as terribly weak and unmanly, and hence as an easy mark for anyone willing to take advantage of him.

Most critics, like most readers and viewers, dismiss both of these speeches as reflective more of Iago's need to justify his villainy than of any real debasement of Othello—a reaction that allows us again to reassert the Petrarchan view, with its essential representation of the play's central character as serious and worthy of our respect. Shakespeare continues to make us squirm, however, by immediately reintroducing Iago's Ascetic view, this time more disturbingly through the actions of the lovers themselves. First, Desdemona reacts to Cassio's plea for help in a way that edges her closer to the traditional view of bad wives:

> My lord shall never rest,
> I'll watch him tame, and talk him out of patience;
> His bed shall seem a school, his board a shrift,
> I'll intermingle every thing he does
> With Cassio's suit.
> (3.3.22–26)

Since we have all along viewed Desdemona as more naive than crafty, most of us prefer not to see this promise as what it would otherwise clearly be: a Wife of Bath–like assertion of control over the husband. And when Desdemona straightway spends thirty lines badgering her husband to say when he will receive the man he has just permanently banished from command, most of us surely see his answer as nothing worse than mere exasperation: "Prithee no more; let him come when he will; / I will deny thee nothing" (3.3.75–76). When she further demands that he give in not as a "boon" but because she has the right to look after his welfare, his response is only slightly less justifiable:

> I will deny thee nothing;
> Whereon, I do beseech thee, grant me this,
> To leave me but a little to myself.
> (3.3.83–85)

Viewed in isolation, this plea, like Desdemona's promise, suggests a domineering wife and a husband too weak to resist. But because Desdemona's badgering seems more that of a disappointed child than that of a crafty adult, and because we never see her follow through with her threat to use her bed to "school" her unsubmissive husband, and because Othello agrees only to see Cassio, not to reinstate him—because of all these reasons, we reject again any suggestion that the relationship is what Iago described: a previously strong and noble man reduced to ignobility by his lust for a woman, who like all women, is deceitful, domineering, irrational, and driven by passions.[11]

Part of the reason we are able to continue to reject this view is that Othello himself continues to project an uncompromising adherence to the one we prefer until well into act 3 scene 3. But the presence of the Ascetic view remains, and even colors such strong Petrarchan statements as Othello's last description of his wife before Iago begins to work his poison:

> Excellent wretch! Perdition catch my soul
> But I do love thee! and when I love thee not,
> Chaos is come again.
> (3.3.90–92)

From the Petrarchan perspective it is Othello's passion for Desdemona that spurs him to be his heroic self; without it, his self disintegrates into chaos. But Othello's statement also uneasily supports the Ascetic perspective, for anyone whose only joy comes from a relationship with a woman has descended into baseness and chaos already. The crucial point here, for us, if not for Othello, is the closeness of the two views: the only real difference is that the Petrarchan view suggests that Othello's passion will lead him to improve his already heroic self; the Ascetic predicts that it will lead to his debasement.

The latter, of course, is what occurs, and very quickly too. The resulting irony is that Othello gives up on love much more quickly than we do, even though our initial identification of the relationship in terms of this system was based mainly on him and his statements. Because we, even more than Othello himself, refuse to accept that love cannot make us better, and because we have more faith in Othello and the love that defines him than he himself does, we still ignore the evidence and believe the less likely view.

In the remainder of the scene (3.3) and in the scenes through act 4 scene 1 Shakespeare makes this affirmation increasingly more difficult for us by giving Othello the same excessive sentiments as Iago spoke before. Under Iago's urging, it is now Othello who speaks of Desdemona's "stol'n hours of lust" and notes:

> O curse of marriage!
> That we can call these delicate creatures ours,
> And not their appetites! I had rather be a toad
> And live upon the vapor of a dungeon
> Than keep a corner in the thing I love
> For others' uses.
> (3.3.268–73)

In the same scene Othello suggests he would not be surprised to hear that his wife had slept with his whole army, and later he falls into a trance because of his inability to tolerate Iago's quibbling on whether Cassio has been lying "with" or "on" Desdemona. All of these extreme speeches and actions—and what could be more extreme in this context than swooning with jealousy—serve partly the same function as Iago's speeches in the first act: to suggest through their grossness the grossness of the conception behind them. The difference now is that the debased view has become internalized in the relationship itself, rather than attached to an outside observer. Instead of simply dismissing the "lying" outsider, we must now take the more difficult approach of viewing the insider as radically altered, indeed as having become his own opposite.[12]

If Shakespeare continued to represent Othello as so debased as to froth at the mouth and to accept whatever Iago says without question, the play would collapse into meaninglessness. Soon, however, the Moor's ravings begin to moderate, and he begins again to describe the relationship as Petrarchan, though abused:

> but, alas, to make me
> The fixed figure for the time of scorn
> To point his slow unmoving finger at!
> Yet could I bear that too, well, very well;
> But there, where I have garner'd up my heart,
> Where either I must live or bear no life;
> The fountain from the which my current runs
> Or else dries up: to be discarded thence!
> Or keep it as a cestern for foul toads
> To knot and gender in!
> (4.2.53–62)

Like many earlier ones, this passage suggests that Othello's love (not his lust) is the very center of his soul; the difference is that he now perceives that center as befouled rather than crystalline and pure.

Othello can claim love but still wish to kill his wife because he now views her as a witchlike creature who has deceived and abused a pure love; if "Heaven mocks itself" for her reality to be so different from her appearance, he does not view himself as weak for having been deceived. His imaging of Desdemona as a foul fountain is reminiscent of numerous Circe figures, beginning, at least most noticeably, with Ovid's Salmacis and proceeding through a dozen or so examples in the *Faerie Queene*. Iago, trying to seduce Othello, makes the first connection of Desdemona to witches:

> She that so young could give out such a seeming
> To seel her father's eyes up, close as oak,
> He thought 'twas witchcraft.
> (3.3.209–11)

Othello himself produces an overtly Circean description two scenes later: "Get me some poison, Iago, this night. I'll not expostulate with her, lest her body and beauty unprovide my mind again. This night, Iago" (4.1.204–6).

The effect of these Emasculating suggestions is to make both Desdemona and Othello seem stronger, since the story of a knight spellbound by a supernaturally powerful witch is a much more heroic representation of both characters than is a story of a man seduced by his own lust to serve a weak and inferior creature. The Emasculating type is like the Petrarchan in that it suggests that the man's passion is the result of the woman's strength, not the man's weakness. In both, the lady is mysteriously powerful, and thus to begin representing the central relationship in terms of the latter helps reestablish the former, especially since we know that Desdemona has not been befouled.[13]

Desdemona has not, however, been all that pure either. Her actions, as we have seen, have always suggested someone at least slightly different from the woman of her husband's initial vision; she has been no more able to live up to his vision than she has to live down to Iago's. But from this point Shakespeare begins to recast her as a more straightforward Petrarchan heroine. This recasting coincides with the elevating in importance of Emilia, who suggests the Petrarchan system both by directly associating her friend with it and by serving as a foil against which Desdemona can be revalued.[14] The first such revaluing comes (in 4.2) when Emilia strongly defends her friend against the Moor's accusations:

> I durst, my lord, to wager she is honest;
> Lay down my soul at stake. If you think other,
> Remove your thought; it doth abuse your bosom.
> If any wretch have put this in your head,
> Let heaven requite it with the serpent's curse!
> For if she be not honest, chaste, and true,
> There's no man happy; the purest of their wives
> Is foul as slander.
>   (4.2.12–19)

Emilia's defense occurs just before Othello's speech linking Desdemona to magic fountains, and like it serves to give Desdemona especial importance, suggesting that she is the very definition of female chastity and virtue—which is, of course, one of the most common assertions made for the ladies of romances or sonnet sequences.

One scene later this same image of unimpeachable virtue is strongly reinforced when Emilia and Desdemona discuss adultery. By now Desdemona senses that her husband will likely kill her, but rather than condemn him, as Emilia does, she asserts that her love prevents her from questioning him, requests that Emilia lay out her wedding sheets, and sings "Willow" while awaiting Othello's return. All of these actions, but especially the last, serve to withdraw Desdemona from the real world of the play. Whereas before she is portrayed as a willing but largely incompetent participant in the decayed world of Venice and Cyprus, her dreamy acceptance of her own destruction, along with her distracted singing (reminiscent of Ophelia's) combine to make her seem now wholly distinct from it—almost as if she had suddenly become a pastoral or romantic figure.

With this distancing as backdrop, Desdemona's question about the existence of adultery sounds completely sincere and reinforces the new representation of her as a Petrarchan heroine completely unable even to comprehend the existence of vice:

> Dost thou in conscience think—tell me, Emilia—
> That there be women do abuse their husbands
> In such gross kind?
>
> (4.3.61–63)

Emilia's responses to this question and to the question of her own willingness to cheat are, not unexpectedly, thoroughly within the ideological framework her husband has given us: "Marry, I would not do such a thing for a joint-ring, nor for measures of lawn, nor for gowns, petticoats, nor caps, nor any petty exhibition; but, for all the whole world—'ud's pity, who would not make her husband a cuckold to make him a monarch? I should venture purgatory for't" (4.3.72–77). She then goes on to explain that since husbands "pour our treasures into foreign laps . . . break out in peevish jealousies . . . or . . . strike us," wives have the right to "revenge": "Then let them use us well; else let them know, / The ills we do, their ills instruct us so" (4.3.102–3). These comments show Emilia well matched with Iago, but much more importantly, they place the Ascetic system he represents in stark opposition to the Petrarchism of Desdemona, thereby strongly emphasizing the newfound validity of the latter. Emilia's understanding of life serves the same function as her husband's similar views earlier in the play. It also helps complete another stunning bit of dramaturgic sleight-of-hand by Shakespeare, for by the conclusion of this scene it is hard to remember that Desdemona was ever associated, even tangentially, with the same type to which she is now so strongly contrasted.

Nor is the magic complete yet, for in the last scene Shakespeare again manages to alter subtly our understanding of the two main characters, producing thereby the final view that most of us take away from the play. The problem to be overcome in this scene has to do with the nature of tragedy: Desdemona now seems morally stronger and more committed to love than her husband, thereby leaving the central character of the play in a rather secondary position. Ending the play in this way would leave us with a tragic hero who is too slight to fill his narrative position properly; we would not feel as though we had seen a "great man" fall.

To reestablish the Moor as such a great man, Shakespeare employs three manipulations, one primarily involving Desdemona, one Othello, and one the opposition of the world of Desdemona's bedroom to the outside world of Cyprus. The first of these involves weakening Desdemona just to the extent that she no longer seems so completely at one with the detached, ethereal world she inhabited (in 4.3). Through her apparent lack of fear of, indeed obliviousness toward, death in that scene, as well as through her unworldly singing and her equally unworldly inability even to conceive of vice, Desdemona firmly associated herself with Petrarchism, and she also created a sort of nonsocial, ideal world where that love can exist away from Iago's world of lust, which has now become synonymous with the world of the play in general. In effect, Iago's world defeats and destroys Othello's, only to have the latter reappear in a removed context, a green world of the mind which Iago's viciously reductive understanding of human actions cannot penetrate. Like Juliet's garden and tomb, or the paradise where, Antony tells us, "souls do couch on flowers," Desdemona's bedroom represents the ideal world of love, the place that revalidates love but at the same time reminds us how little it resembles our own.

This world is reestablished and extended in the final scene, when, after one more scene dominated by Iago (the attack on Cassio), full of noise and deception, we are brought back to the quiet of Desdemona's bedroom. Instead of a cacophony of lights and mistaken identities, we begin with a single taper and with no confusion of identities (though in another sense Othello is, of course, horribly confused). The otherworldliness of the setting is strongly emphasized by Othello's opening speech, which compares the sleeping figure in the center of the room to "monumental alabaster" and to a single, unexcelled rose, images that suggest on the one hand a religious shrine and on the other a garden of love, the latter ever warmed by her "balmy breath."

When Desdemona wakes up, however, she does not quite fit into this world. Instead of submitting nobly to the sacrifice which she describes in act 4 scene 3 and which her husband redescribes in this scene, she attempts once again to justify herself in Iago's world of lost handkerchiefs and false confessions; failing that (as she has always failed before), she is reduced to begging, never an activity with noble connotations: "O, banish me, my lord, but kill me not! . . . Kill me to-morrow, let me live tonight!" (5.2.78, 80). As Othello accurately notes, her refusal to play out her part makes "A murther which I thought a sacrifice" (5.2.65).

For us, this little breakdown has several useful purposes. Most obviously, by making Desdemona seem more human, it makes her ensuing murder seem all the more horrible and pathetic. But probably of more importance is that this distancing of Desdemona from the bedroom world makes her seem weaker in relation to Othello, who at least until the entrance of Emilia seems completely at home in it; the relative weakness of Othello in relation to his wife, then, is reversed, and it is the Moor who finally, as at the beginning, seems most able to exist in a world of total commitment to love.

The second manipulation in the last scene involves a significant extension of an earlier one, the oblique comparisons of Desdemona to a witch. The point of these comparisons was to make Desdemona seem more powerful and heroic (if still evil) than Iago's descriptions or her own actions had suggested, and at the same time to raise as well Othello's seriously declined stature. Desdemona is again compared to Circe in the last scene, but with the difference that the emphasis this time is mostly on her supernatural beauty, rather than on witchlike actions.

The first and most important such comparison is in the opening speech, partially discussed above, where Othello reestablishes the sense of Desdemona's bedroom as a place of magic. Othello does note that the cause of his actions should not be named before the "chaste stars," and he directly tells us that "she must die, else she'll betray more men." But most of his comments suggest either the stunning beauty of Desdemona or the gardenlike quality that she imposes on all around her. Hence her skin is whiter than snow and "smooth as monumental alabaster," and she is the "cunning'st pattern of excelling nature," a perfect rose, and the creator of "balmy breath, that dost almost persuade / Justice to break her sword."

This emphasis on Desdemona's supernatural beauty (rather than on her actions), allows an easy transition back to a Petrarchan representation, which occurs when Othello drops all pretense of viewing the now dead Desdemona as a Circe figure and describes her in terms straight out of Petrarchan love lyrics:

> My wife, my wife! what wife? I have no wife.
> O insupportable! O heavy hour!
> Methinks it should be now a huge eclipse
> Of sun and moon, and that th' affrighted globe
> Did yawn at alteration.
> (5.2.97–101)

Strictly speaking, this statement is absurd for a man who thinks he has just killed a witch masquerading as a wife, but because it fits into the pattern of the scene just before, and because we know Desdemona's innocence and now believe again in the nobility of Othello's love, we can accept the lament without too much of a jar. Amazingly, then, Othello is for us back to a Petrarchan representation even before he learns of his error, the Ascetic and Emasculating portrayals forgotten almost immediately after serving their purposes.

The last manipulation is borrowed from *Romeo and Juliet,* where the lovers' world is made special by making it seem cosmic in comparison to the mundaneness of the ordinary one. In the last scene of *Othello* the main representative of the ordinary world is Emilia, who seeks outside help (and thus the intrusion of the ordinary world) when she hears her dying friend, then has great trouble understanding how the husband she has lived with (in the ordinary world) could have been the one to deceive the Moor, then tries to understand Othello in terms of a Roderigo-like gulled fool: "O gull, O dolt, / As ignorant as dirt" (5.2.163–64). Finally, it is Emilia who explains her husband's use of the handkerchief, which is the ordinary-world situation Othello and Desdemona are least able to comprehend, and generally prepares the way for Montano, Gratiano, and the others to reimpose the rule of the outside.

Ironically, however, it is also Emilia who helps set up the final definition of the cosmic world, at this point closely restricted in place to Desdemona's bedroom (though paralleled by the also detached place where Othello repeated to Desdemona alone the story of his life, and where she expressed her love for him). Emilia makes this world truly cosmic by defining the two lovers in cosmic terms and, more importantly, by helping create a cosmic antagonist for them: her husband. She contributes her part to demonizing Iago by refusing his command of silence after learning what has become of the handkerchief:

> 'Twill out, 'twill out! I peace?
> No, I will speak as liberal as the north:
> Let heaven and men and devils, let them all,
> All, all, cry shame against me, yet I'll speak.
> (5.2.219–22)

Iago, of course, has all along seemed at least as much a Vice as a man, but never is the demonic association as stressed as in this scene. Four times in the next hundred lines he is described as a "damned slave" or a close variant, a combination of motifs often associated with the Vice, suggesting the baseness of evil rather than any weakness in the character. Othello makes the point clear soon after learning of his mistake:

> O ill-starr'd wench,
> Pale as thy smock! when we shall meet at compt,
> This look of thine will hurl my soul from heaven,
> And fiends will snatch at it. Cold, cold, my girl?
> Even like thy chastity. O cursed, cursed slave!
> Whip me, ye devils,
> From the possession of this heavenly sight!
> Blow me about in winds! roast me in sulphur!
> Wash me in steep-down gulfs of liquid fire!
> (5.2.272–80)

Othello expects to roast in hell, led there by one of Satan's emissaries, his "cursed slave." And a few lines later he makes the identification even clearer: "I look down towards his feet; but that's a fable. / If that thou be'st a devil, I cannot kill thee" (5.2.286–87). Othello is correct: modern devils like Iago do not have cloven feet. When the Moor demands to know why he has been "ensnar'd," Iago announces that "From this time forth I will never speak word." Unlike the garrulous man-devil of earlier scenes, he is now the mute embodiment of evil itself: unconcerned with anything but destruction and unaccountable to anyone.

The movement of Iago from the ordinary to the cosmic realm elevates Othello's stature by redefining his failure: rather than just another of a con artist's gulls, like Roderigo, he is now the loser in a struggle with a supernatural being. He has lost, but that he participated in such a battle at all suggests strength and significance. Both of these qualities are then developed in Othello's final speech, as is, again, Othello's separateness from the ordinary world:

> Then must you speak
> Of one that lov'd not wisely but too well;
> Of one not easily jealous, but being wrought,
> Perplexed in the extreme; of one whose hand
> (Like the base Indian) threw a pearl away
> Richer than all his tribe; of one whose subdu'd eyes,
> Albeit unused to the melting mood,
> Drops tears as fast as the Arabian trees
> Their medicinable gum. Set you down this;
> And say besides, that in Aleppo once,
> Where a malignant and a turban'd Turk
> Beat a Venetian and traduc'd the state,
> I took by th' throat the circumcised dog,
> And smote him—thus.
>
> (5.2.343–56)

The Othello of this speech sees himself as the two characters we have seen him enact throughout the play: a base gull who allows a gross, reductive conception of sexual relationships to destroy him, and a strong, self-reliant hero willing to base his life on his idealistic vision of love. But by this point there is no question which of the characters is the dominant one, and the Othello we leave with is much the same as the one with whom we began.

At the end, then, we are left with a sense of Othello as a man of heroic strength who fell heroically, defeated but not beaten by a heroically evil opponent. The play as a whole works because Shakespeare manipulates with extraordinary skill the structural interplay of the Petrarchan and Ascetic interpretations that are always resident in our society's (and thus most individuals') comprehension of sexual relationships. Outside of the final scene, there are very few direct associations of the central relationship with Petrarchism, but by playing on our tendency to value this system and to oppose it to the Ascetic, Shakespeare repeatedly induces us to reassert its validity, even when the lovers themselves no longer fit the pattern. Finally, *Othello* as a whole is less about how little it takes to destroy the Moor's belief in love than it is about how much we will deny to reaffirm our own. But in a larger sense, even this formulation is wrong, for the play is not about anything, whether a character, an idea, or a response; the play *is* our response, or more specifically is whatever response a "we" can be said to share. How this shared response is created and controlled seems to me the only approach that is not mainly a rewriting of the story, and the only one through which we can begin to understand the real "magic in the web."

6

Words, Words, Mere Words:

Troilus and Cressida

Romeo and Juliet and *Othello* are both plays that have produced what is evidently a consistent response over several centuries. Were this not so, the plays could not have had long stage histories: no production can possibly succeed if it does not communicate intelligibly to most of its audience, and repeated successful productions of a single play could not occur unless this same basic communication were continuing to occur. Both plays (but especially *Othello*) have also produced numerous published interpretations, but almost all assume agreement on numerous basic elements: our sympathy with the lovers, our dislike of Tybalt and Iago, the maturing of Romeo and Juliet, the nobility of Othello and faithfulness of Desdemona, and so forth.

Troilus and Cressida, on the other hand, has had almost no stage history at all. It may not have been produced at all before the late nineteenth century, and has been performed with even limited regularity only in the last thirty years. Critics have long agreed that the play contains much powerful poetry, but beyond that they cannot even agree on its genre: comedy, tragedy, history, satire, or some bizarre form created for the nonce. Much of the rest of the commentary debates whether the play supports some very limited value,[1] or is completely nihilistic.[2]

All of this reflects a play that produces no consistent response, an interpretation with which most of my students would certainly agree. Scholars, however, find the play difficult but not meaningless. This suggests that *Troilus and Cressida* does push us toward a coherent vision, but not in any usual or widely applicable way. More than any other Shakespearean play,

Troilus and Cressida depends for its narrative progression on the interplay of complex ideas, and while these ideas are partly structured through their association with love types, the play consistently works to prevent us from sympathizing with or even feeling we understand the characters these types help produce. The result is an unusual subordination of character to ideology and perhaps Shakespeare's most bizarre play.

Three love types are used in *Troilus and Cressida*, but in a way very different from any other of Shakespeare's plays. One type, the Ascetic, is set up to be completely unacceptable, while the other two, each associated with a system of value and with a group of traditionally heroic characters, are used to undermine each other and to portray the characters as depraved and honorless. All we are left with finally is a horrific version of the Ascetic, which in this case is carefully associated with the complete denial of any value whatsoever. To whatever extent we accept this vision as possible the play will force us to confront that most threatening of all perspectives: that all action is meaningless and all value a delusion and lie.

The spokesmen for the Ascetic type are Thersites and Pandarus. The latter, in general, appears in the scenes involving the title characters, where he constantly implies that what the lovers call love is actually nothing but animal lust, and that nothing else is possible for anyone. Thersites, on the other hand, normally concerns himself with the continuing war between the Greeks and the Trojans, asserting that what the antagonists call honor is simple blood lust. In one characteristic attack late in the play he first demolishes the idea that love can motivate honorable action: "Now they are clapper-clawing one another; I'll go look on. That dissembling abominable varlet, Diomed, has got that same scurvy doting foolish young knave's sleeve of Troy there in his helm. I would fain see them meet, that that same young Troyan ass, that loves the whore there, might send that Greekish whoremasterly villain with the sleeve back to the dissembling luxurious drab, of a sleeveless arrant" (5.4.1–9). That done, he immediately extends the denial of honorable action to the war in general, and to all of the famous heroes fighting in it: "A' th' t' other side, the policy of those crafty swearing rascals, that stale old mouse-eaten dry cheese, Nestor, and that same dog-fox, Ulysses, is not prov'd worth a blackberry. They set me up, in policy, that mongril cur, Ajax, against that dog of as bad a kind, Achilles; and now is the cur Ajax prouder than the cur Achilles, and will not arm today; whereupon the Grecians began to proclaim barbarism, and policy grows into an ill opinion" (5.4.9–17). For Thersites, Troilus' attempt to revenge the loss of his lady is equivalent to a brawl over some barroom whore, and the larger war is mere barbarism, fought by men who are little more than the animals to whom they are compared.

An earlier assault on Helen and the war fought over her provides a clearer indication of the basis of Thersites' ideology: "After this, the vengeance on the whole camp! or rather, the Neapolitan bone-ache! for that methinks is the curse depending on those that war for a placket" (2.3.17–20). There are several important ramifications to this brief statement. First of all, Thersites' reduction of the most beautiful woman in the world to the commonality of a placket calls into question any assertion of distinctive feminine beauty. For Thersites, there is nothing to a woman except her sexual function, and all women can serve that function equally well. Thus any assertion of the significance of a particular woman is inherently false and hypocritical. And since women are mere physical objects for Thersites, and all concern for them mere animal lust, the proper payment for wars or adventures or any other activity based on a man's desire for a woman is not honor (as it is in the Petrarchan type) but syphilis.

This radically Ascetic perspective resembles that in some of Iago's speeches, but the difference is that Thersites consistently tries to extend this horrible understanding of women and desire to action in general. For him, not only the Trojan war but everything reflects man's need to glorify his lust and violence: "Lechery, lechery, still wars and lechery, nothing else holds fashion. A burning devil take them!" (5.2.194–96).[3]

Thersites' understanding of man and his motivations is extremely threatening because by denying the possibility of either reason or honor, it undercuts the rationale men generally use to justify their actions and to hold themselves above the animals—to which Thersites compares nearly every character in the play (including himself). Thersites is not, however, an imposing character; Shakespeare, in fact, goes out of his way to portray him as particularly loathsome. If there were any alternative to his nihilistic view, both he and it would be quickly dismissed, much as we dismiss both the persons and the ideologies of Iago and Malvolio in plays where strong positive perspectives are easily discernible. Thersites becomes an important character only because the play refuses to allow validity to any but the view he proposes. *Troilus and Cressida* develops its ability to threaten not through Thersites' assertion that everything is chaos but through the collapse of the structures the play induces us to use to keep the idea of chaos distanced. The real center of the play, then, is not what Thersites says, but how the alternatives to his view are portrayed.

The most obvious alternative is Petrarchism, which holds that proper love results in increased honor. The Petrarchan type is indeed very important in the play, but its presentation in *Troilus and Cressida* is teasingly ambiguous, sometimes serious and straightforward, sometimes satiric. Nowhere is this more apparent than in our first view of the title characters' relationship, where Troilus is sometimes portrayed as a serious Petrarchan lover and sometimes as a parody of one.[4] At least two of the speeches in the first scene, for example, seem like serious representations of the type:

> Patience herself, what goddess e'er she be,
> Doth lesser blench at suff'rance than I do.
> At Priam's royal table do I sit,
> And when fair Cressid comes into my thoughts—
> So, traitor, then she comes when she is thence.
> (1.1.27–31)

> O Pandarus! I tell thee, Pandarus—
> When I do tell thee there my hopes lie drown'd,
> Reply not in how many fadoms deep
> They lie indrench'd. I tell thee I am mad
> In Cressid's love; thou answer'st she is fair,
> Pourest in the open ulcer of my heart
> Her eyes, her hair, her cheek, her gait, her voice,
> Handlest in thy discourse, O, that her hand,
> In whose comparison all whites are ink
> Writing their own reproach; to whose soft seizure
> The cygnet's down is harsh, and spirit of sense
> Hard as the palm of ploughman.
> (1.1.48–59)

Most of the hallmarks of Petrarchism are in these speeches: the lover bewailing the long denial of his suit and praising his own long-sufferance, the description of continuous and uncontrollable domination by love, the blazon of the lady's beauties, and the use of various kinds of excessive rhetoric.

Other parts of the first scene, however, are certainly satiric. The first of these is Troilus' opening description of his love for Cressida, which comes just after a prologue emphasizing the seriousness of the war being fought outside the gates of Troy:

> Call here my varlet, I'll unarm again.
> Why should I war without the walls of Troy,
> That find such cruel battle here within?
> Each Trojan that is master of his heart,
> Let him to field, Troilus, alas, hath none. . . .
> The Greeks are strong and skillful to their strength,
> Fierce to their skill, and to their fierceness valiant,
> But I am weaker than a woman's tear,
> Tamer than sleep, fonder than ignorance,
> Less valiant than the virgin in the night,
> And skilless as unpractic'd infancy.
> (1.1.1–5, 7–12)

This self-portrait is a parody of a Petrarchan lover, for no genuine one could be unwilling to prove himself in combat with a worth enemy, let alone be as weak as a crying woman or as cowardly as a frightened virgin. Serious Petrarchan lovers are dominated and in some ways incapacitated by their love, but the structure of the type demands the ability to engage in an honorable battle or some other proof of manliness and devotion to the lady. It is only through this proof that love can be shown valuable, and only after proof that the narrative of love can be brought to a conclusion.

To see what such worthiness might entail, one has only to look at Chaucer's version of the story. When his Troilus discovers that unless Criseyde "wolden on me rewe, er that I deyde," he responds with an extraordinary display of ferocity in battle, the reason for which is clearly described:

> But for non hate he to the Grekes hadde,
> Ne also for the rescous of the town,
> Ne made hym thus in armes for to madde,
> But only, lo, for this conclusioun:
> To liken hire the bet for his renoun.
> Fro day to day in armes so he spedde,
> That the Grekes as the deth him dredde.
> (*Troilus and Criseyde* 1.477–83)[5]

Chaucer's Troilus becomes much more manly and honorable when he falls in love, and it is love that becomes his prime motivation for fighting. Shakespeare's Troilus, at least the one of the initial speech, is an entirely different creation.

Specifically, he is an Ascetic creation, for it is the Ascetic definition of love as unmanly and dishonorable that is the point of view of the parody. The same type also is used to undercut the treatment of Cressida early in the play. In the first scene, Troilus and Pandarus compare her to wheat that must be ground, bolted, leavened, kneaded, and baked before it is ready to be consumed (1.1.14–26), all of which is more suggestive of Doll Tearsheet than a goddesslike lady.[6] In the next scene, Cressida's bawdy exchanges with Pandarus show how little she fits the Petrarchan ideal of a pure lady who will inspire her lover to perform glorious deeds, and she makes her distance from the role even clearer when she explains in a soliloquy why she resists Troilus even though she finds him attractive:

> Women are angels, wooing:
> Things won are done, joy's soul lies in the doing.
> That she belov'd knows nought that knows not this:
> Men prize the thing ungained more than it is.
> That she was never yet that ever knew
> Love got so sweet as when desire did sue.

> Therefore this maxim out of love I teach:
> Achievement is command; ungain'd, beseech;
> Then though my heart's content firm love doth bear,
> Nothing of that shall from mine eyes appear.
>
> (1.2.286–95)

The woman of most of this speech cares nothing for moving her lover to honor, and she seems to regard his passion as completely physical and irrational, with no basis in a value high enough to survive their first embrace. As a result, the Petrarchan formula of reserving her sexual reward until he has proved himself worthy has no application to the relationship she portrays, and she only puts her lover off to maintain his attention for the longest period of time. And she claims that all other women do the same.

But at the same time that Cressida is calculating the optimum time for bedding down with Troilus, she also asserts that she has "firm love" for him after all, despite leading him on. Given the rest of the speech, the obvious interpretation is that Cressida's view of love is so debased that she cannot even understand what it is. Such a response is itself revealing, for it can only occur if we recognize the separate Ascetic and Petrarchan sections of the speech, and if we regard the latter as the more positive. As in many passages in *Othello*, this one depends on our preferring the Petrarchan to the Ascetic and evaluating characters correspondingly. Because Cressida fails to follow the Petrarchan rules we have a hard time regarding her as a positive character, no matter how sound her Ascetic logic.

The combined (and opposed) use of the Petrarchan and Ascetic types mainly concerns the title relationship, but it appears in other important contexts as well. For example, we are told over and over that the cause of the war is Helen, and the honor to be gained from it dependent on her, but the same woman "Whose price hath launch'd above a thousand ships" and who is "a theme of honor and renown" (2.2.82, 199), is also a simpleminded coquette who has nothing better to do than contemplate the single white hair on Troilus' chin (1.2.107–70).

Hector's challenge to the Greeks (delivered by Aeneas) suggests the same contradiction, though in a different way:

> If there be one among the fair'st of Greece
> That holds his honor higher than his ease,
> And seeks his praise more than he fears his peril,
> That knows his valor and knows not his fear,
> That loves his mistress more than in confession
> With truant vows to her own lips he loves,
> And dare avow her beauty and her worth
> In other arms than hers—to him this challenge!
> Hector, in view of Trojans and of Greeks,

Shall make it good, or do his best to do it:
He hath a lady wiser, fairer, truer,
Than ever Greek did couple in his arms,
And will to-morrow with his trumpet call,
Midway between your tents and walls of Troy,
To rouse a Grecian that is true in love.
If any come, Hector shall honor him;
If none, he'll say in Troy when he retires,
The Grecian dames are sunburnt, and not worth
The splinter of a lance. Even so much.
(1.3.265–83)

In another context this challenge might be taken seriously. Here its formality and artificiality are reminiscent of the ludicrous speeches by Agamemnon and Nestor earlier in the scene. More importantly, Hector's desire to assert the beauty of his lady seems quite out of place in the midst of the Trojan war, which almost every reader will see as important and holding profound implications for several characters present in this scene. When challenges such as Hector's occur in romances (*Lancelot*, for example), care is taken to ensure that the conflict has no value outside of its relevance within the New Comic (and hence Petrarchan) plot. Otherwise the readers would likely see in the scene the Ascetic assertion that love is trivial. When the conflict has important stakes outside of any New Comic plot, the Petrarchan cannot stand alone, and a nonsatiric portrayal is likely to ignore love altogether. A good example is the scene corresponding to Hector's challenge in the *Iliad* (book 7), where the struggle symbolically represents the battle between the warriors' cultures, and whatever honor each man gains will come from his having represented his culture well; no private concerns, such as mistresses or wives, intervene. And in a comparable formal challenge in Shakespeare's works, the quarrel between Bullingbrook and Mowbray in *Richard II*, similar care is taken to make the combatants' concerns seem as public as possible; neither man reduces the seriousness of the proposed battle by claiming that it will only prove whose lady has the fairer skin. When Hector does make such a claim, we are inclined to read it as a parody of Petrarchism (or of epic challenges). But because the challenge is stated so seriously, and is taken seriously by the Greeks, we are also impelled toward a more straightforward reading. Again we have a double view of the Petrarchan type.

The culmination of this curious double vision is the scene in which Troilus and Cressida meet and declare their love. This scene has often been taken as completely satiric, but taken in isolation much of it reads like straightforward Petrarchan love rhetoric. For example, Troilus' actual words in his soliloquy before Cressida's entrance hardly suggest that he is a "sexual gourmet":[7]

> I am giddy; expectation whirls me round;
> Th' imaginary relish is so sweet
> That it enchants my sense; what will it be,
> When that the wat'ry palates taste indeed
> Love's thrice-repured nectar? Death, I fear me,
> Sounding destruction, or some joy too fine,
> Too subtle, potent, tun'd too sharp in sweetness
> For the capacity of my ruder powers.
> I fear it much, and I do fear besides
> That I shall lose distinction in my joys,
> As doth a battle, when they charge on heaps
> The enemy flying.
>
> (3.2.18–29)

Troilus is excited and even "giddy," but then a Petrarchan lover is always similarly affected by even the presence of his lady, to say nothing of an invitation to her bed. In a similar situation, Lancelot falls on his knees before Guinevere's bed and begins to worship her as if she were a saint. And rather than reduce Cressida to ordinary food, Troilus' imagery compares her to nectar, the food of the gods that is beyond the capacity of mortal sensibility. Troilus feels that he is being admitted to the ideal world; he is naturally excited and justifiably worried about the ability of his own gross nature (having in no way proved himself worthy) to withstand such an experience. Similarly, Troilus seems perfectly serious when he tells Cressida that lovers often vow "to weep seas, live in fire, eat rocks, tame tigers; thinking it harder for our mistress to devise imposition enough than for us to undergo any difficulty impos'd. This is the monstruosity in love, lady, that the will is infinite and the execution confin'd, that the desire is boundless and the act a slave to limit" (3.2.78–83). Though the last sentence of this speech carries an unmistakable sexual implication, it seems clear that Troilus' intended meaning is not a complaint about the limitations of male sexual performance; rather, he is directly stating that men cannot accomplish as many heroic tasks as their love leads them to attempt. Because Troilus the lover has been parodied earlier in the play, we are inclined to see continued Ascetic satire in both passages, but it is important to note that Troilus' words (in 3.2) do not support a satiric reading; without the filter of the previous scenes, we would not laugh at Troilus in this one.

Cressida too receives a much more positive presentation in this scene than commentators usually allow her. Particularly, her admission of love expresses both the certainty and modesty that one expects of a Petrarchan lady:

> Boldness comes to me now, and brings me heart.
> Prince Troilus, I have lov'd you night and day
> For many weary months....

> But though I lov'd you well, I woo'd you not,
> And yet, good faith, I wish'd myself a man,
> Or that we women had men's privilege
> Of speaking first. Sweet, bid me hold my tongue,
> For in this rapture I shall surely speak
> The thing I shall repent. See, see, your silence,
> Cunning in dumbness, from my weakness draws
> My very soul of counsel! Stop my mouth.
> (3.2.113–15, 126–33)

And lest we perceive her speech as cleverly designed to inveigle a kiss, she goes on to say

> My lord, I do beseech you pardon me,
> 'Twas not my purpose thus to beg a kiss.
> I am asham'd. O heavens, what have I done!
> For this time will I take my leave, my lord.
> (3.2.136–39)

Thus when Troilus asserts that he is "true as truth's simplicity, / And simpler than the infancy of truth" and Cressida responds that "In that I'll war with you" (3.2.169–71), there is nothing they have said or done in this scene that suggests they should not be believed. They may satirize themselves earlier, but here both their words and their relationship are serious representations of the Petrarchan type.[8]

The Ascetic view in this scene comes not from the lovers but from Pandarus, whose voyeuristic bawdiness defines the relationship very differently than do the lovers' own words. For example, between Troilus' comparisons of Cressida to nectar and to the "eye of majesty" (3.2.39), Pandarus compares her to a "new-ta'en sparrow" (3.2.34), and when Troilus exclaims upon Cressida's entrance that "You have bereft me of all words, lady," Pandarus responds that "words pay no debts, give her deeds; but she'll bereave you a' th' deeds too, if she call your activity in question" (3.2.55–57). Later, Cressida's dedication of her "folly" to the man who pushed her into it provokes Pandarus brazenly to thank her and demand that "if my lord get a boy of you, you'll give him me" (3.2.104–5). And after the lovers have made their vows of faithfulness, Pandarus closes the scene with one more reminder of the physicality of the relationship and of his own contribution to it:

> Amen. Whereupon I will show you a chamber, which bed, because it shall not speak of your pretty encounters, press it to death. Away!
> *Exeunt Troilus and Cressida*
> And Cupid grant all tongue-tied maidens here
> Bed, chamber, Pandar to provide this gear!
> (3.2.207–11)

124 / *The Structure of Love*

Pandarus represents the relationship through the same type that is used to undermine the Petrarchan elsewhere: the Ascetic. But there is a difference. The others are satires, and as such imply the existence of a more honorable course of action. Pandarus makes no such distinctions. Like the tradition through which he is imaged, he sees the nature of all relationships as mere desire, but he nevertheless embraces them as worthy of the attention they receive. To him, Troilus' veneration and Cressida's modesty are just words that hide the actual nature of the relationship, the action in Cressida's bedroom. And as the final comment above indicates, he views all love relationships in exactly the same way. That he does not then go on to condemn sexuality—as do almost all other such strongly Ascetic definitions—suggests that he sees nothing better anywhere else.

Pandarus' grinning reduction of everyone to animalism is as obviously unacceptable as Thersites', but it is also obvious that there are no Petrarchan relationships in the play capable of sustaining that type as an alternative. Honor is an obsessive issue in *Troilus and Cressida*, but no Petrarchan relationship is ever portrayed as producing it. The other possibility offered is the Epic, but in the end it is just as thoroughly demolished as the Petrarchan, and from a similar perspective.

The main Greek supporter of an Epic approach to life and love is Ulysses, which is consistent with his portrayal in the *Odyssey*. Shakespeare's version of the character is also traditional in having considerable intelligence, which he uses to defend his Epic perspective. According to Thersites, all human actions are motivated by pure appetite, and any value attached to these actions is merely hypocrisy. Ulysses defends the possibility of honor by claiming that such "mere oppugnancy" can only occur when men refuse to obey their social superiors, which ultimately means refusing to obey God himself; and when they allow their will and appetite to gain an unnatural dominance over their reason, which again is their link to God. If men ignore these social and intellectual degrees,

> Force should be right, or rather, right and wrong
> (Between whose endless jar justice resides)
> Should lose their names, and so should justice too!
> Then everything include itself in power,
> Power into will, will into appetite,
> And appetite, an universal wolf
> (So doubly seconded with will and power),
> Must make perforce an universal prey,
> And last eat up himself.
>
> (1.3.116–24)

But conversely, if men do respect degree, their rationality and their social superiors will define right and wrong and thus allow the possibility of valuable and honorable action. From this point of view, Thersites' nihilism is wrong because it denies the very element that makes us higher than the beasts: our ability to make moral distinctions. But since this ability is dependent on men preserving degree (which defines the moral distinctions), both in society and in their own minds, chaos is always possible:

> Take but degree away, untune that string,
> And hark what discord follows. Each thing meets
> In mere oppugnancy: the bounded waters
> Should lift their bosoms higher than the shores,
> And make a sop of all this solid globe.
> (1.3.109–13)

Similarly, Petrarchism, though less extreme than nihilism, is also wrong because it tries to locate honor in a double violation of degree: the social absurdity of a man serving a woman, and the intellectual error of an appetite—sexual desire—dominating reason. If Petrarchan love could be honor producing, Ulysses sarcastically tells Achilles, then battles between the sexes could be as significant as battles between men:

> And better would it fit Achilles much
> To throw down Hector than Polyxena.
> But it must grieve young Pyrrhus now at home,
> When fame shall in our islands sound her trump,
> And all the Greekish girls shall tripping sing,
> "Great Hector's sister did Achilles win,
> But our brave Ajax bravely beat him down."
> (3.3.207–13)

Honor exists for Ulysses, but it must come from the rational conflict of socially equal men. A woman might be the reward for winning such a struggle, but making women the stimulus leads only to the kind of enervation shown by Achillles.[9]

Ulysses' rational, hierarchical universe is very attractively presented, but its validity depends on an assumption that can be easily called into question in a play: the innate relationship of quality to social rank, that is, the idea that those of the highest social rank will also represent the best of their society and contribute most to its welfare. Without this relationship there would be no reason for obeying one's social superiors and no clear way of deciding who should be followed in their place. Or as Ulysses puts it, "Degree being vizarded / Th' unworthiest shows as fairly in the mask" (1.3.83–84). And if it is impossible to tell who is worthy and who is not, man will find himself hopelessly alienated from God's will, there will be no basis for determining morality, and Thersites' nihilistic chaos will descend upon society. This equation of quality and social degree does not imply that all aristocrats will be honorable—there will always be a few degenerates—but it does necessarily mean that at least most men must live up to their class.

But no one does, especially in the Greek camp. Most obviously, none of them is distinguished by appearance: Aeneas knows that Agamemnon's "imperial looks" should be different from the "eyes of other mortals," but he does not know that the man to whom he tells this is Agamemnon himself (1.3.215–56). And later in the play Hector mistakes Thersites for one of "blood and honor," instead of the "scurvy railing knave" and "very filthy rogue" that his adversary proudly describes himself to be (5.4.26–35).

Besides not looking their parts, the Greeks are incapable of anything that could be called honorable action. Ulysses knows what honor should be, but he evidently cannot act himself, and his schemes for moving Achilles are no more effective than the commands of the pompous Agamemnon or the silly analogies of the senile Nestor. The one Greek who does seem capable and willing to act, Ajax, is described repeatedly as an idiot or as an animal, as in this account by Cressida's servant: "This man, lady, hath robb'd many beasts of their particular additions: he is as valiant as the lion, churlish as the bear, slow as the elephant; a man into whom nature hath so crowded humors that his valor is crush'd into folly, his folly sauc'd with discretion. There is no man hath a virtue that he hath not a glimpse of, nor any man an attaint but he carries some stain of it" (1.2.19–26). So, while Ajax is certainly willing to fight, that will is no more developed than an animal's.

The most important of the Greeks is Achilles, and it is in the treatment of him that Shakespeare has most significantly manipulated his source material to eliminate any possibility of coexistent class and honor. Like those in the *Iliad*, Shakespeare's Greeks are stymied by the refusal of Achilles to fight, but in the *Iliad*, Achilles' political differences with Agamemnon give him an honorable and class-appropriate, if not altogether acceptable, reason for his lack of action. Shakespeare's Achilles, on the other hand, is never associated with any characteristics suggesting honor, except his legendary but never demonstrated abilities as a warrior. Rather than fight he prefers to make scurrilous amateur theatricals with Patroclus (his "masculine whore"), for which he offers no justification other than that he would prefer to seduce Polyxena than to help in the war effort. When he does take to the field he proves an incompetent warrior and can defeat Hector only when the Trojan is unarmed. Even then, he insists that the actual killing be done by his Myrmidons, after which he has them report this brutal murder as their master's glorious and honorable victory over the Trojan champion. Shakespeare's Achilles, in short, is entirely ignoble, despite his social rank, and yet the Greeks cannot do as Ulysses wishes and expel him from their midst (3.3.95–215): they have no one who can take his place and no one who can claim to be his superior.

Ulysses' response to this paradox of a great knight who is also ignoble is to postulate two Achilleses, the one of the past who became great through noble deeds befitting his aristocratic degree, and the one of the present who has given up the search for honor and thus ceased to be noble or great:

> Time hath, my lord, a wallet at his back,
> Wherein he puts alms for oblivion,
> A great-siz'd monster of ingratitudes.
> Those scraps are good deeds past, which are devour'd
> As fast as they are made, forgot as soon
> As done. Perseverance, dear my lord,
> Keeps honor bright; to have done is to hang
> Quite out of fashion, like a rusty mail
> In monumental mock'ry.
>
> (3.3.145–53)

Ulysses is here telling Achilles that if he refuses to fight he will effectively cease to exist among the nobility and his function as chief warrior will be taken by Ajax. The problem with this position is that it is hard to believe that the man who orders the cowardly murder of Hector could ever have been responsible for deeds glorious enough to make the gods envious, especially since we know that he sometimes lies about his own actions. For his Epic system to operate properly, Ulysses needs the climactic battle between the Trojan champion and the Greek champion to be the heroic struggle of noble adversaries that Homer describes, and to that end he tries to invent an Achilles that we see never has existed nor ever can exist. In *Troilus and Cressida*, the only heroic struggle is within the fiction that Achilles orders his men to report. Among the Greeks, at least, heroism and nobility are the lie; the truth, as Thersites so often reminds us, is the savagery and lust that we see in Achilles.

One way to look at the Greek scenes, then, is as a gradual denunciation of the Epic and ordinary aristocratic conception of honor: Ulysses makes a clear statement of just what that conception is, and then his fellow Greeks fail to measure up to it in any way. Or the Greek scenes might be seen as commentary on the Greeks only, in which case the Epic and aristocratic values must be validated by the Trojans and their counterpart to Achilles, Hector. It is true that the Trojans are in general not so coarse as the Greeks, but that their values are any less corrupt is much less certain.

Our first and best look at Trojan values comes in their long discussion of whether or not they should continue to hold Helen (2.2).[10] As it turns out, this argument essentially amounts to a debate between the Epic and Petrarchan views of love and honor. Despite his challenge to the Greeks two scenes earlier, the main spokesman for the Epic is Hector:

> Let Helen go.
> Since the first sword was drawn about this question,
> Every tithe soul, 'mongst many thousand dismes,
> Hath been as dear as Helen; I mean, of ours.
> If we have lost so many tenths of ours,
> To guard a thing not ours nor worth to us
> (Had it our name) the value of one ten,
> What merit's in that reason which denies
> The yielding of her up? . . .
> Brother, she is not worth what she doth cost
> The keeping.
>
> (2.2.17–25, 51–52)

Hector, with later support from Helenus, does not think Helen is worth the keeping because he does not believe that fighting for a woman can bring him or his country honor; for him, Helen is merely a woman and as such of less value than a single Trojan warrior. And when Troilus responds that Helen is valuable (i.e., honor-producing) because the two armies think she is, Hector asserts that value must be universal to have any meaning:

> But value dwells not in particular will,
> It holds his estimate and dignity
> As well wherein 'tis precious of itself
> As in the prizer.
>
> (2.2.53–56)

Like Ulysses, Hector insists on a system that gives universal significance to individual action. That is possible only if an ultimate authority establishes the value of all things and then passes this value down through the political, ecclesiastical, and intellectual hierarchies of society. Specific actions then have a recognized and defensible value. If value were determined by the individual, society would collapse into a relativistic chaos in which all value, and ultimately, all meaning, would be lost.

Hector believes the Greeks are justified in fighting because they are trying to avenge a grave insult to their culture, and there are many other situations where conflict can define males as men rather than beasts. But there has to be a recognized purpose, and fighting for a stolen woman, whose only value can be her physical person, is absurd:

> 'Tis mad idolatry
> To make the service greater than the god,
> And the will dotes that is attributive
> To what infectiously itself affects,
> Without some image of th' affected merit.
>
> (2.2.56–60)

It is more than absurd: it is an affront to both human reason and the gods.

Troilus and Paris defend their Petrarchan position in a variety of ways. As would be expected, they deny that Helen's worth is limited to her person and challenge Hector for suddenly changing his mind, as in this straightforward argument by Troilus:

> Is she worth keeping? Why, she is a pearl,
> Whose price hath launch'd above a thousand ships,
> And turn'd crown'd kings to merchants.
> If you'll avouch 'twas wisdom Paris went—
> As you must needs, for you all cried "Go, go"—
> If you'll confess he brought home worthy prize—
> As you must needs, for you all clapp'd your hands,
> And cried "Inestimable!"—why do you now
> The issue of your proper wisdoms rate,
> And do a deed that never Fortune did,
> Beggar the estimation which you priz'd
> Richer than sea and land?
> (2.2.81–92)

For Troilus, the theft and keeping of Helen are base only if the Trojans think it so. Following basic Petrarchan ideology, he argues that Helen, like any woman, is of no great innate value, but that serving her and fighting for her are nonetheless honorable. One does not serve or fight for a woman because of her personal value but because she represents and can lead a man toward spiritual values higher than himself. Paris employs much the same position in his emphatic defense of Helen and the Trojan struggle to keep her:

> There's not the meanest spirit on our party
> Without a heart to dare, or sword to draw,
> When Helen is defended; nor none so noble
> Whose life were ill bestow'd, or death unfam'd,
> Where Helen is the subject. Then I say,
> Well may we fight for her whom we know well
> The world's large spaces cannot parallel.
> (2.2.156–62)

According to this argument, Helen's beauty is such that the meanest Trojan will be stirred to honorable action when her life is threatened, and such that even the most noble would gain honor and fame by dying for her. But to return Helen to the Greeks would imply the baseness, not only of the Trojans, but of Helen, for such an action would define her as only a placket after all, valuable for whatever physical pleasure she can provide.

Besides these standard Petrarchan defenses of female beauty as a spur to honorable action, Troilus makes a much more radical attack on the Epic position. Responding to Helenus' charge of irrationality, he argues that reason is inimical to honor and manhood:

> You are for dreams and slumbers, brother priest,
> You fur your gloves with reason. Here are your
>   reasons:
> You know an enemy intends you harm;
> You know a sword imploy'd is perilous,
> And reason flies the object of all harm.
> Who marvels then, when Helenus beholds
> A Grecian and his sword, if he do set
> The very wings of reason to his heels
> And fly like chidden Mercury from Jove,
> Or like a star disorb'd? Nay, if we talk of reason,
> Let's shut our gates and sleep. Manhood and honor
> Should have hare hearts, would they but fat their
>   thoughts
> With this cramm'd reason; reason and respect
> Make livers pale and lustihood deject.
>   (2.2.37–50)

It would be hard to overestimate the threat of this position to Ulysses' rational, continuous universe, for rather than identifying rational with honorable actions, Troilus is arguing that they are contradictory. Troilus does not discuss the implications of his position, but a division between reason and honor could only be possible if they originated in different authorities or in a single but somehow discontinuous one—or if no such authority exists in the first place. For Troilus, honor is always irrational because it always involves danger and going beyond the moderate course. Like Petrarchan love, it is a matter of passion rather than logic; thus Helen is more important than reason because she spurs the Trojans to honorable actions that reason would warn them against:[11]

> She is a theme of honor and renown,
> A spur to valiant and magnaminous deeds,
> Whose present courage may beat down our foes,
> And fame in time to come canonize us,
> For I presume brave Hector would not lose
> So rich advantage of a promis'd glory
> As smiles upon the forehead of this action
> For the wide world's revenue.
>   (2.2.199–206)

Hector's first response to Troilus and Paris is, of course, to accuse them of irrationality, noting that Aristotle thought young men "Unfit to hear moral philosophy" and blandly relegating their arguments to the realms of "hot passion" and "distemp'red blood" (2.2.163–73). He then goes on to define Helen once again in entirely material terms, as a chattel that must be returned to its owner:

> If Helen then be wife to Sparta's king,
> As it is known she is, these moral laws
> Of nature and of nations speak aloud
> To have her back return'd. Thus to persist
> In doing wrong extenuates not wrong,
> But makes it much more heavy.
> (2.2.183–88)

Having made his argument with devastating clarity, Hector shockingly reverses himself and asserts that Helen should be kept after all:

> Hector's opinion
> Is this in way of truth; yet n'er the less,
> My sprightly brethren, I propend to you
> In resolution to keep Helen still,
> For 'tis a cause that hath no mean dependance
> Upon our joint and several dignities.
> (2.2.188–93)

The argument that giving up Helen would adversely affect his honor is contradicted by Hector's own words a few lines before: persisting in a wrong does not extenuate it, but rather makes it heavier. He now says that Helen should be kept because giving her up will make all the Trojans seem cowardly and dishonorable. In making this observation, Hector is admitting to the poverty of his own Epic system, for while he continues to deny the possibility that honor can be earned in an irrational, dishonorable cause, he somehow accepts Troilus' position that a rational course will not produce honor. His continuing to fight shows us that he is far more interested in how he will appear to others than in establishing a defensible reality.

Hector's view of honor, consequently, is really no less superficial and debased than Achilles', for both men are only interested in the appearance of honor. Neither seems to have any confidence in the fundamental Epic assumption that honor is the sign of and reward for a course of action that observes social and psychological degree. As with Achilles, our final and most dramatic indication of Hector's baseness comes on the battlefield. There, his last act before being murdered by the Myrmidons is to chase after a Greek dressed in rich armor that Hector wants to possess:

> Stand, stand, thou Greek, thou art a goodly mark.
> No? wilt thou not? I like thy armor well;

> I'll frush it and unlock the rivets all,
> But I'll be master of it. Wilt thou not, beast, abide?
> Why then fly on, I'll hunt thee for thy hide.
>
> (5.6.27–31)

As he feels toward the concept of honor itself, Hector is only interested in the exterior, material part of this unnamed Greek, as he indicates once he has caught his prey:

> Most putrefied core, so fair without,
> Thy goodly armor thus hath cost thy life.
> Now is my day's work done, I'll take good breath.
> Rest, sword, thou hast thy fill of blood and death.
>
> (5.8.1–4)

When Hector takes off his helmet and begins to toy with his new possession, he is himself captured. Like the Greek, he too is a "goodly mark" with a "putrefied core," there being nothing to him but show. Thus when the Myrmidons trumpet their false account of the Hector-Achilles battle, it is not only Achilles whose honor is wholly a lie, and not only the Greeks who must finally be seen as incapable of validating the Epic and aristocratic system.[12]

Despite the teasingly ambiguous portrayals of the title relationship in the beginning and middle scene, I doubt that many readers hold out much hope that the Petrarchan type will meet a better fate. After all, the story of Cressida's untruth is almost as well known as the story of the war. On the other hand, if Shakespeare could make Achilles and Hector ignoble, he could surely portray Cressida as positive, especially since he would have to look no further than Chaucer for a pattern; she need not necessarily conform to the rabidly Ascetic portrait given by Henryson and later authors.[13] In fact, our first view of the lovers after their one night together reinforces the possibility of a positive presentation. Troilus' displeasure at the shortness of the night is reminiscent of the undeniably positive complaints by Romeo when he and Juliet are also parted by the lark:

> *Tro.* O Cressida! but that the busy day,
> Wak'd by the lark, hath rous'd the ribald crows,
> And dreaming night will hide our joys no longer,
> I would not from thee.
> *Cres.*   Night hath been too brief.
> *Tro.* Beshrew the witch! with venomous wights she stays
> As tediously as hell, but flies the grasps of love
> With wings more momentary-swift than thought.
>
> (4.2.8–14)

And when Cressida learns that she must go to the Greek camp, her protestation of faithfulness sounds sincere, especially since Troilus is not in earshot and there is thus no need for acting:

> I have forgot my father,
> I know no touch of consanguinity;
> No kin, no love, no blood, no soul so near me
> As the sweet Troilus. O you gods divine,
> Make Cressid's name the very crown of falsehood,
> If ever she leave Troilus! Time, force, and death,
> Do to this body what extremes you can;
> But the strong base and building of my love
> Is as the very centre of the earth,
> Drawing all things to it. I'll go in and weep.
> (4.2.96–105)

Many of Shakespeare's heroines could have spoken these words, and the emphatic defense of the husband-figure against all other claims is again especially reminiscent of *Romeo and Juliet*. Whatever she has been in previous speeches, this Cressida is a Petrarchan representation, and to the extent that we as readers are able to believe the scene, Shakespeare makes it difficult for us shortly to follow Ulysses in dismissing her as a whore.[14]

Ironically, the first indication that Cressida's resolve might not hold comes from Troilus, who in the scene where the lovers part, gradually convinces himself that the Greeks might be able to corrupt his lady:

> I speak not "be thou true" as fearing thee,
> For I will throw my glove to Death himself
> That there be no maculation in thy heart. . . .
> The Grecian youths are full of quality;
> Their loving well compos'd with gift of nature,
> Flowing and swelling o'er with arts and exercise.
> How novelty may move, and parts with person,
> Alas, a kind of godly jealousy
> (Which I beseech you call a virtuous sin)
> Makes me afeard. . . .
>   I cannot sing,
> Nor heel the high lavolt, nor sweeten talk,
> Nor play at subtile games—fair virtues all,
> To which the Greeks are most prompt and pregnant—
> But I can tell that in each grace of these
> There lurks a still and dumb-discoursive devil
> That tempts most cunningly, but be not tempted.
> (4.4.62–64, 76–82, 85–91)

Just as Hector's own speech eventually revealed the contradiction in his position, so Troilus now reveals his, for his worries about the "subtile"

Greeks indicate that despite his Petrarchan ideals, Troilus still maintains a fundamentally Ascetic view of women. A true Petrachan lover would be unable to doubt the truth of his lady, not so much because her untruth is impossible, but because doubt would reflect only a partial commitment to love. Troilus has not completely committed himself either to love or to his Petrarchan philosophy, and thus when he describes Cressida as a goddess among mortals and challenges Diomedes to treat her as such, we know that even he does not quite believe what he says:

> I tell thee, lord of Greece,
> She is as far high-soaring o'er thy praises
> As thou unworthy to be call'd her servant.
> I charge thee use her well, even for my charge;
> For by the dreadful Pluto, if thou dost not,
> Though the great bulk Achilles be thy guard,
> I'll cut thy throat.
> (4.4.123–29)

Diomedes' response echoes Hector's earliest attempt to contain value within a logical Epic system: "To her own worth / She shall be priz'd" (4.4.133–34).

The comments of both men suggest that Cressida might be corruptible, but Shakespeare surely startles even her least sympathetic reader by showing her in the next scene kissing each of her Greek captors—symbolically passing from man to man with no apparent thought of her protestations of eternal loyalty only a few lines earlier. She even stoops to a parody of the Petrarchism taken so seriously in the previous scene:

> *Ulyss.* May I, sweet lady, beg a kiss of you?
> *Cres.* You may.
> *Ulyss.*   I do desire it.
> *Cres.*   Why, beg then.
> *Ulyss.* Why then for Venus' sake, give me a kiss
>   When Helen is a maid again and his.
> (4.5.47–50)

Cressida asks Ulysses to beg like a Petrarchan lover for the sexual favor he desires, but he responds instead with sarcasm, for her actions and words have proved to him her whoreishness:

> Fie, fie upon her!
> There's language in her eye, her cheek, her lip,
> Nay, her foot speaks; her wanton spirits look out
> At every joint and motive of her body.
> O, these encounterers, so glib of tongue,
> That give a coasting welcome ere it comes,

> And wide unclasp the tables of their thoughts
> To every ticklish reader! set them down
> For sluttish spoils of opportunity,
> And daughters of the game.
>
> (4.5.54–63)

It might be argued that Cressida does not begin the kissing spree and only comes to enjoy it after a while, and that she later surrenders Troilus' love token (a sleeve) to Diomedes only under considerable pressure and with sincere regret. But the fact that Cressida's infidelities are more a matter of weakness than the deliberate evil Ulysses accuses her of is more damning than the reverse, for if she could be seen as willfully evil, her relationship with Troilus would be interpreted in terms of the Emasculating type, which would make both her and her victim seem more heroic. But Shakespeare's Cressida is not a Circe figure. She is, in fact, not one character at all, for she is equally serious in each of her roles in the play—Petrarchan mistress, faithful wife (when she promises to remain true), and whore. Characterization in terms of mutually exclusive types is not unusual for Shakespeare, but elsewhere we are given logical bridges between them; here they simply occur.

Lacking such textual guidance, readers are forced to develop their own bridges, and in this case I think most of us (male and female) will invoke the Ascetic as a way of naturalizing this radically inconsistent characterization. Understood in terms of that type, Cressida is inconstant because that is the nature of women, and she is untrue and lustful not because she wants to be, but because the solicitations of the Greeks and the callings of her own sexual appetite are too much for her feeble reason to withstand.[15]

Such an interpretation is obviously threatening to Petrarchism, at least as it is seen in this play, for a weak, whorish Cressida suggests that all of the satiric portrayals of the title relationship are correct and that Troilus' love is really no more than lust, as Pandarus and Thersites say. But it is also threatening to the Epic position, as Ulysses suggests when he twice tries to insist that Cressida is not representative of all women, first in the passage above, and second—more directly—in response to Troilus' assertion that a false Cressida makes all women false:

> *Tro.* Let it not be believ'd for womanhood!
> Think we had mothers, do not give advantage
> To stubborn critics, apt without a theme
> For depravation, to square the general sex
> By Cressid's rule. Rather think this not Cresid.
>   *Ulyss.* What hath she done, Prince, that can soil
>   our mothers?
>
> (5.2.129–34)

Ulysses cannot accept Cressida as a model for all women in part because it is uncomfortable for him to think of his mother and, implicitly, his wife as whores. But more importantly, to admit that all women are whores will quickly call into question the "primogenity and due of birth" (1.3.106) which are the foundations of the aristocratic system, and without which Ulysses' concept of order cannot stand. Only a position like Thersites', which denies the nobility of anyone or the possibility of heroic action, could admit to such a view. Ulysses never states directly his understanding of women, but his speech on degree implies that they, though lesser creatures than men, have their own structure of degrees. On the lowest level are women like Cressida, who are born to be "daughters of the game" and who are no more related to noblewomen than are villains to noblemen. This familiar dualistic approach explains away nobly born whores just as it does nobly born villains: as loathsome degenerates who for some reason do not reflect their parentage and who should be shunned even more vigorously than those born to the role. Ulysses eliminates Cressida as a threat by asserting that she is fundamentally different from the women who make up his system.

The problem for us is that we know from earlier scenes that Cressida is neither a born whore nor the saint that Troilus postulates; she is somehow both. Ulysses does not see Cressida as a major threat to his system because he does not see all of the various Cressidas. But we and Troilus do, and his reaction to the final one is the most horrifying and painful speech in the play:

> This she? no, this is Diomed's Cressida.
> If beauty have a soul, this is not she;
> If souls guide vows, if vows be sanctimonies,
> If sanctimony be the gods' delight,
> If there be rule in unity itself,
> This was not she. O madness of discourse,
> That cause sets up with and against itself!
> Bi-fold authority, where reason can revolt
> Without perdition, and loss assume all reason
> Without revolt. This is, and is not, Cressid!
> Within my soul there doth conduce a fight
> Of this strange nature, that a thing inseparate
> Divides more wider than the sky and earth,
> And yet the spacious breadth of this division
> Admits no orifex for a point as subtle
> As Ariachne's broken woof to enter.
> Instance, O instance, strong as Pluto's gates,
> Cressid is mine, tied with the bonds of heaven;
> Instance, O instance, strong as heaven itself,
> The bonds of heaven are slipp'd, dissolv'd, and loos'd,
> And with another knot, five-finger-tied,

> The fractions of her faith, orts of her love,
> The fragments, scraps, the bits and greasy relics
> Of her o'er-eaten faith, are given to Diomed.
> (5.2.137–60)

After originally trying to deny the truth of his senses (5.2.116–25), Troilus in this speech comes to realize that Cressida the whore really exists. But at the same time he cannot doubt the validity of Cressida the Petrarchan lady and faithful wife either, partly because her obvious sincerity earlier makes consistent whorishness seem impossible, and partly because a suddenly whorish Cressida contradicts the basic conception of a Petrarchan lady. As a result, he is left with a logically impossible violation of the principle of identity, the "rule of unity": Cressida is somehow two entirely separate women at the same time that she is one. Cressida "Divides more wider than the sky and earth" to accommodate the distance between Petrarchan lady and whore, and yet remains as indivisible as a single human. From a Petrarchan point of view it is simply impossible that a woman could sincerely pledge love in the morning and then have a new lover by evening, but that is exactly what we and Troilus see. Ariadne's thread pierced and explained the labyrinth and Arachne's tapestry flawlessly explained the myriad shapes of the gods, but the mystery of this paradoxical double Cressida is unpierceable and inexplicable.[16] And since a double Cressida calls into question Troilus' idea of universal order and reason—which is, we can now see, not all that different from Hector's and Ulysses'—he views the destruction of his and Cressida's vows as equivalent to the destruction of heaven itself. The fractions, orts, fragments, scraps, bits, and relics of love that come crashing down upon his head are not merely the evidence of a relationship gone bad; they are the remnants of an entire universe disintegrated, of a system of honor and value dismembered and irretrievably lost.

Troilus' response to the destruction of his universe is to vow unceasing vengeance on the Greeks, not in order to gain honor, but to have some outlet for his fury, now unconstrained by any relationship to humanistic and feminine values:

> For th' love of all the gods,
> Let's leave the hermit pity with our mother,
> And when we have our armors buckled on,
> The venom'd vengeance ride upon our swords,
> Spur them to ruthful work, rein them from ruth....
> Who should withhold me?
> Not fate, obedience, nor the hand of Mars
> Beck'ning with fiery truncheon my retire,
> Not Priamus and Hecuba on knees,
> Their eyes o'ergalled with recourse of tears,

Nor you, my brother, with your true sword drawn,
Oppos'd to hinder me, should stop my way,
But by my ruin.
(5.3.44–48, 51–58)

Hector, who is much more complacent about the corruption of his own system of value, immediately identifies Troilus' attitude for what it is: "Fie, savage, fie!" (5.3.49). Hector wants the upcoming battle to be "in the vein of chivalry" (5.3.32), much like the absurd "maiden battle"—as Achilles derisively calls it (4.5.87)—that he fought with Ajax a few scenes before. Characteristically, he is concerned much more with individual fame than with winning the war—the war having no value for him—and when he learns that he must make an appearance on the field or be considered a coward, he ignores the pleading of his father, wife, and sister that he preserve his position as bulwark of the entire Trojan defense, and ventures out to certain death:

> *Cas.* Farewell; yet soft: Hector, I take my leave.
> Thou dost thyself and all our Troy deceive.
> *Hect.* You are amaz'd, my liege, at her exclaim.
> Go in and cheer the town. We'll forth and fight.
> Do deeds worth praise, and tell you them at night.
> (5.3.89–93)

Cassandra's prophecy is correct: after his day of seeking "chivalry" and other shiny things, Hector is ignominiously butchered by Achilles' surrogates. Meanwhile, Ajax "foams at mouth ... Roaring for Troilus," whose "Mad and fantastic execution" has left scores of Greeks "noseless, handless, hack'd and chipp'd" (5.5.34–38). Darkness and the death of Hector end the carnage, but Troilus leaves us with a final promise that it will soon begin again: "To Troy with comfort go; / Hope of revenge shall hide our inward woe" (5.10.30–31). The Trojans' comfort is their ability to continue the fight, and their only value now is continual revenge; no other action has any meaning.

With the final destruction of Troilus and his Petrarchan system, there is no value left for us either. Shakespeare has provided us two possible ways of attaching honor to some human actions, and then mercilessly torn both apart. Where we have been led to expect the emergence of heroes and spokesmen, we are given instead villains and counterexamples. Eventually, we are forced to accept that the only truth the play supports is the lack of any truth except appetite, and the only candidates possible for its hero and spokesmen roles are its least heroic and least believable characters, Thersites and Pandarus. Pandarus, in fact, directly asserts in the epilogue that he is the tragic hero, and he berates us for both desiring and loathing the service he provides. For him, it is pure hypocrisy for us to distinguish ourselves from "traders in the flesh," for we are actually all alike in appetite. The social and intellectual distinctions that most of us need to justify our actions, indeed our very existence, are just so much empty and worthless rhetoric. We are as villainous as Troilus, Ulysses, and Hector in that regard, and like Thersites before him, Pandarus wishes us all an appropriate reward:

> Brethren and sisters of the hold-door trade,
> Some two months hence my will shall here be made.
> It should be now, but that my fear is this,
> Some galled goose of Winchester would hiss.
> Till then I'll sweat and seek about for eases,
> And at that time bequeath you my diseases.

7

The Gap in Nature:

Antony and Cleopatra

For most of us, *Antony and Cleopatra* is Shakespeare's most effective love tragedy. It is also his least straightforward, for unlike the plays in the three previous chapters, *Antony and Cleopatra* never establishes a particular perspective of the relationship as the true one against which others can be evaluated. It begins with the famous Ascetic image of Antony as a "strumpet's fool," and frequently thereafter portrays the title relationship as foolish and degrading, and love as a dangerous passion that can destroy even the most heroic of men. At other times, however, the relationship is defined in terms of the Etherealized type and thus seems wonderful and worth more than the world it costs. And there are many instances when the relationship is defined in terms of the Epic or its complement, the Emasculating, with no indication of how either of these types is to be reconciled with the two others. So, unlike *Romeo and Juliet,* where we know that the Ascetic view of the relationship is wrong, *Othello,* where we hope it is, and *Troilus and Cressida,* where we know that both the Epic and Petrarchan are defective views of the reality of the play, *Antony and Cleopatra* never conclusively discredits any of its four types, and thus never allows us a confident perspective from which to define the characters and actions before us. By using most of the large variety of traditional views of the historical Antony and Cleopatra but refusing to give priority to any one, or even to any cohesive combination, Shakespeare produces a play that tries to force us to accept the kind of divided unity that destroys Troilus' universe: the idea that a relationship can be a contradiction to itself and that love can be its most decadent at the same time that it is most nearly ideal.[1]

The Gap in Nature: Antony and Cleopatra / 141

The central relationship in *Antony and Cleopatra* is often portrayed in very negative terms, but not always from the same perspective: it can be either Ascetic or Emasculating. Both of these types present relationships that are negative because they are dominated by a woman. The Ascetic tradition, however, views women as naturally unreasonable and as inferior to men in every way, while the Emasculating suggests Circe-like figures who are mysterious and extremely powerful. As noted in the first chapter, this difference in definition of the women determines our view of the men, for a man must be portrayed as exceedingly weak and foolish if he submits himself to an Ascetic woman, but of heroic stature if he battles a Circe figure, who wins domination through magic rather than male weakness. The Ascetic, then, gives us us a whore and a middle-aged fool, while the Emasculating produces us two persons far beyond the ordinary, one endowed with supernatural powers and the other with all the necessary heroic qualities. Cleopatra is either a strumpet and a gypsy or the mysterious creature of "infinite variety" who is somehow most holy when most wanton (2.2.235–39); and Antony is either the "strumpet's fool" (1.1.13) or "the arm / And burgonet of men" (1.5.23–24), the modern counterpart of Hercules and other heroes of the past.

Octavius defines the relationship in the grossest and least heroic terms:

> Let's grant it is not
> Amiss to tumble on the bed of Ptolemy,
> To give a kingdom for a mirth, to sit
> And keep the turn of tippling with a slave,
> To reel the streets at noon, and stand the buffet
> With knaves that smells of sweat: say this becomes him
> (As his composure must be rare indeed
> Whom these things cannot blemish), yet must Antony
> No way excuse his foils, when we do bear
> So great weight in his lightness.
> (1.4.16–25)

Antony's relationship with Cleopatra has naturally associated him with baseness; Octavius does not feel the need even to mention Cleopatra, who is merely the instrument for Antony's self-debasement, and the only reason he stoops to mention the whole sordid affair is the difficulty it is causing in communication. But to Pompey only two scenes later, the relationship is very different:

> But all the charms of love,
> Salt Cleopatra, soften thy wan'd lip!
> Let witchcraft join with beauty, lust with both,
> Tie up the libertine in a field of feasts,
> Keep his brain fuming, epicurean cooks
> Sharpen with cloyless sauce his appetite,

> That sleep and feeding may prorogue his honor,
> Even till a Lethe'd dullness.
>
> (2.1.20–27)

Pompey is wishing rather than describing, but he nevertheless succeeds in introducing the idea of Cleopatra as witch and Circe figure, whose web in this case is the "field of feasts" he wants her to use to "Tie" Antony, who will then sink into a "Lethe'd dullness." Both passages paint a negative portrait of the central relationship, but they are fundamentally different in their definition of the class of the lovers.

The opposition of heroism and baseness is also important to the positive types, the Epic and the Etherealized. The Epic, as we have seen, permits positive relationships, but only if they occur after the male has proved his heroic stature by successfully completing some difficult military task. *Antony and Cleopatra* is full of references to such heroic males and to their relationships. The two most obvious and important past heroes are Julius Caesar and Pompey the Great, who both have been former lovers of Cleopatra and who have present-time descendants in Octavius and Pompey. Each of these men is portrayed as having taken Cleopatra as a lover only after establishing himself as a hero, and as a result she is shown as a sort of trophy for them, a passive symbol of achieved heroism. Cleopatra recounts these male-dominated relationships and her own passivity early in the play:

> Broad-fronted Caesar,
> When thou wast here above the ground, I was
> A morsel for a monarch; and great Pompey
> Would stand and make his eyes grow in my brow;
> There would he anchor his aspect, and die
> With looking on his life.
>
> (1.5.29–34)

Cleopatra is here a piece of food and a mirror, just as one would expect for the woman in an Epic relationship, but not at all like the character who inhabits most of the remainder of the play. Later, she is described as Caesar's "morsel" and Pompey's "fragment" (3.13.116–18), and we hear that Cleopatra was first brought to Caesar by one of his lieutenants as a sort of war prize—rendered uncharacteristically silent and motionless by imprisonment in a rolled mattress (2.6.68–70).

The Antony-Cleopatra relationship is sometimes described in similar terms, as when Cleopatra equates Antony with Atlas and with her two previous Epic lovers, and compares herself to Antony's horse (1.5.18–34). In another instance, the temporary victory over Octavius' forces, Antony represents Scarus—and implicitly himself—as an Epic hero who has earned a reward:

The Gap in Nature: Antony and Cleopatra / 143

> Behold this man,
> Commend unto his lips thy favoring hand.
> Kiss it, my warrior; he hath fought to-day
> As if a god, in hate of mankind, had
> Destroyed in such a shape.
> (4.8.22–26)

Normally, Antony dominates neither Cleopatra nor his military foes, but he still seems heroic through his association with the qualities of what Eugene Waith has called Herculean excessiveness. This technique of characterization, frequently used by Renaissance authors to make their heroes seem godlike and beyond ordinary moral and physical limits, appears in a variety of ways in *Antony and Cleopatra:* physical strength and military prowess, hyperbolic rhetoric, exorbitant generosity, extreme anger, and enormous capacity for sensual pleasures.[2]

The first of these is associated both implicitly and explicitly with the elder Caesar and Pompey, and with Hercules (Antony's ancestor), as well as with Antony, whose generalship, the younger Pompey tells us in referring to the other two triumvirs, is "twice the other twain" (2.1.35), and whose courage and physical strength, Octavius tells us, allowed him to "eat strange flesh / Which some did die to look on" (1.4.67–68). Antony often himself tells us of his physical and military prowess, and when he does he almost always uses hyperbolic rhetoric. As many commentators have noted, Antony's rhetoric and the rhetoric of others who discuss him, even his enemies, is often quite excessive: after all, it is not very likely that Antony could have eaten flesh so horribly rotted that other soldiers died simply from looking at it, but the assertion that he did makes him seem extraordinary nonetheless.[3]

The generosity of Hercules and Julius Caesar was legendary in the Renaissance, and thus implicit in *Antony and Cleopatra,* which goes to some pains to make Antony's generosity, which was also legendary, seem truly amazing—so much so that it kills Enobarbus. But while wonderfully generous, Antony is also prone to attacks of heroic anger, especially when he thinks Cleopatra has betrayed him. In one such attack he seeks an anger hyperbolic enough for Hercules, who set the standard for heroic rage:

> The shirt of Nessus is upon me; teach me,
> Alcides, thou mine ancestor, thy rage.
> Let me lodge Lichas on the horns o' th' moon,
> And with those hands, that grasp'd the heaviest club,
> Subdue my worthiest self.
> (4.12.43–47)

Last and perhaps most important is Antony's sensuality, for it is in terms of this quality that he is most like his heroic forebears. Hercules, of course, was legendary in his wine drinking, and among his amorous adventures was his sleeping with all fifty of Thespius' daughters, all in one night according to some versions. Analogous to Hercules' wine drinking are the prodigious Egyptian feasts that Octavius' lieutenants can only dream about (2.2), which entertained not only the "ne'er-lust-wearied Antony" (2.1.38) but Julius Caesar and Pompey the Great as well. And instead of fifty virgins, the three Romans each have or have had the woman who "makes hungry / Where most she satisfies" (2.2.237).

Heroic excessiveness is an important quality of many epic figures, but it need not always be a positive one. After all, Hercules' outbursts of temper often have unpleasant consequences, as do Orlando's in *Orlando Furioso;* but excessive anger contributes to the heroic characterization of both men just the same. Thus this kind of portrayal is a way of making us see a character as heroic, a way of identifying him as particularly strong but not necessarily either positive or negative. As a result, Antony's heroic excessiveness, especially as it concerns his relationship with Cleopatra, can invoke the Emasculating as well as the Epic type, since both are built around a heroic figure. The difference between the two is the gender of the person who dominates the relationship: if it is Cleopatra, then Antony is losing both his honor and his manhood and the relationship is Emasculating; if it is Antony, then he is merely emulating Julius Caesar and Pompey the Great and the relationship is Epic.

The Etherealized type is in one sense the opposite of the Epic and Emasculating, for where they are constructed on images of dominance, the type always represents a complete merging of two lovers, even to the loss of sexual and other identity. In all of the Etherealized relationships discussed previously, it is this complete union that is stressed, and in fact, the lovers themselves are always viewed as insignificant outside of their affair. In *Antony and Cleopatra,* on the other hand, the significance of the lovers is established outside of their relationship. We are told that Antony has been a great general in battle and is the "triple-pillar of the world," and we know that Cleopatra has had other great men as lovers and has a "hand that kings / Have lipp'd, and trembled kissing" (2.5.29–30). Etherealizing the relationship of figures who are independently heroic makes the lovers seem all the more otherworldly and extraordinary, and their union of cosmic status and importance. Appropriately, the central figures are frequently identified with Mars and Venus, whose union is the usual vehicle in Renaissance art and literature for portraying the discordia concors, the mystical union of warring opposites that will restore Edenic balance and order to the cosmos.[4] So while the Etherealized is diametrically opposed to the Epic and Etherealized in one way, it is also like them in pulling us away from the Ascetic view of the lovers as base.

This opposition of heroism and baseness is the method through which the four relationship types are oriented in this play—as well as the source of a major thematic movement—but in addition there are several subsidiary oppositions. One already apparent is the contrast of Octavius, Pompey, and other Romans of the play's present with Julius Caesar, Pompey the Great, and others of the past. This opposition of present and past is used to show the decline of Roman heroism and of heroism in general: the Romans of the present are associated with luck and political expediency; they are boys to the men of the past, who made their own fortune, preferred battle to political compromise, and are represented as men or demigods. When Pompey meets the triumvirs to negotiate peace, for example, Menas notes that "Thy father, Pompey, would ne'er / Have made this treaty" (2.6.82–83). He means that the old Caesar and Pompey would have risked everything in a single glorious battle, but that their sons are too afraid of the consequences to take such a risk. The fathers were heroic, the sons base. Appropriately, Antony's petulance almost causes the prearranged treaty to come apart, especially his challenge to fight Pompey even on the sea, where his enemy would have the advantage. The irrationality of this kind of bravado will be demonstrated at Actium, but it serves once again to associate Antony with the heroes of the past: like them, compromise is anathema to his nature—at least his nature in this scene.

Octavius and Pompey, of course, do not regard their negotiated peace as indicative of a lack of heroic vigor; rather, for them the treaty represents the victory of rational peace over irrational, unnecessary war, of solid, male friendship over animosity. For these characters and for the Ascetic view of the play's central relationship, the main oppositions are Rome and Egypt, Octavius and Antony, and Octavia and Cleopatra. And behind each of these character oppositions is the basic ideological distinction of the Ascetic tradition: reason versus passion. Thus whereas Egypt is usually portrayed as the place of continual feasting and lovemaking among the people and of mysterious and uncontrollable fertility in the land and the Nile, Rome is preeminently the place of politics and rational order, the intellectual center of the earth, where even sexual relationships are carefully and unemotionally arranged. And whereas Antony prefers Cleopatra's love to everything, including even his own life, Octavius never reveals any regard for women and sexuality, his only departure from constant political calculation being a drinking party with the boys, which he obviously does not enjoy. Finally, whereas Cleopatra usually refuses to be submissive to Antony or anyone else and is reserved in nothing, Octavia perfectly fits the Ascetic model of ideal womanhood: reserved in all things and submissive to men in all respects, including the arrangement of her own marriage.[5]

The Ascetic provides a readymade way of understanding the reason-passion, positive-negative orientation of each pair of characters, but it is not the only type through which the oppositions are viewed. Although Egypt, Antony, and Cleopatra are irrational and negative in the Ascetic scheme, they are fertile, natural, and timeless in the Etherealized, with their opposites correspondingly impotent, artificial, and imprisoned in a particular time. Octavius especially is often described as a boy—hence impotent in comparison with men—and as "Fortune's Knave" (5.2.3). He is less significant than Antony, from the Etherealized point of view, because he absents himself from his own nature in order to achieve material possessions. Passion is natural, according to this scheme, the key to man's higher nature and the ideal world, while strict rationality is unnatural and inherently worldly and materialistic. Thus while Antony is materialistic in terms of the Ascetic tradition because he worships Cleopatra's body, Octavius is materialistic in terms of the Etherealized because his cool logic can never transcend the corrupted earth. And like all such materialists in this idealistic view, Octavius is doomed to the uncertainty of Fortune's wheel, which eventually overturns all the plans of man, no matter how carefully wrought. Antony, on the other hand, escapes the tumult of earthly affairs by dedicating himself to the achievement of an ideal state, his vehicle a sexual relationship that somehow transcends the earthly and the changeable. From the Etherealized point of view both men eventually achieve the goals they seek: for Octavius, Egypt and Cleopatra—ironically reduced by death to the complete physicality that all along marks the Ascetic definition of the whore—and for Antony, a garden of love "Where souls do couch on flowers" (4.14.51), where love may exist undisturbed by the tumult of Fortuna's world.

Throughout this study I have chosen not to speculate about the possible social and psychological motivations behind our continued use of the various types. Though such motivations certainly exist, and hence are part of our response, they are much more difficult to identify than the exterior systems they (in one sense) produce. Psychoanalytic and other critics have sought to unmask these motivations directly, but it seems to me that the first step has to be to determine the exterior systems, since it is only through them that any deeper structures can be seen. And even without any recourse to motivational deep structures, surely most of our understanding and enjoyment of any narrative comes from recognizing exterior systems and turning them into the interior ones which control the story.

Deeper structures are there, however, and play an especially important part in narratives we find especially powerful. Such must be the case in *Antony and Cleopatra*, since its unconventional and in many respects incoherent use of plot and character suggest that the response of those of us who find the play one of Shakespeare's best cannot derive mostly from an excellent use of familiar plotting and characterization—as in, for example,

Romeo and Juliet. The exterior systems in this play produce contradictory interior ones. When the play works, it must do so more than usually in terms of structures one or more removes from the level of exterior systems.

A full consideration of any structure deeper than exterior systems is far beyond the range of this study, but it seems clear that in *Antony and Cleopatra* Shakespeare arranges his use of the Ascetic and Etherealized types so as to emphasize an important opposition behind not only these systems, but many others as well. Basically, the Ascetic in this play is used in such a way as to reinforce the value of rationality and the individual's responsibility to himself, while the Etherealized glorifies emotion and unrestrained, unrestricted union. This opposition might be restated as reason versus emotion, but since the idea of the individual implies separation from other humans and from physical nature, it could just as accurately be self versus union. And since union in this sense represents merger with a changeless, all-providing ideal state, the same deep structure is often expressed as freedom-security, individual-state, or even world-womb. Still others might be added, such as free will—determinism, representation-ideal, change-stasis, and corruption—perfection. Behind all of these are our contradictory drives toward both maintenance of self and merger with our fellow humans and ultimately with a god figure. Or, put in different terms, we desire to feel we control our own actions and our own sense of reality while at the same time we long to have both validated by some outside force.

The tension created by this contradictory desire for both individuality and merger has extensive ramifications within our culture, and to the extent that the conflict between the Ascetic and Etherealized views of the central relationship in *Antony and Cleopatra* makes the self-union conflict as clear for us as possible, we are forced to contend with this tension.

Such coercion, however, is not the method of most other works that represent ideal states. In *Romeo and Juliet*, for example, there is also a conflict between the Ascetic and the Etherealized, but in that play the Ascetic is clearly discredited, and at least as it is expressed by Mercutio, not even concerned with the same relationship as the Etherealized view. There is no tension created by the two types because the choice between them is never really ours to make. In other Etherealized portraits, such as Donne's "The Canonization" or the Amoret-Scudamour union in the *Faerie Queene*, there is not even a perfunctory representation of the Ascetic or any other view emphasizing self rather than union: the author in each case simply plays upon our attraction to ideals and union and ignores the potential threat to the sense of self implicit in such representations. The Judeo-Christian heaven and other outright evocations of an ideal world avoid this implicit threat in a different way, by simply asserting that there is no contradiction between maintenance of self and merger with a changeless and perfect world. One may accept these representations as paradoxically true or reject them as impossible, but in either case the representation itself works to diminish rather than increase tension, though with the inevitable result of also diminishing our possible emotional reaction to the ideal, the basis for such a reaction—the distinction-union conflict—having been artificially eliminated.

In *Antony and Cleopatra*, on the other hand, the contradiction between the Ascetic and Etherealized views—and thus between self and union—is actively forced upon us. Unlike *Romeo and Juliet*, *Antony and Cleopatra* makes it impossible for us to disregard or dismiss the Ascetic, for it is not just motivated outsiders who describe the relationship as vile; the relationship itself sometimes insists on such an interpretation, sometimes insists that we see its irrationality and the debilitating effect it has on the lovers. And it is not just the commentary of Octavius and his followers but the conduct of the lovers themselves that makes us sometimes view them as vain, untruthful, lustful, exploitative, foolish, and degenerate. In other words, the Ascetic view of the relationship is part of the actual stage representation, not just a secondary description.

But if the lovers are sometimes undeniably negative, they are also sometimes undeniably positive, particularly in the Etherealized portraits of the last two acts. What Shakespeare does, then, is stretch us uncomfortably between two poles: if we wish to follow Octavius and denigrate the relationship, we must reject the possibility of love and accept Octavius as the best of men. But if we choose instead to accept the relationship as positive, we are forced to confront its absolute rejection and contradiction of many of the values that we hold as essential for our social fabric: moderation, rationality, moral law, simple manners. Most of us do finally accept the relationship as positive, I think, but we are forced to do so only in the face of the overwhelming otherness of what we embrace.[6]

I have, of course, overstated my case, for in fact Shakespeare does distance us significantly from a truly threatening presentation of the lovers' final union. He has the lovers themselves speak of an afterlife in a garden of love, which, like the Judeo-Christian heaven, is a nonthreatening combination of idealization and individuality, and he presents Octavius so unsympathetically that we naturally sympathize with—and thus humanize—his opponents. And in addition, Shakespeare uses the two types not overtly concerned with distinction and union, along with the two that are, to work out the theme of heroism versus baseness, a theme that eventually stresses the individuality of Antony—though individuality of a very alien kind.

But despite these distancing techniques, much of the threat implicit in the Etherealized union still comes through, and comes through more strongly than in almost any similar narrative. Critics have long had trouble explaining their reactions to *Antony and Cleopatra*, especially when these reactions take the form of affirmation of the lovers. Ultimately, it is this sense of threat that makes the play troublesome and makes us want to pull back from—and even vilify—the same relationship that we also wish to embrace. How the play makes us feel this contradictory reaction is the key issue in what makes *Antony and Cleopatra* powerful drama.

Shakespeare is usually an economical playwright and almost always produces effective introductions, so it is not surprising to see two of the four types and the important past-present opposition established in the first ten lines of the play:

> Nay, but this dotage of our general's
> O'erflows the measure. Those his goodly eyes,
> That o'er the files and musters of the war
> Have glow'd like plated Mars, now bend, now turn
> The office and devotion of their view
> Upon a tawny front; his captain's heart,
> Which in the scuffles of great fights hath burst
> The buckles on his breast, reneges all temper,
> And is become the bellows and the fan
> To cool a gipsy's lust.
> (1.1.1–10)

The Antony of the past is here a heroic Epic figure, a man whose past military exploits can only be understood as like a god's. But the Antony of the present, Philo's real interest, has been so diminished by his relationship with Cleopatra that he is no longer even a man, let alone a god; he is merely an instrument used to satisfy the lusts of a whore. This Antony is, of course, strictly Ascetic.[7]

But when the lovers actually appear, they do not present themselves in terms of either of these types, but especially not the Ascetic; rather, their first dialogue is a hyperbolic attempt to assert their love's transcendence over all human activity whatsoever:

> *Cleo.* If it be love indeed, tell me how much.
> *Ant.* There's beggary in the love that can be
>   reckon'd.
> *Cleo.* I'll set a bourne how far to be belov'd.
> *Ant.* Then must thou needs find out new heaven, new
>   earth.
> (1.1.14–17)

This dialogue begins what will become the Etherealized view of the relationship by defining it as the opposite of earthly materialism (i.e., as ethereal or ideal), and when a messenger follows with news from Rome—which Antony naturally rejects as too material for such a moment—another frequent element of the Etherealized type is added: an adversary relationship with some outside force, in this case Fulvia and "scarce-bearded Caesar," whom Cleopatra represents as commanding that Antony "Take in that kingdom, and enfranchise that; / Perform't, or else we damn thee" (1.1.23–24). This establishment of an opposing outside force helps define and isolate the relationship, and it sparks Antony to give the first truly Etherealized portrait of his love:

> Let Rome in Tiber melt, and the wide arch
> Of the rang'd empire fall! Here is my space,
> Kingdoms are clay; our dungy earth alike
> Feeds beast as man; the nobleness of life
> Is to do thus—when such a mutual pair
> And such a twain can do't, in which I bind,
> On pain of punishment, the world to weet
> We stand up peerless.
>
> (1.1.33–40)

The basis of this description is again the ethereality and ideality of the relationship in comparison to the materialism of everything else, but the Etherealized view is now much more complete. The sexuality of the relationship (the passage suggests the lovers embrace on stage) is now more clearly and favorably compared to a nonideal activity (collecting kingdoms), and the singularity of both the lovers and their relationship is stressed. This is the last complete Etherealized portrait before the fourth act, but the framework of the type is clearly established here, thus enabling its values to continue to function. One of these values is the sexual merger which the lovers hold more valuable than the whole world but which already in this scene is opposed by the view that such complete lack of restraint makes even the best of men a "strumpet's fool."[8]

Scene 1, then, establishes three of the play's four relationship types, and by describing Antony in heroic terms suggests the possibility of the fourth, the Emasculating. This introduction is followed by the first of several units of scenes. In the early scenes (1.2–2.2), the play presents us with representations of the central relationship in terms of each of the four types, but in such a way that these contradictory portrayals do not seem logically incompatible. Although there are suggestions of the Ascetic throughout this group of scenes, act 1 scenes 2 and 3 and the first part of four consistently portray not only the relationship but Egypt itself as the epitome of Ascetic decadence. Most of scene 2, for example, shows Antony's reproaching of his own "idleness" (1.2.130) and his consequent resolve to leave Cleopatra and return to Rome, but it also includes a look at Cleopatra's attendants, especially the women, who are portrayed as concerned with only such trivial wantonness as jokes about oily palms, cuckolds, and male "inches"—the effect of which is to associate not just the lovers but everyone in Egypt with Ascetic decadence.

This established, the next two scenes provide expanded portraits of each of the lovers. Cleopatra is presented as a typical Ascetic woman, so changeable and dishonest that she tells Charmian that should she find Antony sad she should "Say I am dancing; if in mirth, report / That I am sudden sick" (1.3.4–5). The next scene then begins with the Ascetic denunciation of Antony by Octavius noted earlier, in which Antony is portrayed as having given a "kingdom for a mirth" (1.4.18)—an analysis that stands in direct contrast with the "Kingdoms are clay" of the first scene.

Having damned the present Antony as the "abstract of all faults" (1.4.9), Octavius goes on to describe an Antony of the past who was the abstract of virtue, and in the process to mark the transition from Ascetic to Epic:

> Antony,
> Leave thy lascivious wassails. When thou once
> Was beaten from Modena, where thou slew'st
> Hirtius and Pansa, consuls, at thy heel
> Did famine follow, whom thou fought'st against
> (Though daintily brought up) with patience more
> Than savages could suffer. Thou didst drink
> The stale of horses and the gilded puddle
> Which beast would cough at; thy palate then did deign
> The roughest berry on the rudest hedge;
> Yea, like the stag, when snow the pasture sheets,
> The barks of trees thou brows't. On the Alps
> It is reported thou didst eat strange flesh,
> Which some did die to look on; and all this
> (It wounds thy honor that I speak it now)
> Was borne so like a soldier, that thy cheek
> So much as lank'd not.
> (1.4.55–71)

With this description we are back to Antony as "plated Mars," completely remarkable and beyond ordinary bounds. Indeed, in this portrait Antony is heroic because he is entirely unaffected by the laws that govern all other men and beasts: because Antony can drink urine and calmly eat rotted meat, he is viewed as better than all of us who could not endure such refreshment. The analogy for such a person, according to the system the play sets up, must be to a god, as Cleopatra claims when she described Antony as the "demi-Atlas of this earth, the arm / And burgonet of men" (1.5.24) and describes herself as his horse, the toy of Antony just as she was the toy of Julius Caesar and Pompey the Great. This is, of course, the Epic Antony, and it is significant to note that the necessary heroic nature for this part is associated wtih alienness, with complete difference from the ordinary.

This Epic Antony is clearly incompatible with the Ascetic one, but Shakespeare maintains his illusion of psychological coherence by playing one in the past and one in the present. In act 2, however, the heroic Antony is brought into the present through Pompey's Emasculating description of Cleopatra as the witch whose powers are keeping Antony's brain "fuming" (2.1.23). But before portraying Cleopatra as a witch, Pompey gives us a capsule description of the three triumvirs:

> Mark Antony
> In Egypt sits at dinner, and will make
> No wars without-doors. Caesar gets money where
> He loses hearts. Lepidus flatters both,
> Of both is flatter'd; but he neither loves,
> Nor either cares for him.
> (2.1.11–16)

This thoroughly nonheroic representation of Antony is paired with equally nonheroic representations of Octavius and Lepidus, who are always described in that way. But while Pompey's assessment of Octavius and Lepidus may be correct, he is wrong about their being in Rome, as he soon learns from a messenger. Shocked to find two of his enemies already in the field, he must suddenly place all his trust in Cleopatra's ability to hold Antony in Egypt, and therefore he turns to Cleopatra as a sort of military ally:

> He dreams; I know they are in Rome together,
> Looking for Antony. But all the charms of love,
> Salt Cleopatra, soften thy wan'd lip!
> (2.1.19–21)

The Emasculating description that follows (quoted earlier) seems realistic to us because Shakespeare has established a context in which such a viewpoint is necessary for Pompey. But at the same time, the description goes beyond Pompey, for it calls into question two aspects of characterization that had seemed firmly established: the scope of Cleopatra's power, which is never before represented as going beyond the usual Ascetic list of feminine wiles (such as pouting, abusing logic, and constantly changing); and Antony's present relation to the heroic ideal. It is important to note that early on the love relationship is portrayed as wholly banal (in 1.2, 1.3, and 1.4); it is only later (in 2.1) that it begins to have any especial power, either as an evil or a good. Thus when Pompey goes on to assert that Antony's "soldiership / Is twice the other twain" (2.1.34–35), the heroic Antony slips quietly from the past to the present, and the play from careful realism to direct, if understated, contradiction.

This contradiction is understated because the exoticism of Cleopatra, her servants, and everything else Egyptian has already helped establish the sense of mystery and fluctuation that prevails throughout the play. This atmosphere, the sense of magic created by Pompey (in 2.1) and the sense of the Epic created by Cleopatra (in 1.5) all combine to prepare for one of the most magical moments in the play, Enobarbus' description of Cleopatra's barge:

> The barge she sat in, like a burnish'd throne,
> Burnt on the water. The poop was beaten gold,
> Purple the sails, and so perfumed that
> The winds were love-sick with them; the oars were
>   silver,
> Which to the tune of flutes kept stroke, and made
> The water which they beat to follow faster,
> As amorous of their strokes. For her own person,
> It beggar'd all description: she did lie
> In her pavilion—cloth of gold, of tissue—
> O'er-picturing that Venus where we see
> The fancy outwork nature. . . .
>   At the helm
> A seeming mermaid steers; the silken tackle
> Swell with the touches of those flower-soft hands,
> That yarely frame the office. From the barge
> A strange invisible perfume hits the sense
> Of the adjacent wharfs.
>   (2.2.191–201, 208–13)

This description would seem about as far removed as possible from that of Antony's activities in the Alps, but they are alike in one important respect: both are attempts to give a sense of otherness, of a character and a scene completely beyond ordinary experience and limitations. One scene is more beautiful than we can experience, the other more horrible, but both make the described character seem wonderful because he or she is beyond our various laws.

As many have noted, Enobarbus' description clearly associates Cleopatra with Venus. Since this Venus figure is about to meet an equally Mars-like Antony, the whole description takes on Etherealized connotations: the goddess of beauty and love is about to meet the god of destruction and war, and the sexual union of such an elemental opposition must represent something more than mere lust. As if to emphasize the point, Enobarbus goes on to describe Cleopatra's amazing sexuality:

> Age cannot wither her, nor custom stale
> Her infinite variety. Other women cloy
> The appetites they feed, but she makes hungry

> Where most she satisfies; for vildest things
> Become themselves in her, that the holy priests
> Bless her when she is riggish.
>
> (2.2.234–39)

Ordinary women wither, and sex with them can be only temporarily satisfying, but everything about Cleopatra is eternal and—though unabashedly sexual—holy. She is Venus or mother earth, the universal female force than channels man's vitality into fertility rather than destruction. As Agrippa puts it, "She made great Caesar lay his sword to bed; / He ploughed her, and she cropp'd" (2.2.227–28). The similar bedding of Antony can hardly be seen from this viewpoint as the trivial and unsavory antics of a degenerate with a whore.

The meeting of Antony and Cleopatra is set in the past, and the present, the meeting of Antony and Octavius and the arrangement of Antony's marriage with Octavia (2.2), suffers considerably in comparison to it. This type of past-present comparison becomes one of the important techniques in the middle scenes (2.3–3.9), where the emphasis is on a series of negative portraits of individuals, rather than on describing the central relationship. For example, we are given one of our least appealing portrayals of Cleopatra, who opens the scene by defining music as the "moody food / Of us that trade in love" (2.5.1–2)—the significant term here being "trade"—and then goes on to demonstrate typical Ascetic female irrationality and instability by badgering a messenger from Rome. But before the messenger enters, Cleopatra gives us a nostalgic portrait of the recent past:

> That time? O times!
> I laugh'd him out of patience; and that night
> I laugh'd him into patience; and next morn,
> Ere the ninth hour, I drunk him to his bed;
> Then put my tires and mantles on him, whilst
> I wore his sword Philippan.
>
> (2.5.18–23)

In one sense, the basis of this speech is as much Ascetic as the rest of the scene: Antony's excessive lust and drinking have made him so unmindful of his honor that he has placed himself under the control of a woman, who not only wears the pants in their relationship, but the sword as well.

At the same time, however, the literary allusions implicit in the speech reassociate both characters with heroic figures. The exchange of clothing is reminiscent of a similar incident involving Hercules and Omphale, and is part of the standard Renaissance representation of the Mars-Venus union. And when the heroes in Renaissance epic-romances fall under the spell of a Circe figure, their domination is shown as feminization, usually involving involving loss of control of the sword. These allusions make Cleopatra's nostalgia a kind of pun, signifying both the banal and the heroic, and both degradation and the mysterious union of cosmic opposites. As before, both visions are portrayed as true, and the text suggests no way for us to bridge the contradiction.[9]

Then the focus shifts to the Romans and yet another recharacterization of Antony (2.6–3.2). In the first two of these four scenes the treaty between Pompey and the triumvirs is settled and then celebrated on board Pompey's galley. One scene takes place in an atmosphere of conflict, the other of amity, but in both we are clearly told that the Romans of the past would not have done things the same as do their descendants. Antony begins as heroic (2.6), preferring to fight than to sign a treaty giving away land to an enemy, but by the end of the scene he has agreed not only to the treaty but to drawing lots with the others to see who entertains first. Instead of a victory celebration, the next scene presents an aimless party in which Antony is as silly as the other drunks. By act 3 scene 1 Antony has changed from the heroic urine-drinker of the past to a better-mannered but less noteworthy politician who marries as a method of political compromise. Even his past heroism is now questionable, at least according to Ventidius:

> Caesar and Antony have ever won
> More in their officer than person. . . .
> I could do more to do Antonius good,
> But 'twould offend him; and in his offense
> Should my performance perish.
>   (3.1.16–17, 25–27)

This Antony is hardly the same soldier that Octavius and Pompey revere; he is not a soldier at all but rather a politician who keeps soldiers in his hire. The same character appears in the next scene, where, in the process of satirizing Lepidus, Agrippa and Enobarbus imply how far short their masters fall of heroic description:

> *Agr.*   'Tis a noble Lepidus.
> *Eno.* A very fine one. O, how he loves Caesar!
> *Agr.* Nay, but how dearly he adores Mark Antony!
> *Eno.* Caesar? Why, he's the Jupiter of men.
> *Agr.* What's Antony? The god of Jupiter.
> *Eno.* Spake you of Caesar? How, the nonpareil!
> *Agr.* O Antony! O thou Arabian bird!
>   (3.2.6–12)

It is worth noting that the Antony of several previous scenes is at least as rare as an "Arabian bird," but just as Cleopatra separated from Antony becomes trivial and base, so he becomes base when separated from her, and is lumped with Lepidus and Octavius into a banal present bereft of heroes.

Antony, however, is not the main representative of the present in this unit of scenes, or the main character denounced through it; those distinctions belong to Octavius. Unlike Antony, Octavius is represented with consistency throughout the play, beginning in the first scene. There Cleopatra's description of him as "scarce-bearded" (1.1.19) suggests that he is a boy compared to Antony. This boy-man opposition is expanded and explained when the Soothsayer—perhaps the only unbiased character in the play—explains why Antony should avoid Octavius:

> Thy daemon, that thy spirit which keeps thee, is
> Noble, courageous, high unmatchable,
> Where Caesar's is not; but near him, thy angel
> Becomes a fear, as being o'erpow'r'd: therefore
> Make space enough between you. . . .
> If thou dost play with him at any game,
> Thou art sure to lose; and of that natural luck,
> He beats thee 'gainst the odds. Thy luster thickens
> When he shines by. I say again, thy spirit
> Is all afraid to govern thee near him;
> But he away, 'tis noble.
> (2.3.20–24, 26–31)

The Soothsayer states what will soon be apparent, that Antony becomes as ignoble as Octavius when with him rather than Cleopatra. But more importantly, he gives us insight into Octavius' nature. In effect, he is saying that Antony cannot challenge Octavius because Octavius is not a person; he is merely a tool of the fortune that allows "The very dice [to] obey him" (2.3.34). Much later, Cleopatra makes a similar observation:

> My desolation does begin to make
> A better life. 'Tis paltry to be Caesar;
> Not being Fortune, he's but Fortune's knave,
> A minister of her will: and it is great
> To do that thing that ends all other deeds,
> Which shackles accidents and bolts up change,
> Which sleeps, and never palates more the dung,
> The beggar's nurse and Caesar's.
> (5.2.1–8)

This speech, which comes just after Octavius has explained how he wrote his memoirs instead of fighting during the last battle against Antony, goes further than the Soothsayer's: it asserts that Octavius' dependence on fortune—here given its frequent Christian association with earthly corruption—makes him no better, indeed no different from a beggar. Because he lacks the heroic nature to establish his own destiny, Octavius is stuck on

Fortune's wheel, and no more responsible for his excess of luck than a beggar is for his lack of it. Antony cannot challenge Octavius because Fortuna is ultimately unchallengeable on the corrupted earth. But like Cleopatra, Antony will eventually triumph in the "better life" that will come with death and reunite the lovers in an eternal, nonearthly, Etherealized relationship. Octavius, then, is associated not only with fortune rather than heroic assertion but with earthly corruption rather than ideality.

He is also associated with time (as opposed to stasis), the idea that makes Fortuna's wheel and earthly corruption possible, and the idea that for most in the Renaissance signifies man's ever-increasing distance from God and Eden. As Janet Adelman has shown, the passage of time in Octavius' Rome is several times opposed to the slow or nonexistent alteration of either Cleopatra or Egypt before Actium.[10] Then as this battle approaches, many short scenes begin to crowd themselves onto the stage, and even the larger ones are broken up by numerous reports of the rapid passage of time—shown as the advance of Octavius:

> *Ant.* Is is not strange, Canidus,
> That from Tarentum and Brundusium
> He could so quickly cut the Ionian Sea,
> And take in Toryne?
> (3.7.20–23)
>
> *Mess.* The news is true, my lord: he is descried;
> Caesar has taken Toryne.
> *Ant.* Can he be there in person? 'Tis impossible
> Strange that his power should be.
> (3.7.54–57)

It is as time that we can see Octavius' clearest relation to the middle scenes. The basic opposition in this unit is between a decayed present and a past at least heroic, if not unquestionably good. Octavius is certainly a representative of the nonheroic present, but he also represents the process that forced the change, the advance of time and the attendant progressive corruption of the human spirit. The middle scenes suggest that true heroism lies only in the past, where it is represented in terms of the Epic, Emasculating, and Etherealized types; the present in these scenes is exclusively Ascetic and base.

While the middle scenes are concerned with individuals as they are constituted by the present, the late scenes (3.10–4.12) concentrate again on the central relationship and its effect on the lovers. But the relationship as it is represented in the late scenes is no longer viewed strictly in terms of itself: it is now inextricably tied up in the dominant past-present and heroic-base oppositions so important in the middle scenes. Most obviously, the resumption of the relationship just before Actium represents the past brought into the present and the heroic lovers directly opposed to the base Octavius. The heroic-base opposition is not, however, completely outside of the relationship, that is, between it and Octavius, but inside as well, for the relationship has itself sometimes been as closely associated with the Ascetic as Octavius, and thus is as much an emblem of the decayed present as he is. Antony sometimes views the relationship as advancing him beyond time, fortune, and corruption, but he and others also sometimes view the relationship as marking Antony's very real descent from heroic stature to base. Thus it is not surprising that just after we hear of Octavius' incredibly fast approach to Egypt, the central relationship is again strongly associated with the Ascetic, through Scarus' description of the first battle:

> Yon ribaudred nag of Egypt
> (Whom leprosy o'ertake!) i' th' midst o' th' fight,
> When vantage like a pair of twins appear'd,
> Both as the same, or rather ours the elder—
> The breeze upon her, like a cow in June—
> Hoists sails and flies. . . .
>   She once being loof'd,
> The noble ruin of her magic, Antony,
> Claps on his sea-wing, and (like a doting mallard),
> Leaving the fight in heighth, flies after her.
> I never saw an action of such shame;
> Experience, manhood, honor, ne'er before
> Did violate so itself.
>   (3.10.10–15, 17–23)

Despite his ascription of "magic" to Cleopatra, Scarus' description of her as a "ribaudred nag," a "cow in June," and a potential leper (like Cressida in Ascetic versions of her story) is clearly Ascetic. And Antony, though once capable of godlike heroism, is now a "ruin."

In the next scene, Antony himself echoes Scarus, declaring that the land "is asham'd to bear me" and that

> I have fled myself, and have instructed cowards
> To run and show their shoulders. Friends, be gone,
> I have myself resolv'd upon a course
> Which has no need of you. Be gone.
> My treasure's in the harbor; take it. O,
> I follow'd that I blush to look upon.
>   (3.11.2, 7–12)

But even in the midst of this self-denunciation, Antony's generosity suggests the heroic figure of previous scenes: a truly base Antony would not offer to give away all of his possessions. The heroic Antony also comes out a few lines later when he compares himself and Octavius in terms of their respective contributions to the battle at Philippi:

> Yes, my lord, yes; he at Philippi kept
> His sword e'en like a dancer, while I strook
> The lean and wrinkled Cassius, and 'twas I
> That the mad Brutus ended. He alone
> Dealt on lieutenantry, and no practice had
> In the brave squares of war; yet now—No matter.
> (3.11.35–40)

Antony's disgrace now seems less that he fled the battle than that he lost to a base foe, the Octavius who used proxies to fight at Philippi and has just used them again at Actium. And when Cleopatra asks forgiveness for her part in the military debacle, Antony is again portrayed as fully heroic:

> Fall not a tear, I say, one of them rates
> All that is won and lost. Give me a kiss.
> Even this repays me. We sent our schoolmaster,
> Is 'a come back? Love, I am full of lead.
> Some wine, within there, and our viands! Fortune knows
> We scorn her most when most she offers blows.
> (3.11.69–74)

In challenging Fortuna, Antony is asserting his difference from men like Octavius, all of whom are merely her pawns and tools. He, on the other hand, scorns Fortuna as an unworthy foe, and though he may be beaten by her, never admits her sovereignty. In calling for wine, Antony makes another separation between himself and Octavius, for while his enemy prepares for battle by calmly figuring which troops should bear the brunt of the fight, Antony is here beginning his last prebattle "gaudy night" (3.13.182) of massive drinking and celebration. For him, battle is the place for displaying great personal strength and valor rather than mastery of modern military tactics, and thus the best preparation for it is Herculean excess.

But at the same time that Antony reasserts his heroism and his superiority to Octavius, he makes a clear allusion to a previous speech that precedes the full development of the heroic-base theme: the single previous Etherealized portrait of the lovers, where Antony declares that his and Cleopatra's love is worth more than all the kingdoms of "dungy earth" (1.1.35) that he owns. Before, he would let "Rome in Tiber melt" (1.1.33) rather than give up his love; now he asserts that one of Cleopatra's tears is worth "All that is won and lost." And most noticeably of all, the centerpiece of both speeches is an embrace signifying the superiority of the relationship to everything else in the world. The difference between the speeches is the situation, for whereas in the first scene he had both his love and his kingdoms, by this time (3.11)

Antony has had to choose between them, and his assertion that one kiss "repays" him for what he has given up to follow Cleopatra's galley away from the battle carries considerable significance. Now, for Antony, his love justifies his flight from the battle and represents, not cowardice (as it did only a few lines earlier), but the choice of love over kingdoms, the ideal instead of "dungy earth." And just as important, Antony's statement clearly associates the Etherealized vision of scene 1 with the heroic values developed since then. The Etherealized relationship is now equated with heroic excess and the rejection of Fortuna and earthly corruption; indeed, Etherealization now becomes one of the chief avenues for heroic endeavor—and once Octavius finally defeats Antony's little band of warriors, it will be the only one.

Before Octavius can impose his "time of universal peace" (4.6.4), Antony and his men "drown consideration" (4.2.45) in a night of revel and then soundly beat their much more numerous enemy; Scarus, and doubtlessly Antony as well, fights "As if a god, in hate of mankind, had / Destroyed in such a shape" (4.8.25–26). But eventually Antony can no longer come "smiling from / The world's great snare uncaught" (4.8.17–18) and is defeated, again through the desertion of Cleopatra's forces. Antony's response, as after his first defeat, is to berate Cleopatra, this time calling her a "triple-turn'd whore," the "false soul of Egypt," a "right gypsy," and a "witch" (4.10.13, 25, 28, 47). But as after the first battle, and as after he found Cleopatra entertaining Octavius' messenger (in 3.13), Antony is ready to forgive. The price he exacts for forgiveness, however, grows with each apparent treachery. After the first battle, all Cleopatra must do to reassure Antony that she has not renounced their love is produce a tear and ask forgiveness, but after entertaining Thidias, he responds only to a truly hyperbolic assertion of loyalty:

> Ah, dear, if I be so,
> From my cold heart let heaven engender hail,
> And poison it in the source, and the first stone
> Drop in my neck; as it determines, so
> Dissolve my life! The next Caesarion smite,
> Till by degrees the memory of my womb,
> Together with my brave Egyptians all,
> By the discandying of this pelleted storm,
> Lie graveless, till the flies and gnats of Nile
> Have buried them for prey!
> (3.13.158–67)

After her third treachery, all that is left is hyperbolic action—or at least what Antony thinks is hyperbolic action—to reassure him of her love. This apparent action is, of course, her reported suicide, which Antony takes first as the proof of heroic nature and then as the basis for Etherealization:

> I will o'ertake thee, Cleopatra, and
> Weep for my pardon. So it must be, for now
> All length is torture; since the torch is out,
> Lie down and stray no farther. Now all labor
> Mars what it does; yea, very force entangles
> Itself with strength. Seal then, and all is done.
> Eros!—I come, my queen!—Eros!—Stay for me!
> Where souls do couch on flowers, we'll hand in hand,
> And with our sprightly port make the ghosts gaze.
> Dido and Aeneas shall want troops,
> And all the haunt be ours. Come, Eros, Eros!
> (4.13.44–54)

This passage begins the concluding scenes, which establish the new and permanently heroic world that the lovers will inhabit after their death. What Antony suggests for us is that his present world is no longer appropriate for heroic action, for in its valor and love, self and union are contradictory. He has found that it is impossible to maintain his position in the world and his own view of self yet still commit himself to love; the result is that heroic labor is self-defeating, "Mars what it does," and "force" paradoxically "entangles / Itself with strength."

Antony's solution is a positive Garden of Love, where there will be no contradiction between love and heroic action. He implies as much by placing Dido and Aeneas in this garden as well, for Aeneas would seem to be the direct opposite of Antony, he having given up love for the world, rather than the other way around. Antony, however, suggests that he and Aeneas are alike in that both are exemplary as lovers as well as soldiers, and that any contradiction in the roles signifies a defective world, not a defective hero. But in making such a suggestion, Antony is simply deferring the conflict, for as the whole play shows, there is an irresolvable contradiction between the assertion of individual strength implicit in Antony's brand of heroic soldiership and the necessary de-emphasis of individuality in the type of commitment he wants to make to Cleopatra. The tragedy of the play, then, is not Antony's mistakes or character flaws but this inevitable contradiction between two positive goals. Antony wants to establish his individual worth through soldiership and to demonstrate his scorn of fortune and corruption through giving himself completely to a transcendent sexual union, but while he accomplishes both goals separately, he demonstrates that eventually they contradict each other.[11]

Cleopatra's feigning of suicide calls into question her motives, as many have noted, but it also allows the same death sequence as in *Romeo and Juliet*: each lover gets to lament the demise of his or her mate. Cleopatra's death, though, is delayed much longer than Juliet's, and she is placed in firm opposition to Octavius, that model of baseness who helped make Antony seem so heroic. Ironically, then, Cleopatra's lie about her suicide finally helps make her a more positive character, because with Antony dead she becomes the main opposition to Octavius. This opposition is first established in the speech quoted earlier, where Cleopatra asserts that " 'Tis paltry to be Caesar" and then compares her future "better" life to Octavius' life of fortune and its attendant earthly corruption (5.2.1–8). Later in the same scene she baffles another of Octavius' proxies with a well-known, hyperbolic description of an Antony whose "legs bestrid the ocean," whose "voice was propertied / As all the tuned spheres," and whose "delights / were dolphin-like, they showed his back above / The element they liv'd in" (5.2.82–90). The base Dolabella does not believe that such a person could exist, but Cleopatra does and seems more heroic to us for making the assertion. And when Octavius himself attempts to seduce Cleopatra into staying in his world rather than traveling to Antony's, her crushing analysis firmly establishes who is deceiving whom: "He words me, girls, he words me, that I should not / Be noble to myself" (5.2.191–92).

She then goes on to describe the two worlds from which she has to choose, the vulgar Rome of Octavius, or the ideal world of Antony—which she calls "Cydnus":

> Now, Iras, what thinks't thou?
> Thou, an Egyptian puppet, shall be shown
> In Rome as well as I. Mechanic slaves
> With greasy aprons, rules, and hammers shall
> Uplift us to the view. In their thick breaths,
> Rank of gross diet, shall we be enclouded,
> And forced to drink their vapor. . . .
>   Saucy lictors
> Will catch at us like strumpets, and scald rhymers
> Ballad 's out a' tune. The quick comedians
> Extemporally will stage us, and present
> Our Alexandrian revels: Antony
> Shall be brought drunken forth, and I shall see
> Some squeaking Cleopatra boy my greatness
> I' th' posture of a whore. . . .
>   Now, Charmian!
> Show me, my women, like a queen; go fetch
> My best attires. I am again for Cydnus
> To meet Mark Antony. Sirrah Iras, go.
> Now, noble Charmian, we'll dispatch indeed,
> And when thou has done this chare, I'll give thee leave
> To play till doomsday.
>
> (5.2.207–21, 226–32)

And finally, Cleopatra opposes in one last passionate speech her coming Etherealized world to Octavius' impotent Ascetic one:

> Give me my robe, put on my crown, I have
> Immortal longing in me. Now no more
> The juice of Egypt's grape shall moist this lip.
> Yare, yare, good Iras; quick. Methinks I hear
> Antony call; I see him rouse himself
> To praise my noble act. I hear him mock
> The luck of Caesar, which the gods give men
> To excuse their after wrath. Husband, I come!
> Now to that name my courage prove my title!
> I am fire and air; my other elements
> I give to baser life. So, have you done?
> Come then, and take this last warmth of my lips.
> Farewell, kind Charmian, Iras, long farewell.
> (5.2.280–92)

In a sense, here Cleopatra gives both Antony and Octavius what they want. Octavius gets the base part of Cleopatra, the only part he ever thought existed, and Antony gets his eternal merger with the fire and air she has now become.

What the concluding scenes do, then, is provide a double Etherealization of the central relationship, first by Antony, then by Cleopatra. This Etherealization serves two purposes. First, it powerfully concludes the opposition between the heroic and the base. It is the last in a series of representations that make us feel as well as see the loss of the heroic world. In this sense, *Antony and Cleopatra* enacts for us one of the basic Elizabethan conceptions of society: the Christian and classical idea that current society is but the deteriorated shell of an ideal past. The lovers are not portrayed as ideal, faultless characters, but they are clearly made to seem more heroic—thus closer to the ideal—than Octavius, who like Bolingbroke in *Richard II* is the efficient but soulless politician of the modern age. The result, as Cleopatra puts it at the moment of Antony's death, is the reduction of society to the lowest common denominator:

> The crown o' th' earth doth melt. My lord!
> O, wither'd is the garland of the war,
> The soldier's pole is fall'n! Young boys and girls
> Are level now with men; the odds is gone,
> And there is nothing left remarkable
> Beneath the visiting moon.
> (4.15.63–68)

Her later portrait of the Rome to which Octavius wants to take her gives a graphic view of just such an undifferentiated and chaotic world. Cleopatra's

Rome is, of course, Shakespeare's London and our even more chaotic twentieth-century world, as well as *Antony and Cleopatra* itself. And Octavius is the Elizabethan view of "progress," and our view of modern leadership. The Antony and Cleopatra of the last scenes, on the other hand, are Shakespeare's attempt—via "quick comedians" and a "squeaking Cleopatra"—to intimate the lost Eden, the world that the lovers represent and eventually return to, the perfect world that all of us yearn to touch.

But at the same time that *Antony and Cleopatra* pushes us toward the ideal world, it also makes that world too alien and threatening to be fully accepted. Octavius' world may be chaotic in its lack of true heroes, but it is the only one that the play represents as practical. Octavius himself is mean-spirited in comparison with Antony, but he is also moderate and consistent. Antony, on the other hand, stands at the extremes of heroic individualism and all-consuming sexual union, and the play suggests that he cannot be emulated at either. His heroic individualism is attractive because it allows the breaking of basic moral and physical limitations, but a character who can eat meat that others die to look on and who can fight like a god even after a night of heroic drinking and feasting is not one who can be sympathized with or even understood. As with the Greek god and demigod upon whom he is based, we can only stand in awe of him.

Nor, finally, can we accept the cost of the Etherealized view of the central relationship. It is not the lovers' deaths or their loss of worldly power and possessions that makes the completeness of their final union threatening; death and rejection of materialism are easily valorized through our ethical system. Rather, the threat comes from the loss of individual control that the relationship produces. This loss is especially evident in Antony, who wants to be free even of fortune, but demonstrates throughout the play that his profoundest emotions and reactions are under the control of Cleopatra. Even in the first scene Cleopatra is able to play upon Antony's fear of domination by Fulvia and Octavius to elicit an Etherealized statement of devotion to her and their union. Two scenes later she tells us that she controls Antony by deliberately taking the opposite mood from his, and then proceeds quite obviously to manipulate his emotions throughout the scene. Other examples of Cleopatra's manipulative power abound, a particularly noticeable one being the exchange of clothing (recounted in 2.5). It is these manipulations, much more than the Ascetic denunciations by Octavius and others, that make us distrustful of the relationship, for they directly contradict our desire to see Antony as an heroic individual.

What we would like to see is the lovers enacting an Epic relationship, thereby neutralizing all the Ascetic descriptions. Instead, Antony seems to show just the weakness that Octavius ascribes to him. Antony, of course, also controls Cleopatra, as is shown by her lethargy and irrationality when he is gone, but the real point is that throughout the play, a weakened individual control is shown to be the product of the lovers' relationship. Try as they will, these two confident and powerful individuals cannot maintain complete hold on their identities and still love, as Antony proves at Actium by shockingly violating what seemed the most fixed aspect of his nature—his courage and soldiership. Even Antony does not know why he deserted the battle, but he does know that his only recourse is either rejection of his love—the Ascetic option—or an even more complete affirmation of it, the option he chooses (in his Etherealized speech ending 3.11). The result of this choice is continued personal dissolution, so much so that Antony eventually comes to compare his personal identity to a cloud that is one moment distinctly shaped, the next

> indistinct
> As water is in water. . . .
> My good knave Eros, now thy captain is
> Even such a body. Here I am Antony,
> Yet cannot hold this visible shape, my knave.
> (4.14.10–14)

Antony finds that love is dangerous to individuality and that the more complete the union, the less surely is one able to call himself his own. For Antony, as finally for us, the movement toward the final ecstatic union is too compelling to be resisted. But *Antony and Cleopatra* makes us understand that such a union can only be purchased at a terrible price.

Conclusion

Like any other Shakespearean, I hope that my readings contribute to our growing understanding of the love tragedies. But besides adding to what is in most cases a developing consensus, I hope that I have shed new light on how it is that we arrive at readings in the first place, how it is that a literary work induces readers to form similar meanings. Whatever light I have shed, however, is necessarily over only a small part of the procedure. There are many kinds of exterior systems that I have not treated, and the complex series of rules governing how we turn exterior systems into interior ones seems to me largely a mystery, except in vague outline. Even the systems I have examined deserve a treatment that better accounts for their historical development.

In setting up such categories as exterior and interior systems, I do not mean to imply that New Criticism is defective. It seems to me that the current opposition of this approach to structural and poststructural ones is false, since it is New Criticism that has returned us to the Aristotelian quest for the rules that control the reading process. Whatever ability we currently have to understand each other's response is largely in terms of New Critical insights, and future developments will be on this base. I see this work, then, as within a developing tradition, and hence as neither new nor static.

My contribution (and that of others involved in similar enterprises) is to work toward a more precise methodology for understanding the relationship of historical documents to language and to literary works. As it stands now, scholars often assume that historical influences on a play are straightforward and easily isolated. I hope that I have demonstrated that the most significant historical influences on a work (or more accurately, on the reader of a work) are the ones built into the conceptual systems without which reading could not proceed at all.

I wish, of course, that my understanding of the identity and interaction of the systems within the plays were more complete, or even somewhat less elementary, for if it were it would be possible to make a broader and more defensible analysis of how each text controls our response. But no matter how much we learn of this interaction, we will never completely define the process of reading literature, never completely close the mystery of the continual recreation of literature within the mind. Few of us would want it any other way, but at the same time few of us would deny the need to map out whatever part of the labyrinth we can discern. For the attraction of the labyrinth is that it is not just the story of great art, but of ourselves as well.

Notes

Index

Notes

Introduction

1. Roland Barthes, *S/Z,* tr. Richard Miller (New York: Hill and Wang, 1975). The more important works by the authors listed are described in numerous recent bibliographies, anthologies, and critical summaries.
2. The translation is from S. H. Butcher, tr., *Aristotle's Theory of Poetry and Fine Art,* 4th ed. (New York: Dover, 1955); other translations are similar, though the section is sometimes numbered 9 instead of 6.
3. I. A. Richards, *Practical Criticism* (New York: Harcourt, Brace, 1929).
4. Cleanth Brooks, *The Well Wrought Urn: Studies in the Structure of Poetry* (New York: Harcourt, Brace and World, 1947), p. 201.
5. The best study of semiotics is still Umberto Eco, *A Theory of Semiotics* (Bloomington: Indiana Univ. Press, 1976). Some of the more important semiotic approaches to literature are Vladimir Propp, *The Morphology of the Folktale,* tr. Lawrence Scott (Austin: Univ. of Texas Press, 1968); A. J. Greimas, *Semantique Structural* (Paris: Larousse, 1966); Roland Barthes, *The Pleasure of the Text,* tr. Richard Miller (New York: Hill and Wang, 1975); Jurij Lotman, *The Structure of the Artistic Text,* tr. Ronald Vroon, *Michigan Slavic Contributions,* 7 (1977); Tzvetan Todorov, *The Poetics of Prose,* tr. Richard Howard (Ithaca: Cornell Univ. Press, 1977); and Jacques Derrida, *Of Grammatology,* tr. Gayatri Chakravorty Spivak (Baltimore: Johns Hopkins Univ. Press, 1976). Among the best examples of semiotic approaches to specific literary works are the various essays in Umberto Eco, *The Role of the Reader* (Bloomington: Indiana Univ. Press, 1979) and *S/Z.*
6. On the use of cultural documents to establish the conceptual systems used in literature, see Stephen Greenblat, *Renaissance Self-Fashioning: From More to Shakespeare* (Chicago: Univ. of Chicago Press, 1980), as well as other works of the "new historiography."
7. For examples of this tendency gone wild, see Wallace Martin, *Recent Theories of Narrative* (Ithaca: Cornell Univ. Press, 1986).

8. Northrop Frye, *Anatomy of Criticism* (Princeton: Princeton Univ. Press, 1957), p. 172.

9. For other extended treatments of the love tragedies, see Franklin M. Dickey, *Not Wisely But Too Well* (San Marino, Calif.: Huntington Library, 1966); Lenora Leet Brodwin, *Elizabethan Love Tragedy, 1587–1625* (New York: New York Univ. Press, 1971); Roger Stilling, *Love and Death in Renaissance Tragedy* (Baton Rouge: Louisiana State Univ. Press, 1976); and Derik R. C. Marsch, *Passion Lends Them Power* (New York: Barnes and Noble, 1976).

10. Among many works by Holland arguing that meaning is mostly centered in the reader, see *Poems in Persons: An Introduction to the Psychoanalysis of Literature* (New York: Norton, 1973), *5 Readers Reading* (New Haven: Yale Univ. Press, 1975), and "Unity, Identity, Text, Self," *PMLA*, 90 (1975), 813–22. Two works by Bleich taking a similar position are *Subjective Criticism* (Baltimore: Johns Hopkins Univ. Press, 1978) and "The Logic of Interpretation," *Genre*, 10 (1977), 363–94. See also the collection of essays mostly from this perspective in Shoshana Felman, ed., *Literature and Psychoanalysis: The Question of Reading: Otherwise* (Baltimore: Johns Hopkins Univ. Press, 1982).

11. Fish's recent position is shown in several essays in *Is There a Text in This Class? The Authority of Interpretive Communication* (Cambridge: Harvard Univ. Press, 1980). His earlier text-centered approach can be seen in the two best examples of sustained reader-response criticism: *Surprised by Sin: The Reader in Paradise Lost* (New York: St. Martins, 1967), and *Self-Consuming Artifacts: The Experience of Seventeenth-Century Literature* (Berkeley: Univ. of California Press, 1972). Wolfgang Iser and Georges Poulet also locate meaning in the text: Iser, *The Act of Reading: A Theory of Aesthetic Response* (Baltimore: Johns Hopkins Univ. Press, 1978) and *The Implied Reader: Patterns of Communications in Prose Fiction from Bunyan to Beckett* (Baltimore: Johns Hopkins Univ. Press, 1974); Poulet, "Criticism and the Experience of Interiority," in Richard A. Macksey and Eugenio Donato, *The Structuralist Controversy: The Languages of Criticism and the Sciences of Man* (Baltimore: Johns Hopkins Univ. Press, 1972), pp. 56–72. For an excellent introduction to reader-response criticism, selection of essays, and annotated bibliography, see Jane P. Tompkins, *Reader Response Criticism: From Formalism to Post-Structuralism* (Baltimore: Johns Hopkins Univ. Press, 1980).

1/ *The Structure of Love: Then*

1. Augustine, *The City of God*, tr. Gerald Walsh and Grace Monahan, in Roy Joseph Deferrari, gen. ed., *The Fathers of the Church* (Washington: Catholic Univ. of America Press, 1952), 7:393–404 (bk. 14). On Early Christian views on women and sex, see Katherine M. Rogers, *The Troublesome Helpmate: A History of Misogyny in Literature* (Seattle: Univ. of Washington Press, 1966), pp. 14–22; Vern Bullough, *Sexual Variance in Society and History* (Chicago: Univ. of Chicago Press, 1976), pp. 159–204; John Boswell, *Christianity, Social Tolerance, and Homosexuality* (Chicago: Univ. of Chicago Press, 1980), pp. 61–168; and Reay Tannahill, *Sex in History* (New York: Stein and Day, 1980), pp. 136–61.

2. On the history of misogyny, see Rogers, *Troublesome Helpmate*.

3. Tertullian, "On the Apparel of Women," *The Ante-Nicene Fathers,* ed. A. C. Coxe (New York: Charles Scribner's Sons, 1925), 4:19; Chrysostom, "An Exhortation to Theodore after His Fall," *Nicene and Post-Nicene Fathers,* ed. Phillip Schaff (Grand Rapids, Mich.: Eerdmans, 1956), 9:104.

4. Aquinas, *Summa Theologia,* tr. Fathers of the English Dominican Province, 3

vols. (New York: Benziger Brothers, 1947): on marriage and sexuality, Suppl., q.41–42; on women, 1:q.92 and 1:q.99, a.1; on the formation of children, II–II, q.26, a,10. On the relation of women and sex to medieval asceticism, see Rogers, *Troublesome Helpmate*, pp. 65–77; Tannahill, pp. 256–82; C. S. Lewis, *The Allegory of Love* (1936; rpt. Oxford: Oxford Univ. Pres, 1975), pp. 113–240; Joan M. Ferrante, *Woman as Image in Medieval Literature* (New York: Columbia Univ. Press, 1975), pp. 17–64, 101–5; and Charles and Katherine George, *The Protestant Mind of the English Reformation, 1570–1640* (Princeton: Princeton Univ. Press, 1961), pp. 261–63.

5. Bromyard, "Luxuria," from *Summa Predicantium* (c. 1350), excerpt translated in G. R. Owst, *Literature and Pulpit in Medieval England*, 2d ed. (New York: Barnes and Noble, 1961), p. 395.

6. Heinrich Kramer and James Sprenger, *Malleus Maleficarum* (1486), tr. and ed. Montague Summers (1928; rpt. New York: Dover, 1971), p. 47. On the number of German women accused of witchcraft, see H. C. Erik Midelfort, *Witch Hunting in South-western Germany: The Social and Intellectual Foundations* (Stanford: Stanford Univ. Press, 1972), pp. 89–137; see also Jeffrey Burton Russell, *Witchcraft in the Middle Ages* (Ithaca: Cornell Univ. Press, 1972); Keith Thomas, *Religion and the Decline of Magic* (New York: Charles Scribner's Sons, 1971) pp. 435–83; and Lawrence Stone, "Magic, Religion and Reason," *The Past and the Present* (London: Routledge and Kegan Paul, 1981), pp. 154–74.

7. More, *Utopia*, tr. H. V. S. Ogden (Northbrook, Ill.: Crofts Classics, 1949), pp. 51–52.

8. Bacon, *Essays* (London: Oxford Univ. Press, 1947), pp. 39–40.

9. Burton, *The Anatomy of Melancholy* (London: Dent, 1932), 2:3, 49.

10. Heywood, *Of Actors and the True Use of Their Quality*, in *English Literary Criticism: The Renaissance*, ed. O. B. Hardison (New York: Appleton-Century-Crofts, 1963), p. 228.

11. Lyly, *Euphues: The Anatomy of Wit and Euphues and His England*, ed. M. W. Croll and Harry Clemons (London: Routledge, 1916), p. 10.

12. Graham Hough, ed., *Sir John Harington's Translation of Orlando Furioso* (Carbondale: Southern Illinois Univ. Press, 1962), 28.21, 73.

13. For descriptions of these and other tracts on the virtues of women, see Louis B. Wright, *Middle-Class Culture in Elizabethan England* (Ithaca: Cornell Univ. Press, 1958), pp. 465–507; and Chilton Lathan Powell, *English Domestic Relations, 1487–1653* (New York: Columbia Univ. Press, 1917), pp. 147–78.

14. Citations are to Thomas Middleton and William Rowley, *The Changeling*, ed. N. W. Bawcutt (Cambridge: Harvard Univ. Press, 1958).

15. Citations are to John Webster, *The Duchess of Malfi*, ed. John Russell Brown (Cambridge: Harvard Univ. Press, 1964). Other editions mark these lines as 1.2.152–54 and place the other quotations in scene 2 as well.

16. Line 6; all citations to Shakespeare's works are to G. Blakemore Evans, ed., *The Riverside Shakespeare* (Boston: Houghton Mifflin, 1974).

17. All citations are to Fredson Bowers, ed., *The Complete Works of Christopher Marlowe* (Cambridge: Cambridge Univ. Press, 1973), vol. 2.

18. Walter R. Davis, ed., *The Works of Thomas Campion* (London: Faber and Faber, 1969), p. 22.

19. I (A), 3275, in F. N. Robinson, *The Works of Geoffrey Chaucer*, 2d ed. (Boston: Houghton Mifflin, 1957); all Chaucer citations are to this edition.

20. Hugh MacDonald, ed., *Englands Helicon* (Cambridge: Harvard Univ. Press, 1950), p. 193.

21. Camoëns, *The Lusiads,* tr. William C. Atkinson (Middlesex, Eng.: Penguin Books, 1952), p. 216. See A. Bartlett Giamatti, *The Earthly Paradise and the Renaissance Epic* (Princeton: Princeton Univ. Press, 1966), pp. 215–26. For a view of the Island of Venus as allegory only, see Norwood H. Andrews, Jr., "An Essay on Comoës' Concept of the Epic," *Revista de Letras de Faculdade de Filosofia Ciencias e Letras de Assis,* 3 (1962), 61–93.

22. See Lewis, pp. 26–32; and Ferrante, pp. 65–97.

23. Andreas Capellanus, *The Art of Courtly Love,* tr. John Jay Parry (New York: Columbia Univ. Press, 1941), p. 73; all citations to Andreas are to this edition. On the question of Andreas's seriousness, see N. K. Coghill, "Love and 'Foul Delight': Some Contrasted Attitudes," in *Patterns of Love and Courtesy,* ed. John Lawlor (Evanston: Northwestern Univ. Press, 1966), pp. 141–56).

24. Baldassare Castiglione, *The Book of the Courtier,* tr. Charles S. Singleton (Garden City, N.Y.: Anchor Books, 1959), p. 354.

25. Sixteenth-century neoplatonism was, of course, much more complicated and varied than my brief comment suggests. Specifically, scholars such as Varchi, Equicola, and Betussi denied the absolute distinction between the spirit and sexuality; the most prominent of this school was Leone Ebreo, who in his influential *Dialoghi d'Amore* (1535) went so far as to claim that "with the correspondence of the bodily union, the spiritual love is augmented and made more perfect." This view did not, however, have much noticeable impact on Continental literature, and the idealized sexuality it suggests is only found in some Elizabethan literature, as will be discussed shortly. The quotation from Leone is from A. J. Smith, "The Metaphysic of Love," in Frank Kermode, ed., *Discussions of John Donne* (Boston: Heath, 1962), pp. 150–60; see especially T. Antony Perry, *Erotic Spirituality: The Integrative Tradition from Leone Ebreo to John Donne* (University: Univ. of Alabama Press, 1980). On the subjects of Dante's and Petrarch's relationship to the courtly love tradition, see Colin Hardie, "Dante and the Tradition of Courtly Love," in Lawlor, pp. 26–44; L. F. Mott, *The System of Courtly Love Studied as an Introduction to the Vita neuova of Dante* (Boston: Ginn, 1896); Robert M. Durling, tr. *Petrarch's Lyric Poems* (Cambridge: Harvard Univ. Press, 1976), pp. 1–35; J. W. Lever, *The Elizabethan Love Sonnet* (London: Methuen, 1956), pp. 1–13; and Lisle Cecil John, *The Elizabethan Sonnet Sequences* (New York: Russell and Russel, 1964), pp. 26–32.

26. For an analysis of how one English sequence differs from Petrarch's, see David Kalstone, *Sidney's Poetry* (Cambridge: Harvard Univ. Press, 1965), pp. 105–32. See also John, pp. 1–78; and Lever, pp. 1–13.

27. For a description of the standard Petrarchan relationship, see Richard B. Young, "English Petrarke: A Study of Sidney's *Astrophel and Stella,*" *Yale Studies in English,* 138 (1958), 10–15.

28. Daniel, *"Poems" and "A Defence of Rhyme",* ed. Arthur C. Sprague (Cambridge: Harvard Univ. Press, 1930); all citations to Daniel are to this edition.

29. All citations are to *The Poems of Sir Philip Sidney,* ed. William A. Ringler, Jr. (Oxford: Clarendon Press, 1962).

30. Wyatt citations are to Kenneth Muir, ed., *Collected Poems* (Cambridge: Harvard Univ. Press, 1950).

31. This poem is in imitation of a *baiser,* a flamboyant poetic form popularized after Petrarch's time; like the other songs, this one is usually dismissed by critics as inferior because of its difference from the rest of the sequence. See Ringler, pp. xiv and 480; Kalstone, pp. 175–76; and Jane G. Scott, *Les Sonnets elisabethains* (Paris: Champion, 1929), pp. 58–62.

32. See *Orlando Furioso,* canto 6. Young, pp. 73–76, discusses Stella as violating

her responsibilities as a lover and cites Ficino's commentary on the subject. According to Ficino, "Anyone who is loved ought in very justice to love in return, and he who does not love his lover must bear the charge of homocide, nay rather, the triple charge of thief, homocide and desecrator" (*Symposium*, tr. S. R. Jayne [New York: Columbia Univ. Press, 1944], p. 145). See Ringler, p. 484, on the possibility that this song was composed earlier than the sonnets.

33. This and other poems addressed to the young man have received considerable biographical attention; for examples, see Stephen Booth, *Shakespeare's Sonnets* (New Haven: Yale Univ. Press, 1977), pp. 447–48. For other types of analyses, see Murry Krieger, *A Window to Criticism* (Princeton: Princeton Univ. Press, 1964), pp. 80–117; James Winney, *The Master-Mistress* (London: Chatto and Windus, 1968), pp. 145–69; Katharine M. Wilson, *Shakespeare's Sugared Sonnets* (New York: Barnes and Noble, 1974), pp. 146–71; and Booth, pp. 145–61.

34. For commentary on sonnet 131, see Winny, pp. 95–96; Wilson, pp. 93–95; and especially Booth, pp. 455–57, and for more general information on the "Dark Lady" group, pp. 434–533.

35. *Aeneid*, tr. H. Rushton Fairclough (Cambridge: Harvard Univ. Press, 1950), 2.261–64.

36. Torquato Tasso, *Jerusalem Delivered*, tr. Edward Fairfax (1600; rpt. New York: Capricorn Books, n.d.); all citations to Tasso are to this edition.

37. All citations to Spenser are to J. C. Smith and E. de Selincourt, eds., *Spenser: Poetical Works* (London: Oxford Univ. Press, 1912). See Giamatti, pp. 150–61, 202–8, 277–80; Lewis, pp. 319–30; Harry Berger, Jr., *The Allegorical Temper* (New Haven: Yale Univ. Press, 1957), pp. 211–40; and Merritt Y. Hughes, "Spenser's Acrasia and the Circe of the Renaissance," *Journal of the History of Ideas*, 4 (1943), 331–99.

38. See Edgar Wind, *Pagan Mysteries of the Renaissance* (New Haven: Yale Univ. Press, 1958), pp. 84–96; and Janet Adleman, *The Common Liar* (New Haven: Yale Univ. Press, 1973), pp. 80–101. For citations to the comments of Ficino, Boccaccio, Pico, Comes, Hesiod, Pausanias, Ovid, and Statius, see James Nohrnberg, *The Analogy of the Faerie Queene* (Princeton: Princeton Univ. Press, 1976), pp. 458–59. On Venus' role as a generative force, see Nohrnberg, pp. 519–68.

39. William Perkins, *Works* (Cambridge, 1616), 1:391. For fuller treatments of the Elizabethan attitude toward sex and marriage, see especially Lawrence Stone, *The Family, Sex, and Marriage in England, 1500–1800* (New York: Harper and Row, 1977), pp. 123–218; see also idem, *The Crisis of the Aristocracy, 1558–1641* (Oxford: Oxford Univ. Press, 1965), pp. 589–671; Wright, pp. 201–27; Powell, pp. 28–48, 101–46; George, pp. 257–76; and William and Malleville Haller, "The Puritan Art of Love," *Huntington Library Quarterly*, 5 (1941–42), 235–72.

40. Daniel Rogers, *Matrimoniall Honoure* (London, 1642), p. 148.

41. William Whately, *The Bride-Bush* (London, 1617), pp. 70–71, 31.

42. *A Defence of Poetry*, ed. Jan Van Dorsten (Oxford: Oxford Univ. Press, 1966), pp. 32, 23–24.

43. The commentary on this episode is enormous, but on the sexual implications of the Garden and their relationship to various classical, medieval, and Renaissance traditions, see especially Nohrnberg, pp. 519–68.

44. See Lewis, pp. 344–45; T. P. Roche, *The Kindly Flame: A Study of the Third and Fourth Books of Spenser's Faerie Queene* (Princeton: Princeton Univ. Press, 1964), pp. 133–36; Mark Rose, *Heroic Love: Studies in Sidney and Spenser* (Cambridge: Harvard Univ. Press, 1968), pp. 127–28; and A. J. Smith, *The Metaphysics of Love: Studies in Renaissance Love Poetry from Dante to Milton* (Cambridge:

Cambridge Univ. Press, 1985), pp. 178–80. On the relationship of marriage and the Hermaphrodite, see Nohrnberg, pp. 599–604.

45. All citations to Donne's Poetry are to Helen Gardner, ed. *John Donne: The Elegies and The Songs and Sonnets* (Oxford: Clarendon, 1965).

46. Cleanth Brooks, "The Language of Paradox," *The Well Wrought Urn* (New York: Harcourt, Brace and World, 1947), pp. 3–21. On Donne and Leone, see note 20; Smith, *The Metaphysics of Love*, pp. 195–204; and Helen Gardner, "The Argument about 'The Ecstacy,'" in Herbert Davis and Helen Gardner, eds., *Elizabethan and Jacobean Studies Presented to F. P. Wilson* (Oxford: Clarenden, 1974), pp. 279–306.

47. On the Elizabethan understanding of flies, see A. B. Chambers, "The Fly in Donne's 'Canonization,'" *JEGP*, 65 (1966), 252–59; on hermaphroditic figures, see Nohrnberg, pp. 599–604. On the poem and platonic love, see Donald L. Guss, "Donne's Conceit and Petrarchan Wit," *PMLA*, 78 (1963), 308–14. See also Clay Hunt, *Donne's Poetry: Essays in Literary Analysis* (1954; rpt. Hamden, Conn.: Archon Books, 1969), pp. 79–95; Murry Roston, *The Soul of Wit: A Study of John Donne* (Oxford: Clarendon, 1974), pp. 1–20, 108–49; and Rosalie Colie, "The Rhetoric of Transcendence," *Philological Quarterly*, 43 (1964), 145–70.

2/ *The Structure of Love: Now*

1. Citations are to John Milton, *Complete Poems and Major Prose*, ed. Merritt Y. Hughes (Indianapolis: Bobbs-Merrill, 1957).
2. M. Lafayette Byrn, *The Book of Nature* (New York: Hurst, 1875), p. 57.
3. B. G. Jefferis and J. L. Nichols, *Search Lights on Health: Light on Dark Corners, a Complete Sexual Science* (1895; rpt. Naperville, Ill.: J. L. Nichols, 1920), p. 114.
4. Joseph Johnson, *Willing Hearts and Ready Hands, or the Labours and Triumphs of Earnest Women* (London: T. Nelson and Sons, 1869), pp. 39–40.
5. William Walling, *Sexology* (Philadelphia: Puritan, 1904), p. 120.
6. Charles Kingsley, *Yeast* (London: Macmillan, 1908), p. 18. My discussion of the Ascetic in nineteenth- and twentieth-century literature is indebted to the parallel discussions of misogyny in Katharine M. Rogers, *The Troublesome Helpmate: A Study of Misogyny in Literature* (Seattle: Univ. of Washington Press, 1966); on representations of women in nineteenth-century fiction, see Françoise Basch, *Relative Creatures: Victorian Women in Society*, tr. Antony Rudolf (New York: Schocken, 1974).
7. Quoted in Elizabeth Cady Stanton, Susan B. Anthony, and Matilda Joslyn Cage, eds., *History of Women's Suffrage* (New York: Fowler and Wells, 1881), 1:556.
8. H. L. Mencken, *In Defense of Women* (1918), in *A Mencken Chrestomathy* (New York: Knopf, 1949), p. 37.
9. Ernest Hemingway, *For Whom the Bell Tolls* (New York: Charles Scribner's Sons, 1940), p. 349.
10. D. H. Lawrence, *Fantasia of the Unconscious* (New York: Thomas Seltzer, 1922), pp. 280–81, 284.
11. D. H. Lawrence, *Lady Chatterley's Lover* (1928; rpt New York: Grove, 1959), p. 149.
12. D. H. Lawrence, *Studies in Classic American Literature* (1923; rpt. New York: Viking, 1964), pp. 88–89.
13. William Faulkner, *The Hamlet*, 3d ed. (New York: Random House, 1964), pp. 100, 115.

14. William Faulkner, *Mosquitoes* (New York: Liveright, 1927), p. 241.
15. William Faulkner, *Sanctuary* (New York: Random House, 1931), pp. 182, 287–88.
16. William Faulkner, *Sartoris* (New York: Random House, 1929), pp. 178, 257.
17. Written by Otis Blackwell and Elvis Presley (Unart Music Company, 1957).
18. F. Scott Fitzgerald, *The Great Gatsby* (New York: Charles Scribner's Sons, 1925), pp. 149, 154.
19. P. 288.
20. Philip Wylie, *Generation of Vipers* (New York: Farrar and Rinehart, 1942), pp. 188–89; see also Mencken, p. 35.
21. Norman Mailer, *The Short Fiction of Norman Mailer* (New York: Howard Fertig, 1980), p. 252.
22. Marie Stopes, *Married Love* (1918; rpt. Garden City, N.Y.: Sundial Press, 1943), p. 22.
23. Erica Jong, *Fear of Flying* (New York: New American Library, 1973), p. 11.
24. Marabel Morgan, *The Total Woman* (1973; rpt. New York: Pocket Books, 1975), p. 128.

3/ Creating the Heroine

1. On the subject of Shakespeare's women and their relationship to modern representations of women, see Juliet Dusinberre, *Shakespeare and the Nature of Women* (New York: Barnes and Noble, 1975) and various essays in Carolyn Ruth Swift Lenz, Gail Greene, and Carol Thomas Neely, eds., *The Woman's Part: Feminist Criticism of Shakespeare* (Urbana: Univ. of Illinois Press, 1980). For psychoanalytic approaches to the representation of Shakespeare's women, see Coppelia Kahn, *Man's Estate: Masculine Identity in Shakespeare* (Berkeley and Los Angeles: Univ. of California Press, 1981); and W. Thomas MacCary, *Friends and Lovers: The Phenomenology of Desire in Shakespearean Comedy* (New York: Columbia Univ. Press, 1981).
2. All Citations to Lodge's *Rosalynde* are to Geoffrey Bullough, *Narrative and Dramatic Sources of Shakespeare*, 8 vols. (New York: Columbia Univ. Press, 1957–63), 2:158–256.
3. On Rosalind, see C. L. Barber, "The Use of Comedy in *As You Like It*," *Philological Quarterly*, 21 (1942), 353–67; Helen Gardner, "As You Like It," in John Garrett, ed., *More Talking of Shakespeare* (London: Longmans, Green, 1959), pp. 17–32; and Marco Mincoff, "What Shakespeare Did to Rosalynde," *Shakespeare Jahrbuch*, 96 (1960), 79–89; Alexander Leggatt, *Shakespeare's Comedy of Love* (London: Methuen, 1974), pp. 184–219; and Hugh Richmond, *Shakespeare's Sexual Comedy* (Indianapolis: Bobbs-Merrill, 1971), pp. 137–46.
4. On Orlando, see Thomas Kelly, "Shakespeare's Romantic Heroes: Orlando Reconsidered," *SQ*, 24 (1973), 12–24; and Mark Bracher, "Contrary Notions of Identity in *As You Like It*," *SEL*, 24 (1984), 228–32.
5. On the parodic love relationships in this play, see C. L. Barber, "The Use of Comedy in *As You Like It*, " pp. 353–67.
6. Barber, *Shakespeare's Festive Comedy* (Princeton: Princeton Univ. Press, 1959), pp. 232–39.
7. See note 3.
8. Dusinberre, pp. 5–19.
9. Herbert Ellis, *Shakespeare's Lusty Punning in Love's Labour's Lost* (Paris: Mouton, 1973); for a more comprehensive view of the language of the play, see

William Carroll, *The Great Feast of Language in Love's Labour's Lost* (Princeton: Princeton Univ. Press, 1976). See also E. A. M. Coleman, *The Dramatic Use of Bawdy in Shakespeare* (London: Longman, 1974), pp. 13–45.

10. See, for example, Peter G. Phialas, *Shakespeare's Romantic Comedies* (Chapel Hill: Univ. of North Carolina Press, 1966), pp. 78–83; and J. Dennis Huston, *Shakespeare's Comedies of Play* (New York: Columbia Univ. Press, 1981), pp. 52–57. Marilyn French's feminist reading makes essentially the same point: *Shakespeare's Division of Experience* (New York: Summit Books, 1981), pp. 93–96. For a contrasting view, see Leggatt, pp. 85–88.

11. On the Claudio question, see Nadine Page, "The Public Repudiation of Hero," *PMLA*, 50 (1935), 739–44; T. W. Craik, "Much Ado about Nothing," *Scrutiny*, 19 (1953), 297–316; Kerby Neill, "More Ado about Claudio: An Acquittal for the Slandered Groom," *SQ*, 3 (1952), 91–107; Robert G. Hunter, *Shakespeare and the Comedy of Forgiveness* (New York: Columbia Univ. Press, 1965), pp. 98–105; and Leggatt, pp. 153–67. For a different perspective on Don Pedro, see William G. McCollom, "The Role of Wit in *Much Ado about Nothing*," *SQ*, 29 (1968), 165–74.

12. *Orlando Furioso*, bk. 5. On the sources in general, see Charles T. Prouty, *The Sources of Much Ado about Nothing* (New Haven: Yale Univ. Press, 1950); and Bullough, 2:61–142.

13. Hunter, pp. 104–5. For a relation of the ending to sacrificial and other religious motifs, see Arthur Kirsch, *Shakespeare and the Experience of Love"* (Cambridge: Cambridge Univ. Press, 1981); see also Delora G. Cunningham, "Wonder and Love in the Romantic Comedies," *SQ*, 35 (1984), 262–64.

14. See Carol Thomas Neely, *Broken Nuptials in Shakespeare's Plays* (New Haven: Yale Univ. Press, 1985), pp. 45–46.

15. See ibid., pp. 46–49.

16. The best extended study of this play is David P. Young, *Something of Great Constancy* (New Haven: Yale Univ. Press, 1966). Essays relating to my analysis include Ernest Schanzer, "The Central Theme of *A Midsummer Night's Dream*," *University of Toronto Quarterly*, 20 (1951), 233–38; Barber, *Festive Comedy*, pp. 119–57; Paul Olsen, "*A Midsummer Night's Dream* and the Meaning of Court Marriage," *ELH* 24 (1957), 95–119; Paul Siegel, "*A Midsummer Night's Dream* and the Wedding Guests," *SQ*, 4 (1953), 139–44; Frank Kermode, "The Mature Comedies," in *Early Shakespeare*, Stratford Upon Avon Studies, 3 (New York: St. Martins, 1961), pp. 214–20; and Charles R. Lyons, *Shakespeare and the Ambiguity of Love's Triumph* (Paris: Mouton, 1971), pp. 21–43.

17. When Artegal defeats Britomart in *F.Q.* 4.6, he splits open her helmet, immediately falls in love with her, and then begins to act like a Petrarchan lover; this scene is an expansion of Rogero and Bradmante's first meeting, in *Orlando Furioso*, canto 4.

18. Several critics view Theseus as the moral center of the play, for example, H. B. Charlton, *Shakespearean Comedy* (London: Methuen, 1938), p. 122; and Olsen, pp. 101–3. Young, pp. 137–40, and Lyons, pp. 28–35, present more balanced analyses.

19. On the lovers in the woods, see especially Young, pp. 61–108.

20. On the relationship of the marriages to the structure of the play and to the play's possible original purpose as a marriage entertainment, see Siegel and Olsen. On oppositions and transformations in the play, see Young, pp. 151–66, and Barber, *Festive Comedy*, pp. 135–37.

4 / The Paradise of Flesh

1. See, for example, H. A. Mason, *Shakespeare's Tragedies of Love* (New York: Barnes and Noble, 1970), pp. 3–23.
2. Hence the frequent claim that the play is an immature work. See Mark Van Doren, *Shakespeare* (1939; rpt. New York: Doubleday, 1953), pp. 51–61; H. B. Charlton, *Shakespearean Tragedy* (Cambridge: Cambridge Univ. Press, 1948), pp. 49–63; and G. I. Duthie's introduction to the New Cambridge edition of the play, Duthie and John Dover Wilson, eds. (Cambridge: Cambridge Univ. Press, 1963).
3. On the parody of the feud in this scene, see James H. Seward, *Tragic Vision in Romeo and Juliet* (Washington: Consortium Press, 1973), pp. 59–63.
4. On the use of comic patterns throughout the play, see Susan Snyder, *The Comic Matrix of Shakespeare's Tragedies* (Princeton: Princeton Univ. Press, 1979), pp. 56–70. On the mixture of comedy and threat in this scene, see Derik R. C. Marsch, *Passion Lends Them Power* (New York: Barnes and Noble, 1976), pp. 53–54.
5. On balanced scene design in this and other Shakespearean plays, see Mark Rose, *Shakespearean Design* (Cambridge: Harvard Univ. Press, 1972).
6. For more complete analyses of Romeo's love melancholy, see Franklin M. Dickey, *Not Wisely But Too Well* (San Marino, Calif.: Huntington Library, 1966), pp. 75–82; and Seward, pp. 63–69.
7. Harry Levin similarly contrasts the lovers' mutuality to earlier polarities in "Form and Formality in *Romeo and Juliet*," *SQ*, 11 (1960), 3–11.
8. The most useful studies of the play's imagery are Caroline F. E. Spurgeon, *Shakespeare's Imagery and What It Tells Us* (Cambridge: Cambridge Univ. Press, 1935), pp. 310–16; Donald A. Stauffer, *Shakespeare's World of Images* (New York: Norton, 1949), pp. 53–59; W. H. Clemen, *The Development of Shakespeare's Imagery* (London: Methuen, 1951), pp. 63–73; and M. M. Mahood, *Shakespeare's Wordplay* (London: Methuen, 1957), pp. 56–72.
9. This idea is from Denis de Rougemont, *Love in the Western World*, tr. Montgomery Belgion (New York: Random House, 1956). On the possible application of the *Liebestod* myth to *Romeo and Juliet* especially, see Mahood, pp. 56–72.
10. For two other perspectives on Romeo's refusal to fight, see Curtis Brown Watson, *Shakespeare and the Renaissance Concept of Honor* (Princeton: Princeton Univ. Press, 1960), p. 356, and Raymond V. Utterback, "The Death of Mercutio," *SQ*, 24 (1973), 107–12.
11. Levin, p. 5.
12. Geoffrey Bullough, *Narrative and Dramatic Sources of Shakespeare*, 8 vols. (New York: Columbia Univ. Press, 1957), 1:357, line 2788.
13. *Shakespeare's Living Art* (Princeton: Princeton Univ. Press, 1974), p. 145.
14. See Norman Rabkin, *Shakespeare and the Common Understanding* (New York: Free Press, 1967), pp. 181–84; Stauffer, pp. 57–58; and Siegel, pp. 383–92.

5 / Magic in the Structure

1. Carol McGinnis Kay, "Othello's Need for Mirrors, *SQ*, 34 (1983), 261–70.
2. G. B. Shaw, "A Word More about Verdi," *Anglo-Saxon Review*, March 1901, pp. 221–29; and T. S. Eliot, "Shakespeare and the Stoicism of Seneca," reprinted in *Elizabethan Essays* (New York: Haskell House, 1964), pp. 38–40. Their view was forcefully expanded by William Empson, "Honest in *Othello*," in *The Structure of Complex Words* (London: Chatto and Windus, 1951), pp. 218–49; F. R. Leavis,

"Diabolic Intellect and the Noble Moor," in *The Common Pursuit* (London: Chatto and Windus, 1952), pp. 152–59; D. A. Traversi, *An Approach to Shakespeare*, 3d ed. (New York: Doubleday, 1960); and Leslie Fiedler, *The Stranger in Shakespeare* (New York: Stein and Day, 1972), pp. 134–95. Leavis and Traversi both specifically contrast themselves with the heroic view of Othello by A. C. Bradley in *Shakespearean Tragedy*, 2d ed. (London: MacMillan, 1905), 186–98. Two others who take this view are H. Granville-Barker, *Prefaces to Shakespeare* (London: B. T. Batsford, 1958), 2:3–149; and G. Wilson Knight, *The Wheel of Fire* (London: Oxford Univ. Press, 1930), pp. 107–31. E. K. Chambers also uses this approach, but with a bizarre definition of heroism, in *Shakespeare: A Survey* (New York: Hill and Wang, 1925), pp. 218–25. Overall studies of the play include Robert B. Heilman, *Magic in the Web* (Lexington: Univ. of Kentucky Press, 1956); G. R. Eliot, *Flaming Minister: A Study of Othello* (Durham: Duke Univ. Press, 1953); and Jane Adamson, *Othello as Tragedy: Some Problems of Judgment and Feeling* (London: Cambridge Univ. Press, 1980).

On the critical history of this play, see Helen Gardner, "*Othello*: A Retrospective, 1900–1967," *Shakespeare Survey*, 21 (1968), pp. 1–11; Norman Sanders, ed., *The New Cambridge Shakespeare: Othello* (Cambridge: Cambridge Univ. Press, 1984), pp. 17–30; and Carol Thomas Neely, *Broken Nuptials in Shakespeare's Plays* (New Haven: Yale Univ. Press, 1985), pp. 105–8.

3. For example, see E. E. Stoll, *Shakespeare and Other Masters* (Cambridge: Harvard Univ. Press, 1940), pp. 190–280; Bernard Spivack, *Shakespeare and the Allegory of Evil* (New York: Columbia Univ. Press, 1958), pp. 3–27, 415–53; Stanley Edgar Hyman, *Iago: Some Illusions of His Motivation* (New York: Atheneum, 1970); and Stephen Greenblat, *Renaissance Self-Fashioning: From More to Shakespeare* (Chicago: Univ. of Chicago Press, 1980), pp. 222–54.

4. Othello's 861 lines represent 26% of the 3,272 lines in *Othello*; in contrast, Hamlet has 39% of his play's lines (1,509 out of 3,832), and Macbeth has 33% of his (691 out of 2,095).

5. For a provacative view of the overall relationship of *Othello* to comedy, especially Shakespeare's comedies, see Susan Snyder, *The Comic Matrix of Shakespeare's Tragedies* (Princeton: Princeton Univ. Press, 1979), pp. 70–90; see also Neely; Fiedler, pp. 139–45; Barbara H. C. de Mendonca, "Othello: A Tragedy Built on a Comic Structure," *Shakespeare Studies*, 21 (1968), pp. 31–38; Roger Stilling, *Love and Death in Renaissance Tragedy* (Baton Rouge: Louisiana State Univ. Press, 1976), pp. 145–54; and Norman Rabkin, *Shakespeare and the Common Understanding* (New York: Free Press, 1967), pp. 63–64.

6. See Rabkin, pp. 64–68.

7. For character-based studies of Desdemona as less than perfect, see Robert Speaight, *Nature in Shakespearean Tragedy* (London: Hollis and Carter, 1955), p. 74; Richard Flatter, *The Moor of Venice* (London: Heinemann, 1955), pp. 102–7; and M. L. Renald, "The Indiscretions of Desdemona," *SQ*, 14 (1965), 127–39. See also Neely, pp. 105–35.

8. For an example of the usual explanation that Desdemona is worrying about Othello and not really paying much attention to the conversation, see John Bayley, *The Characters of Love: A Study of the Literature of Personality* (London: Chatto and Windus, 1960), pp. 153–54.

9. Two obvious uses of "eye" in this way are in *Love's Labor's Lost* and *The Changeling*:

> [A woman is] A whitely wanton with a velvet brow,
> With two pitch-balls stuck in her face for eyes,

> Ay, and, by heaven, one that will do the deed
> Though Argus were her eunuch and her guard.
> (3.1.196–99)

> a woman, they say, has an eye more than a man.
>
> (3.3.79–80)

10. For a similar account of the two views of love in the play, see Bayley, pp. 129–36; and Rabkin, pp. 64–71.

11. For a way to see this scene as building, rather than destroying, love and communication, see Bayley, *Characters of Love*, pp. 164–71.

12. For a discussion of Othello's depravity in these scenes, see Leavis, pp. 144–48.

13. For a different view of Desdemona as witch, see Fiedler, pp. 141–42.

14. For a related discussion of Emilia's structural function, see Howard Felperin, *Shakespearean Representation* (Princeton: Princeton Univ. Press, 1977), pp. 81–82.

6/ Words, Words, Mere Words

1. Kenneth Muir, for example, sees the play as a rejection of the foolishness and evil of some men, but not of value in general; Nevil Coghill sees support for the Trojans and their idealism; Carolyn Asp sees a rejection of idealism and courtly love and an affirmation of a "realistic, moral, and rational view of life"; Norman Council sees the rejection of one form of honor as implying support for another; and Juliet Dusinberre sees the play as condemning an understanding of beauty based on a person, but supporting the beauty of creation itself. (Muir, "Troilus and Cressida," *Shakespeare Survey*, 8 [1955], 28–39; Coghill, *Shakespeare's Professional Skills* [London: Cambridge Univ. Press, 1964], pp. 76–126; Asp, "Th' Expense of Spirit in a Waste of Shame," *SQ*, 22 [1971], 345–57; Council, *When Honour's at the Stake: Ideas of Honor in Shakespeare's Plays* [New York: Barnes and Noble, 1973], pp. 75–88; and Dusinberre, "*Troilus and Cressida* and the Definition of Beauty," *Shakespeare Survey* 36 [1983], 85–95).

2. Two convincing arguments for a nihilistic thesis are Una Ellis-Fermor, *The Frontiers of Drama* (London: Methuen, 1945), pp. 56–76; and Alice Shalvi, "Honor in *Troilus and Cressida*," *SEL*, 5 (1965), 283–302. Others who stop just short of nihilism include L. C. Knights, "*Troilus and Cressida* Again," *Scrutiny*, 18 (1951), 144–57; Robert Ornstein, *The Moral Vision of Jacobean Tragedy* (Madison: Univ. of Wisconsin Press, 1960), pp. 240–49; and Camille Slights, "The Parallel Structure of *Troilus and Cressida*," *SQ*, 25 (1974), 42–51.

3. For discussion of Thersites and his function in the play, see Ellis-Fermor, pp. 68–69; and Oscar J. Campbell, *Comicall Satyre and Shakespeare's Troilus and Cressida* (San Marino, Calif.: Huntington Library, 1938), pp. 201–5.

4. For other discussions of the first scene, see W. W. Lawrence, *Shakespeare's Problem Comedies* (1931; rpt. New York: Frederick Ungar, 1960), pp. 142–43; Elias Schwartz, "Tonal Equivocation and the Meaning of *Troilus and Cressida*," *Studies in Philology*, 49 (1972), 305–7; Asp, pp. 350–51; and French, pp. 162–64.

5. F. N. Robinson, ed., *The Works of Geoffrey Chaucer*, 2d ed. (Boston: Houghton Mifflin, 1957). For a comparison of Shakespeare's and Chaucer's approaches to the story, see M. C. Bradbrook, "What Shakespeare Did to Chaucer's *Troilus and Criseyde*," *SQ*, 9 (1958), 311–19.

182 / Notes

6. See 2 *Henry IV* 2.4.125–26, where Doll tells Pistol that "I am meat for your master."
7. Campbell, p. 212.
8. Two of those whose interpretations I do not agree with are Campbell, pp. 211–13, and Asp, pp. 52–56. Slights, pp. 46–47, is much closer to my view.
9. See G. Wilson Knight, *The Wheel of Fire* (London: Oxford Univ. Press, 1930), pp. 54–56.
10. Some of the many discussions of this scene are Campbell, pp. 205–7; Knight, pp. 56–60; Muir, pp. 34–35; Ornstein, pp. 242–44; Asp, p. 353; Slights, pp. 44–46; and Rosalie Colie, *Shakespeare's Living Art* (Princeton: Princeton Univ. Press, 1974), pp. 326–28.
11. See Ornstein, pp. 242–43.
12. For an excellent discussion of Hector, see Shalvi, pp. 288–96.
13. See Bradbrook, pp. 313–19, and Lawrence, pp. 145–54.
14. For other views of the way Shakespeare manipulates our understanding of Cressida, see Colie, pp. 325–26, John Bayley, *Shakespeare and Tragedy* (London: Routledge and Kegan Paul, 1981), pp. 105–6; Linda LaBranche, "Visual Patterns and Linking Analogues in *Troilus and Cressida*," *SQ* 37 (1986): 440–50.
15. For a different but somewhat parallel approach to Cressida, see Howard Felperin, *Shakespearean Romance* (Princeton: Princeton Univ. Press, 1972), pp. 79–81. See also Colie, pp. 340–41.
16. For a discussion of "Ariachne" and of the dissolution of Troilus' universe, see J. Hillis Miller, "Ariachne's Broken Woof," *Georgia Review*, 31 (1977), 44–60. Other discussions of this scene include Campbell, pp. 216–17; Ornstein, pp. 248–49; and Knight, pp. 75–77.

7/ *The Gap in Nature*

1. For an examination of the disparate traditions behind Antony and Cleopatra, see Janet Adelman, *The Common Liar: An Essay on Antony and Cleopatra* (New Haven: Yale Univ. Press, 1973), pp. 53–68; and J. L. Simmons, *Shakespeare's Pagan World: The Roman Tragedies* (Charlottesville: Univ. Press of Virginia, 1973), pp. 124–33. See also, John F. Danby, *Poets on Fortune's Hill* (London: Faber and Faber, 1952), pp. 145–46; and Howard Felperin, *Shakespearean Representation* (Princeton: Princeton Univ. Press, 1977), pp. 108–9.
2. Eugene M. Waith, *The Herculean Hero* (New York: Columbia Univ. Press, 1962), pp. 39–45.
3. See especially Rosalie Colie, "*Antony and Cleopatra:* The Significance of Style," in *Shakespeare's Living Art* (Princeton: Princeton Univ. Press, 1974), pp. 168–207; and Adelman, pp. 157–68.
4. For a fuller discussion of the relationship of Mars and Venus to the play and to Renaissance tradition, see Adelman, pp. 78–101.
5. On Octavia, see Danby, pp. 142–43.
6. For a different views of the union-distinction opposition, see Adelman, pp. 142–60; Simmons, pp. 109–67; and Peter Erickson, *Patriarchal Structures in Shakespeare's Drama* (Berkeley and Los Angeles: Univ. of California Press, 1985), pp. 133–47.
7. Gordon P. Jones argues that the interpretation of Antony as depraved is so strong in this scene that in the original production he and Cleopatra entered in exchanged clothes ("The 'Strumpet's Fool' in *Antony and Cleopatra*," *SQ*, 34 [1983], 62–68).

8. For other useful analyses, see Danby, pp. 132–36, and Bernard Beckerman, "Past the Size of Dreaming," in Mark Rose, ed., *Twentieth Century Views of Antony and Cleopatra* (Englewood Cliffs, N.J.: Prentice-Hall, 1977), pp. 101–4.

9. See Adelman, pp. 90–96.

10. See ibid., pp. 151–54.

11. See Barbara C. Vincent, "Shakespeare's *Antony and Cleopatra* and the Rise of Comedy," *ELR,* 12 (1982), 53–86, and William D. Wolf, "'New Heaven, New Earth': The Escape from Mutability in *Antony and Cleopatra,*" *SQ,* 33 (1982), 328–35.

Index

Adam, 3, 33–34, 40, 47, 62
Adelman, Janet, 157
Aeneid, 11, 23
Albee, Edward, 43
Alther, Lisa, 40
Anatomy of Melancholy, 4
Andreas Capellanus, 13–15, 18–19, 24
Angel of the Hearth, 36–40
Antony: as debased wastrel, 141, 144–52, 154, 157–58, 163–65; as Etherealized lover, 140, 142, 144, 146–50, 153, 157–65; as Herculean hero, 141–44, 151–54, 159–62; as Mars, 144, 149, 151, 153–54, 161; as politician, 155; as unmanned by Cleopatra, 141–42, 152, 154, 160; see also *Antony and Cleopatra;* Cleopatra
Antony and Cleopatra, xix, xxi, 24, 110, 140–65; Actium, 145, 157, 159, 165; discordia concors, 144, 153–54; distinction-union opposition, 146–48, 161, 164–65; Egypt, 145–46, 150–52, 157–58, 160, 163; Hercules, 143–44; Julius Caesar, 142–45, 151; Octavia, 145, 154; Octavius, 145–46, 148, 155–59, 162–64; past vs. present, heroism vs. baseness, 142–45, 154–60, 163–64; Rome, 145, 149–50, 152, 154, 157, 159, 162–64; *see also* Antony; Cleopatra; *the* Ascetic, Ethealized, Emasculating, *and* Epic *types*
Aquinas, St. Thomas, 3
Ariosto, Ludovico, 5, 18, 23–24, 28, 60–61
Aristotle, x–xi, xvi, 3
Art of Courtly Love, 13–15, 18–19, 24
Ascetic type, 1–8, 32–41; *Antony and Cleopatra*, 141, 144–52, 154, 157–58, 163–65; *As You Like It*, 48–54; *Changeling, The*, 6; *Duchess of Malfi, The*, 6–8; *Euphues: The Anatomy of Wit*, 4–5; *Love's Labor's Lost*, 55–58; *Midsummer Night's Dream, A*, 65, 69–71; *Much Ado about Nothing*, 61–62, 64; *Orlando Furioso*, 5; *Othello*, 99–106, 109, 111, 113, 114; *Paradise Lost*, 33–34; *Romeo and Juliet*, 73, 75–79, 82–84, 88–89, 92–93; *Troilus and Cressida*, 116–17, 119–24, 132, 134–35
Astrophel and Stella, 17–19, 30
Augustine, St., 2

186 / Index

Austen, Jane, 41, 55

Bacon, Francis, 4
Barber, C. L., 53
Barthes, Roland, x–xi, xiv
Beauty, female: as derived from God, 14–15, 17, 33–34; as snare, 2–5, 59–60, 89–90, 107, 117; as spur to heroic action, 12–15, 80–81, 96, 120–21, 129; perception of controlled by God, 26
Bentley, Thomas, 5
Bleich, David, xix
Boccaccio, Giovanni, 10, 21
Botticelli, Sandro, 25
Bromyard, John, 3
Brontë, Charlotte and Emily, 55
Brooke, Nickolas, 90–91
Brooks, Cleanth, xi, xix, 29
Burton, Robert, 4
Byrn, M. Lafayette, 34, 36

Camoëns, 12, 25
Campbell, Oscar, 121
Campion, Thomas, 9
Castiglione, Baldassare, xv, 14–15
Catullus, xiv
Changeling, The, 6
Chaucer, Geoffrey: *Canterbury Tales*, 10, 21, 105; *Troilus and Criseyde*, 55, 119, 132, 158
Chevalier de la Charrette, Le (*Lancelot*), 12–13, 20–22, 121–22
Chrétien de Troyes, 12–13, 20–22, 121–22
Christianity, xiv, 1–3, 147–48, 156, 163
Chrysostom, St. John, 2, 35
Church, early, 1–2
Circe figure, xv, 8, 18–25, 37–38, 42–43; *see also* Emasculating type
Claudian, 24
Cleopatra: as Circe figure, 141–42, 152, 154, 160; as Etherealized lover, 140, 144, 146, 148, 153, 157, 159–65; as Venus, 141, 144, 153–54; as whore, 141–42, 148–49, 154, 158, 163–65; *see also* Antony; *Antony and Cleopatra*
Colie, Roselie, 91

Colse, Peter, 5
Conrad, Joseph, 42
Courtier, The, 14–15
Cressida: as whore, 119–20, 123–24, 134–37; as Petrarchan Lady, 118, 122–23, 132–33; as image of chaos, 136–37; *see also Troilus and Cressida*

Daniel, Samuel, 17, 19
Dante, 14–15
Decameron, 10
Deep structures, 146–48
Dekker, Thomas, 9
Delia, 17
Deloney, Thomas, 5
Derrida, Jacques, x, xix
Desdemona: as Ascetic whore, 99, 103, 107; her bedroom as garden, 108–12; as Petrarchan Lady, 101–2, 106, 108; as realistic, 100–102, 105, 108; *see also Othello*
Dickens, Charles, 36, 41
Discordia concors, 64–65, 67, 144, 153–54
Donne, John, 11, 29–30, 79, 84, 93, 147
Duchess of Malfi, The, 6–8

Ebreo, Leone, 29
Eco, Umberto, x
Eden, 27, 164
Eliot, T. S., 98
Elizabethan theater history, 54
Emasculating type, 8, 18–25, 38–39, 42–43, 73; *Aeneid*, 23; *Antony and Cleopatra*, 140–42, 144, 150, 152, 157, 160; *As You Like It*, 51–52; *Astrophel and Stella*, 18–19; *Faerie Queene*, 24; *Gerusalemme liberata*, 24; *Love's Labor's Lost*, 58; *Midsummer Night's Dream, A*, 69; *Much Ado about Nothing*, 60–61; *Odyssey*, 22–23; *Orlando Furioso*, 23–24; *Othello*, 107–8, 111; *Romeo and Juliet*, 73, 77–78, 81–84; Shakespeare's *Sonnets*, 20–21; *Troilus and Cressida*, 132, 135
Epic type, 11–12, 25, 42; *Antony and Cleopatra*, 140–44, 149–54, 157,

164; *Lusiads*, 12; *Troilus and Cressida*, 124–36
Etherealized type, 25–30, 44–45; *Antony and Cleopatra*, 140, 142, 144, 146–50, 153, 157–65; "Canonization, The," 29; *Faerie Queene*, 27–28; *Midsummer Night's Dream, A*, 64–70; *Romeo and Juliet*, 84–93
Euphues, 4, 5
Eve, 3, 33–34, 38, 67
Exterior systems, xii–xv, xix–xxi, 8, 16, 30–31, 49, 53–54, 146–47, 166

Fabliaux, 1, 6, 10–11, 21, 46, 57, 73–74
Faerie Queene, xv, 12, 24, 28, 30, 64, 84, 91–93, 107, 147
Faulkner, William, 37–39, 43
Female characters: Circe figure, 8, 18–25, 37–38, 42–43; Epic prize, 11–12; Griselda figure, 5, 33–36; history of representation, 39–41, 54–55; misogynistic influences, 2–4, 9–10, 36–37; mixed type, 46–55, 62–64; Petrarchan Lady, 12–22; Petrarchan refuser of love, 13–19, 58; Seduction quarries, 8–11
Fertility, 25, 27, 65, 80–84, 96, 145, 154
Fielding, Henry, 54
Fish, Stanley, xix
Fitzgerald, F. Scott, 42
Fleming, Ian, 42
Frye, Northrop, xiv, xvi–xvii, xxi

Gardens of love, 25, 27, 91–96, 110–11, 157, 161
Gataker, Thomas, 26
Gerusalemme liberata, 24
Givson, Anthony, 5
Gouge, William, 26
Gray, Zane, 42
Greece, ancient, x, xvii, 2–3, 11, 22, 42–43, 121, 124, 126–27, 143–44, 164
Greimas, A. J., x

Hemingway, Ernest, 37, 43
Henryson, Robert, 132

Hero and Leander, 8–9
Heroic characters, xxi, 18, 21–23, 42, 79, 98–102, 106–13, 127, 141–64
Heroic literature, 5–8, 11–12, 142–44
Herrick, Robert, 11
Heywood, Thomas, 54
Hierarchical structure, 124–25
Hieron, Samuel, 26
Holland, Norman, xix
Homer, 11, 22, 42–43, 121, 124, 126–27
Honor, 12–13, 59–62, 116–19, 124–32, 135–37, 142–44
Horace, x, xiv, xix
Hunter, R. G., 61

Idealism: beauty as ideal, 33–34, 106; heroic action as ideal, 23, 125, 152; ideal worlds, 27, 53, 66–67, 84–85, 108–11, 122, 146–48, 162–64; love as ideal, 14–15, 41, 67, 90–91, 102, 110–13, 140, 160; sex as ideal, 27–30, 44–45, 64–66, 84–85, 91–93, 149–50
Iliad, 11, 121, 126–27
Impotence and infertility, 65, 73–76, 78, 80–84, 88, 90
Interior systems, xii–xv, xix–xxi, 8, 16, 30, 49, 53–54, 146–47, 166

James, Henry, 43
Jean de Meun, 24
Jefferis, B. G., and J. L. Nichols, 34–35
Johnson, Joseph, 35
Jong, Erica, 40, 45
Jonson, Ben, 11, 54

Kay, Carol M., 98
Kingsley, Charles, 36
Kramer, Heinrich, and James Sprenger, 3

Lancelot (Chevalier de la Charrette, Le), 12–13, 20–22, 121–22
Lawrence, D. H., 37–38, 43–44
Lewis, Sinclair, 37, 43
Lodge, Thomas, 47–49
Love, *see* Petrarchan type
Lusiads, 12, 25

Lust, *see* Ascetic type; Emasculating type
Lyly, John, 4, 5

Mailer, Norman, 43–44
Malleus Maleficarum, 3
Marlowe, Christopher, 8–10
Marriage, views of: Ascetic, 1–5, 36–37, 50–52; Epic, 11–12; nineteenth-century, 34–37; Puritan, 25–27, 33–34; twentieth-century, 37–39
Marriage manuals, 34–36
Mars, 4, 24–25, 29, 137, 144, 149, 151, 153–54, 161
Marvell, Andrew, 11
Menander, xiv
Mencken, H. L., 37, 43
Middle ages, xvii, 3, 6, 10, 21, 24–25, 29, 37, 40, 91
Middleton, Thomas, and William Rowley, 6
Miller, J. Hillis, xix
Milton, John, 9, 33–34
Misogyny, 2, 4, 10, 36–37
More, Thomas, 3
Morgan, Marabel, 45
Morris, William, 43
Motion pictures, 39–44

Narrative structure, xiii–xiv, xvi, xviii, xx–xxi, 73; Ascetic type, 4–6, 35–36; Emasculating type, 23; Epic type, 11–12; Etherealized type, 27–29; Petrarchan type, 12–16; Seduction type, 8–10
New Comedy, xiv, xviii; *Midsummer Night's Dream, A,* 64, 67–69; *Much Ado about Nothing,* 60–61; *Othello,* 100–101; related to Petrarchan type, 21–22; *Romeo and Juliet,* 72–75, 79, 82–84, 87, 93; *Troilus and Cressida,* 121
New Criticism, x–xi, 166
Nineteenth century, xi, xv, xviii, 9, 32–35, 37, 40, 43, 54–55, 115

Odyssey, 11, 22, 42–43, 124
Orlando Furioso, 5, 18, 23–24, 144
Othello, 98–114, 115, 120, 140; Brabantio, 98–101; Emilia, 102, 108–10, 112; New Comic plot, 100–101; ordinary world–extraordinary world opposition, 108–11; Roderigo, 98–99, 103, 112–13; *see also* Ascetic type; Desdemona; Gardens of love; Petrarchan type
Ovid, xiv, 41, 107

Paradise Lost, 33–34
Pastoral, xv, 10–11, 23, 43, 66, 109
Perkins, William, 26
Petrarch, 14–15
Petrarchan Lady, 12–22; *see also* Petrarchan type
Petrarchan type, xv, 12–22, 25–26, 32–35, 41–42; *As You Like It,* 46–54; *Love's Labor's Lost,* 55–58; *Midsummer Night's Dream, A,* 66–69; *Much Ado about Nothing,* 58–64; *Othello,* 99–111, 113–14; *Paradise Lost,* 33–34; *Romeo and Juliet,* 75–78, 80–87, 90; *Troilus and Cressida,* 117–25, 129–30, 132–37
Plato, x, xix
Poststructuralism, xii, xix, xxi
Presley, Elvis, 41
Propp, Vladimir, xiv
Psychoanalytic criticism, xix
Puritans, 26, 33–34

Rape type and rape, 9–10, 17, 42–44, 47, 64, 75
Reader–audience response criticism, ix, xvii–xxi
Richards, I. A., xi, xix
Richardson, Samuel, 41, 54
Rogers, Daniel, 26
Rome, ancient, x, xiv, xvii, xix, 1–2, 11, 21, 23–25, 41, 73, 107; *see also Antony and Cleopatra*
Romeo and Juliet, 72–97, 101, 111, 115, 133, 140, 147–48, 161; Benvolio, 74–77, 81, 83, 85, 88; Capulet, 74–75, 79–82, 86–87, 93–95; feud, 72–79, 81–82, 84–90, 93, 95; Friar Lawrence, 84–88, 90, 94, 97; imagery, patterns of, 85–87; impotence-fertility opposition, 73–76, 78, 80–84, 88, 90; Juliet's garden as garden of love, 91–96;

Mercutio, 74, 79, 83, 85, 87–88, 147; mutuality-conflict opposition, 82, 84, 92, 96; New Comedy, use of, 72–75, 79, 82–84, 87, 93; ordinary world–extraordinary world opposition, 84–96; Paris, 87, 93–96; Rosaline, 75, 77–83, 85–86; Tybalt, 74–75, 78, 81, 85, 88–89, 93–94, 115; see also Ascetic, Emasculating, Petrarchan, and Etherealized types
Rosalynde, 47–49
Roth, Philip, 42

Satan, devils, and demons, 2–3, 103, 113, 117, 133
Seduction type, 8–11, 43–44, 50, 54, 65–66, 68, 71
Semiotics, ix, xii–xiv, xvii–xix, xxi
Sensuality, 3–4, 14, 28, 49, 143; see also Ascetic and Emasculating types
Shakespeare: *All's Well That Ends Well*, 61, 64; *As You Like It*, 5, 30, 40, 46–54, 58, 63, 90; *Cymbeline*, 30; *Hamlet*, 72, 98, 109; *1 Henry IV*, 119; *King Lear*, 5; *Love's Labor's Lost*, 55–58, 62; *Measure for Measure*, 61, 64; *Merchant of Venice*, 64; *Midsummer Night's Dream, A*, 64–71, 79; *Much Ado about Nothing*, 58–64; *Rape of Lucrece*, 9; *Richard II*, 121, 163; *Sonnets*, 19–21, 77; *Titus Andronicus*, 30; *Twelfth Night*, xiii, 64, 117; *Venus and Adonis*, 8, 11
Shaw, G. B., 98
Shoemaker's Holiday, 9
Sidney, Sir Philip, 17–19, 27, 30
Sin and evil, *see* Ascetic type
Smith, Henry, 26
Sonnet sequences, 15–21, 23, 56, 77, 82, 108
Spenser, Edmund, xv, 12, 24–25, 27–30, 64, 84, 91–93, 107, 147

Statius, 24
Stopes, Marie, 44–45
Structuralism, ix–xii, xiv, xvii–xix, xxi
Summa Theologia, 2

Tasso, Torquato, 24, 28
Television, 39, 42, 44
Tennyson, Alfred, Lord, 36
Tertullian, 2
Thackeray, W. M., 55
Thurber, James, 43
Troilus and Cressida, xiv, 99, 115–39, 140; Ajax, 116, 125–27, 138; Hector, 120–21, 125–34, 137–39; honor and value, 116–19, 124–32, 135–37; nihilism, 115–17, 124–25; Pandarus, 116, 118, 119, 123, 124, 135, 138, 139; Thersites, 116–17, 124–27, 135–39; *Troilus and Criseyde*, comparison with, 119; Ulysses, 116, 124–28, 130, 133–37, 139; see also Cressida, the Ascetic, Petrarchan, Epic, and Emasculating types
Twentieth century, xv–xvi, xviii, 37–45, 54–55, 163–64

Utopia, 3, 4

Venus, 8, 11, 24–29, 60, 91–92, 134, 144, 153–54
Virgil, 11, 23

Waith, Eugene, 143
Walling, William, 35
Warren, Robert Penn, xi
Webster, John, 6
Wertmuller, Lina, 43
Whately, William, 26
Wife of Bath, 105
Williams, Tennessee, 43
Woman Killed with Kindness, A, 54
Wylie, Philip, 43